Managing Sport Development

Sport development has become a significant part of the international sport industry. The development *of* sport (creating pathways for participation and talent development) and sport *for* development (using sport as a tool to achieve outcomes beyond sport) are now fundamental aspects of the organisation and governance of sport around the world. Consequently, any manager working in sport today needs to understand what sport development is and how sport development programs can be managed, implemented and evaluated. This is the first undergraduate textbook to offer a complete introduction to sport development, covering theory and its application to managerial practice, with examples from international contexts.

The book integrates discussion of the development *of* sport and sport *for* development in every chapter, with international case studies to illustrate the significance and application of both. Each chapter introduces key theory, examines the implications of theory for practice and critically analyses practical managerial issues. Discussions of both able-bodied and disability sport are embedded throughout, and the book includes a range of useful features to aid understanding, such as learning objectives, real-world data and examples, key terms, review questions and a companion website containing slides and a test bank for instructors.

Managing Sport Development is an essential text for any introductory sport development course, and invaluable reading for any course on international sport management, sport policy, sport governance, sport and social issues, or coach education.

Emma Sherry is a Senior Lecturer within the La Trobe University Centre for Sport and Social Impact, specialising in the area of sport development. Emma's PhD studies investigated conflict of interest in the Australian Football League. Emma's current research interests include community development through sport activities, undertaking a broad range of research projects with national and regional sport organisations in Australia and Oceania, including Netball Australia, National Rugby League, Australian Football League, Tennis Australia and Hockey Victoria. Other recent research has included access and equity in sport participation, sport in correctional facilities, and sport and recreation for at-risk and marginalised communities. Emma is co-editor for the *Journal of Sport for Development* and is on the editorial board of *Communications and Sport Journal*. Emma has worked in roles in the area of sport facility and event management and recreation management within the local government and university sport sectors. Emma also sits as a director on the Vicsport board.

Nico Schulenkorf is Senior Lecturer for Sport Management at the University of Technology Sydney (UTS). His research focuses on the social, cultural and health-related development outcomes of sport and event projects, and he is the author of several peer-reviewed journal articles. Nico is co-founder and editor of the *Journal of Sport for Development*.

Pamm Phillips is an Associate Professor in Sport Management at Deakin University. Pamm's research is focused on understanding sport organisation development, including formulating and testing intervention strategies that optimise an organisation's effectiveness and enhance the quality of life for individuals who participate and work in sport.

www.routledge.com/cw/sherry

Managing Sport Development

An international approach

**Edited by
Emma Sherry, Nico Schulenkorf
and Pamm Phillips**

LONDON AND NEW YORK

First published 2016
by Routledge
2 Park Square, Milton Park, Abingdon, Oxon OX14 4RN

and by Routledge
711 Third Avenue, New York, NY 10017

*Routledge is an imprint of the Taylor & Francis Group,
an informa business*

British Library Cataloguing-in-Publication Data
A catalogue record for this book is available from the British
Library

Library of Congress Cataloging in Publication Data
Managing sport development: an international approach/edited by
    Emma Sherry, Nico Schulenkorf & Pamm Phillips.
    pages cm
    Includes bibliographical references and index.
    1. Sports administration. I. Sherry, Emma.
    GV713.M3616 2016
    796.06'9–dc23
    2015033272

ISBN: 978-1-138-80270-4 (hbk)
ISBN: 978-1-138-80271-1 (pbk)
ISBN: 978-1-315-75405-5 (ebk)

Typeset in Berling and Futura
by Florence Production Ltd, Stoodleigh, Devon, UK

Contents

List of figures and tables   *vii*

List of contributors   *ix*

Acknowledgements   *xv*

List of abbreviations   *xvii*

SECTION 1 Introduction and theory   **1**

1   What is sport development?   3
    Nico Schulenkorf, Emma Sherry and Pamm Phillips

2   Theory of development *of* and *through* sport   12
    Matthew T. Bowers and B. Christine Green

SECTION 2 Policy and international differences   **29**

3   International sport development   31
    Laura Misener and Kylie Wasser

4   Sport development policy   45
    Iain Lindsey, Ruth Jeanes and Henry Lihaya

SECTION 3 High performance and community   **61**

5   High performance development pathways   63
    Popi Sotiriadou, Jessie Brouwers and Veerle De Bosscher

6   Community sport   77
    Pamm Phillips and Stacy Warner

SECTION 4 Support networks for sport development **91**

7 Inter-organisational relationships in sport development 93
   Geoff Dickson and Emma Sherry

8 Coaches, officials and change agents in sport development 107
   Pamm Phillips and Nico Schulenkorf

SECTION 5 Sport and social change **119**

9 Sport and health promotion 121
   Katie Rowe and Katja Siefken

10 Sport and social inclusion 135
   Jon Welty Peachey and Emma Sherry

11 Sport for conflict resolution and peace building 147
   Nico Schulenkorf, John Sugden and Jack Sugden

SECTION 6 Monitoring and evaluation **159**

12 Evaluating sport development 161
   Emma Sherry, Nico Schulenkorf and Pamm Phillips

   Glossary 177
   Index 187

Figures and tables

FIGURES

1.1	Defining sport development	7
3.1	The global-local nexus	33
3.2	The global-local nexus, the IOC and the IPC	41
5.1	The seven pathways of sport development	66
5.2	HP services – strategies, policies and people – for success	67
5.3	Integrated network of high performance partners	70
7.1	Patterns of relationships	94
7.2	Factors facilitating inter-organisational relations	98
12.1	Program logic model	164

TABLES

7.1	Social network analysis: organisational attributes	96
7.2	Social network analysis: network attributes	96
7.3	Social network analysis: relationship attributes	96
9.1	Initiatives to improve health through sport and physical activity	127

Contributors

Kylie Bellesini
Kylie is a Lecturer in the School of Exercise and Nutrition Sciences at Deakin University. She has published in the *Journal of Strength and Conditioning Research* and *ICSSPE Bulletin*, among others.

Matthew T. Bowers
Matt is a Clinical Assistant Professor of Sport Management at the University of Texas at Austin. His research examines the management of systems for athlete development. His work has been published in a variety of journals, including *Journal of Sport Management* and *Sport Management Review*.

Jessie Brouwers
Jessie graduated in 2009 at the Vrije Universiteit Brussel, Belgium, with a master's in Physical Education and Movement Sciences (specialising in sports management) with the highest distinction. In her master's thesis, she examined the talent identification process based on youth tournaments in tennis. Currently, Jessie is undertaking a PhD at Griffith University, Queensland, Australia, on the subject of elite sport policies and elite athlete pathways in tennis. Jessie has several publications in peer-reviewed journals and has presented her research at international conferences.

Ben Corbett
Ben is a PhD candidate at Griffith University. His thesis is on the subject of strategic change in response to an environmental jolt for rugby and the Olympics.

Veerle De Bosscher
Veerle is Professor at the Department of Sports Policy and Management (Faculty of Physical Education) in the Vrije Universiteit Brussel (VUB), Belgium, and Visiting Professor at Utrecht University (the Netherlands). Her research expertise is in the area of elite sport, sport development, sport policy and management, effectiveness, benchmarking and competitiveness. She has published her work in diverse refereed journals, written book chapters, and edited and authored several English and Dutch books (including *The Global Sporting Arms Race* and *Managing High Performance Sport*). She is leading a worldwide international network on research in high performance sport, SPLISS (Sports Policy factors Leading to International Sporting Success), which was also the subject of

her PhD in 2007. Veerle is a board member of the *European Sport Management Quarterly* (*ESMQ*), co-editor of the *International Journal of Sport Policy and Politics* (*IJSPP*), board member of the European Association of Sport Management (EASM) and of the Steering Committee of elite sport in Belgium (Flanders). She has worked with elite sport development sport organisations internationally.

Geoff Dickson

Geoff is an Associate Professor at Auckland University of Technology. His research interests include inter-organisational relationships and sport governance. He has been a director of AFL New Zealand since 2006 and President of the Sport Management Association of Australia and New Zealand between 2013 and 2016.

B. Christine Green

Chris Green studies the intersection of sport and development at the University of Illinois. Her work examines the growth and development of sport programs and systems, and their relationship to the development of individuals, groups, communities and organisations. The intellectual aim of her work is to elaborate a model that identifies factors that facilitate or inhibit the development of sport at each level, and that describes the separate, cumulative and interactive effects of those factors within and across levels. The practical objective of this work is enhanced effectiveness in the governance, administration, marketing and policymaking for sport programs and sport systems. In this way, sport settings can be created and maintained in ways that assist the development of a wide range of individuals, groups and communities.

Ruth Jeanes

Ruth is a Senior Lecturer in Sports Coaching and Community Development within the Faculty of Education at Monash University. Ruth is a social scientist whose research interests focus on the use of sport and recreation as a community development resource, particularly to address social exclusion among acutely marginalised groups. Ruth earned her PhD at Loughborough University and has authored several books, including *Sport and Social Exclusion in Global Society* and *The Socioecological Educator: A 21st Century Renewal of Physical, Health, Environment and Outdoor Education*, as well as numerous journal articles and chapters.

Henry Lihaya

Henry has bachelor's and master's degrees from the University of Dar es Salaam. He is currently Secretary General of the National Sports Council of Tanzania. Previously, he has been employed as Sports Officer in Tanzania's Ministry of Information, Culture and Sports and a Visiting Lecturer at the National Sports Development College, Malya.

Iain Lindsey

Iain is a Lecturer in Sport Policy in the School of Applied Social Sciences at Durham University. Iain's research has primarily examined sport policy and development, especially youth sport policy in the UK and the use of sport for development in Africa. In doing so, particular issues that are of interest to Iain are governance and partnership working, evidence-based policy and sustainable development. Iain has published widely in sport, development and politics journals, and has co-authored a book on *Sport Policy in Britain* with Professor Barrie Houlihan (Loughborough University). He has received research grants from the Leverhulme Trust, Comic Relief and UK Sport, an organisation that he works closely with in the field of sport for development. Iain is also co-editor of the *International Journal of Sport Policy and Politics*.

Laura Misener

Laura is an Associate Professor in the School of Kinesiology at Western University. She teaches in the areas of sport for development, globalisation and event management. Her research focuses on how sport and events can be use as instruments of social change. Her current research program is focusing on the role of sport events for persons with a disability in influencing community accessibility and perceptions of disability. Her work has been published in scholarly outlets such as *Journal of Sport Management*, *European Sport Management Quarterly* and *Journal of Sport and Social Issues*, and she recently co-edited a special issue of *Sport Management Review of Managing Disability Sport*.

Brianna Newland

Brianna is a Research Fellow in the College of Business and has published in *Managing Leisure* and *Journal of Physical Activity and Health*, among others.

Angela Osborne

Angela is a researcher for the Centre for Sport and Social Impact at La Trobe University, Melbourne. She has been involved in several sport development projects and has published in *Soccer & Society*, *Sex Roles* and *Media International Australia*.

Pamm Phillips

Pamm is an Associate Professor in Sport Management at Deakin University. Pamm's research is focused on understanding sport organisation development, including formulating and testing intervention strategies that optimise an organisation's effectiveness and enhance the quality of life for individuals who participate and work in sport.

Katherine Raw

Katherine is a PhD candidate at La Trobe University. Her doctoral thesis is on the subject of sport for development.

Katie Rowe

Katie is a Lecturer in the Sport Management Program at Deakin University, and currently teaches units in Sport Development, Sport Performance and Sport Practicum. She completed her PhD in 2013 with a focus on women's cycling participation in Australia. Katie's research interests include sport and recreation participation, women's s engagement in sport and the ways in which sport can be used as a tool to improve community health and well-being (sport for development). Her research to date has focused on participation issues in sports such as cycling, table tennis and netball, and she is interested in exploring opportunities for development through sport initiatives in local government contexts. Katie has presented at sport management and physical activity conferences both nationally and internationally.

Nico Schulenkorf

Nico is Senior Lecturer for Sport Management at the University of Technology Sydney (UTS). His research focuses on the social, cultural and health-related development outcomes of sport and event projects, and he is the author of several peer-reviewed journal articles. Nico is co-founder and editor of the *Journal of Sport for Development*.

Emma Sherry

Emma is a Senior Lecturer within the La Trobe University Centre for Sport and Social Impact, specialising in the area of sport development. Emma's PhD studies investigated conflict of interest in the Australian Football League. Emma's current research interests include community development through sport activities, undertaking a broad range of research projects with national and regional sport organisations in Australia and Oceania, including Netball Australia, National Rugby League, Australian Football League, Tennis Australia and Hockey Victoria. Other recent research has included access and equity in sport participation, sport in correctional facilities, and sport and recreation for at-risk and marginalised communities. Emma is co-editor for the *Journal of Sport for Development* and is on the editorial board of *Communications and Sport Journal*. Emma has worked in roles in the area of sport facility and event management and recreation management within the local government and university sport sectors. Emma also sits as a director on the Vicsport board.

Katja Siefken

Katja is Senior Researcher for Public Health at the Medical School Hamburg. She currently leads research projects funded by FIFA that investigate the interplay of physical activity and mental health. Katja is particularly interested in reducing non-communicable disease risk through sport and development initiatives, especially in low- and middle-income countries. She is consulting the World Health Organization and collaborates with government bodies (e.g. Ministry of Health) in various countries around the world. Here, she provides technical input for NCD prevention and control initiatives, ranging from rural and urban community project evaluations to workplace health policy development. Katja has published research findings in high-impact academic journals; she has authored book chapters and compiled reports for the WHO. She further co-founded the *Journal of Sport for Development*.

Popi Sotiriadou

Popi is a Senior Lecturer at Griffith Business School, Griffith University, Australia. The areas of her research expertise include sport development, high performance management, club management and sport policy. Dr Sotiriadou started her career as a professional athlete in sailing and built on that experience with her PhD on sport development processes and practice in Australia. Her research has gained such acceptance that she has been invited to consult for the Australian Sports Commission, Sarawak (Malaysia), Cycling Australia, Basketball Queensland and the Queensland Academy of Sport on sport development and high performance management. Popi was the guest editor for a special issue of *Sport Management Review* on sport development published in 2008, and is the author of books, including *The Sport Development Processes and Practices in Australia: The Attraction, Retention, Transition and Nurturing of Participants and Athletes* and *Managing High Performance Sport*.

Jack Sugden

Jack is a PhD candidate at the University of Technology Sydney (UTS). His research focuses on the role of sport for integration in divided societies. Jack has been working as a coach and researcher at numerous sport-for-development projects around the world.

John Sugden

John is Academic Leader of the Sport and Leisure Cultures subject group at the University of Brighton's School of Sport and Service Management. He is well known for his work on sport and peace building in divided societies, and for his investigative research into football's underground economy.

Stacy Warner

Stacy's research is focused on the roles that sport and sport culture play in the lives of individuals through families, communities and work environments. Warner's work often critically examines sport in an effort to consider if sport can be managed in such a way that it positively impacts an individual's life quality.

Kylie Wasser

Kylie is a PhD student at Western University in London, Ontario, studying under the supervision of Dr Laura Misener. Before Western, Kylie completed her undergraduate degree in Kinesiology at McMaster University and her master's in Human Kinetics at the University of Windsor. Kylie's research interests include sport events and their impacts, sport for social change and the leveraging of events. She has consulted for provincial sport organisations both in the planning and leveraging of events, as well as the management of parasports within able-bodied organisations. Her dissertation research will examine the leveraging of sport events by cities for regeneration and revitalisation purposes.

Jon Welty Peachey

Jon is an Associate Professor in the Department of Recreation, Sport and Tourism at the University of Illinois, whose research centres upon sport for development and social change. Dr Welty Peachey is the author of more than 60 peer-reviewed journal articles and book chapters.

Acknowledgements

The editors would like to thank the contributing authors for sharing their theoretical knowledge and applied expertise in this increasingly significant field of sport development. Their insights provide a solid foundation for readers new to the topic. We are also grateful to the authors of the case studies whose practical experience provide relevant and useful examples of the theory in application and to Angela Osborne for editorial assistance. Finally, the authors would like to thank the many sport development practitioners, volunteers, participants and academics around the world for their tireless efforts to establish, develop and consolidate this exciting, contemporary and important field of sport management.

Abbreviations

ABCD	Autoridade Brasileira de Controle de Dopagem
ACF	advocacy coalition framework
ACHPER	Australian Council for Health, Physical Education and Recreation
ACU	Australian Catholic University
ADM	athlete development model
AF	Australian Rules football
AFL	Australian Football League
AFLNZ	Australian Football League New Zealand
AGSEP	Asian-German Sport Exchange Program
ARTN	attraction, retention/transition and nurturing
ASADA	Australian Sports Anti-Doping Agency
ASC	Australian Sports Commission
BP	blood pressure
CALD	culturally and linguistically diverse
CBPR	community-based participatory research
CGC	Commonwealth Games Canada
DPAS	Global Strategy on Diet, Physical Activity and Health
ECB	England and Wales Cricket Board
FARE	Football Against Racism in Europe
FFA	Fijian Football Association
FFSA	Football Foundation of South Africa
FIFA	Fédération Internationale de Football Association
FIY	Future in Youth Program
F-MARC	FIFA Medical Assessment and Research Centre
FTEM	Foundations, Talent, Elite, Mastery framework
GAVI	Global Alliance for Vaccination and Immunisation
GDP	gross domestic product
GNI	gross national income
HIC	high-income country
HWC	Homeless World Cup
IDS	International Development through Sport
IF	international federation
IGO	international governing organisation
INGO	international non-governmental organisation

IOC	International Olympic Committee
IOR	inter-organisational relationship
IPC	International Paralympic Committee
IRC	International Relations Committee
ITF	International Tennis Federation
KPI	key performance indicators
LGA	local government authority
LIC	low-income country
LMIC	lower middle-income country
LTAD	long-term athlete development
LTTE	Liberation Tigers of Tamil Eelam (Tamil Tigers) (Sri Lanka)
M&E	monitoring and evaluation
MLB	Major League Baseball
MOU	memorandum of understanding
NA	national academy
NADO	National Anti-Doping Organizations
NCAA	National Collegiate Athletic Association (USA)
NCD	non-communicable disease
NGB	national governing body
NGO	non-governmental organisation
NOC	National Olympic Committees
NPC	National Paralympic Committees
NRL	National Rugby League (Australia)
NSA	national sporting association
NSC	National Sports Council (Tanzania)
NSO	national sporting organisation
NV	Netball Victoria
NZRU	New Zealand Rugby Union
NZSSSC	New Zealand Secondary School Sports Council
ODA	Olympic Development Academy
OTC	Olympic Training Centre
PA	physical activity
PE	physical education
RBI	Reviving Baseball in Inner Cities Program
RBV	resource-based view
SD	sport development
SDP	sport for development and peace
SFD	sport for development
SFDT	sport-for-development theory
SME	sporting mega-event
SNA	social network analysis
SSA	state sporting association
SSO	state sporting organisation
SSUSA	Street Soccer USA
TA	Tennis Australia
UMIC	upper middle-income country

UN	United Nations
UNGA	United Nations General Assembly
UNICEF	United Nations International Children's Emergency Fund
UNOSDP	United Nations Office on Sport for Development and Peace
US	United States
USADA	United States Anti-Doping Agency
USAR	USA Rugby
USOC	United States Olympic Committee
USSDA	US Soccer Development Academy
UYA	Urban Youth Academy
WADA	World Anti-Doping Agency
WCA	Women's Cricket Association (England)
WHO	World Health Organization

SECTION 1

Introduction and theory

CHAPTER 1

What is sport development?

Nico Schulenkorf, Emma Sherry and Pamm Phillips

INTRODUCTION

Sport development is an area of exponential growth in the international sport industry. The significance of sport development is felt on the sporting fields around the world where professional sport managers, development officers, program coordinators, coaches and volunteers are focusing on growing the potential of athletes and their sport communities to affect positive development outcomes. Against this background, graduates of sport studies and sport management programs are increasingly required to have expertise in the area of sport development, and thus sport development has been established at universities as an important part of sport and sport management degrees.

In this textbook, we invite readers to explore, learn and discuss the latest concepts and trends in managing sport development. This is important because only when appropriately conceived and managed, can sport development make a significant difference for professional athletes, as well as grass-roots clubs and local communities.

OUTLINE OF THE CHAPTER

This introductory chapter begins with a brief historical review of sport development and briefly shows its evolution over time. The chapter then discusses what we describe as the two arms of sport development, that is: development *of* sport and development *through* sport. In doing so, the sport development field is introduced and analysed in the context of the wider sport management theory and practice. Next, the chapter briefly introduces the policy tensions in sport development, where differences in ideologies and political priorities result in struggles for funding and support between professional sport clubs and community sport initiatives. Finally, this first chapter introduces the remaining 11 chapters that make up this textbook and identifies career opportunities in the sport development space. These should be of particular significance for young and aspiring university graduates on their way towards securing employment in the sport development sector.

After completing this chapter, you should be able to:

- understand the history and evolution of sport development;
- recognise the two arms of sport development and their specific contributions;

- critically analyse ongoing tensions between the two arms of sport development;
- appreciate the complexity of the sport development sector; and
- consider and reflect on career opportunities in sport development.

HISTORICAL BACKGROUND OF SPORT DEVELOPMENT

In essence, sport development is about providing opportunities for individuals and communities to engage and grow in different types of physical activity (Shilbury *et al.* 2008). Sport development happens at different levels and in different social contexts; it spans from young children who are introduced to sport and play in schools and sport clubs, to professional athletes who are trying to improve their skill levels to win medals at world championships and Olympic Games. Sport development even applies to the growing number of masters sport initiatives where the focus is placed on keeping our aging population active and healthy. Overall, sport development is an important space for everyone involved in sport – from the young to the old, from grass roots to elite. However, as will be discussed in this book, the specific goals and objectives of sport development initiatives vary, and professionally educated sport managers are required to provide the most relevant and meaningful services and experiences needed for people to maximise their sport and community goals.

In the nineteenth century, reforms that took place in elite English public schools resulted in what we know today as modern, codified sports (Schulenkorf and Adair 2012). The undisciplined, often violent behaviour of schoolboys was at odds with the goal of producing young men who, by virtue of their social position, were set to assume leadership roles in English society. They often had status on account of birth and privilege, but too many lacked commitment to study and respect for authority. Sweeping reforms to this elite educational system were introduced during the mid-nineteenth century, part of which involved developing both the mind and the body of pupils (Holt 1990). Sport, in the reformers' view, was much more than a mere game: it provided important lessons for life, such as striving for victory and accepting defeat – both with good grace. Similarly, sport was thought to build character and provide a productive outlet for young boys to express themselves physically and represent their schools, and in the process create feelings of community among students and promote a sense of loyalty to the institution (Chandler 1991). These early forms of junior sport development, therefore, were about purposeful physical activity in the interests of inculcating moral values. The health dimensions of sport – that is, appropriate levels of exercise – were a secondary consideration.

Since then, much has changed. In the early twentieth century, the rise of the amateur ideal in sport – which became a cornerstone of the modern Olympic Games – provided an emphasis on *participation for its own sake* with a focus on selflessness and community spirit (Jobling 2000; Obel 2005; Seynard 2002). At that time, sport was understood as a *common good* that provided people of varying ages and backgrounds with valuable social experiences. However, the boundaries around the amateur ideal began to loosen by the last quarter of the twentieth century (Schulenkorf and Adair 2012) and the commercialisation of sport began. This development towards the commercialisation of sport led to a new value system for sport within which community development is no longer inconsistent with commercial sponsorship, business-like operation and remuneration of club representatives (Owen and Weatherston 2002). Winning and elite performance became the new currency for sport.

While the professionalisation of sport organisations and the management of them has been documented at length elsewhere (Dowling *et al.* 2014), it is useful at this point to explore the place of sport development within the increasingly professional sport landscape. As Dowling *et al.* (2014) explain, professionalisation has occurred from a systemic, organisational and occupational perspective. That is, professionalisation of sport has occurred due to: system changes – such as when an external force impacts sport; organisational factors internal to the organisation – such as governance, structure and policy; and in terms of personnel where occupations become professions.

From a systemic perspective, many governments around the world have been a catalyst for the commercial development of sport and therefore the professionalisation of sport management in a range of ways. First, by increasing financial commitment to sport, some governments have invested in sports – albeit in many cases only a limited number of sports in which it is believed there will be international success – with the aim that the investment will lead to the development of athletes who can compete successfully nationally and internationally. Through doing so, governments anticipate that athletic successes will lead to national pride, as well as international prestige when nations can embrace the victories and triumphs of their successful athletes. Governments have contributed to sport development through a range of activities that include building of community and elite facilities or providing direct funding to programming; in addition, some governments have also invested in hosting international-level high-profile sport events through which they seek to increase social, economic and environmental rewards for host cities and communities. Of course, in addition to government investment in sport, corporate businesses have increasingly invested in sport to enhance their own business success. In other words, as government investment has led to a more lucrative and popular sport market, businesses have sought to use sport to engage their customers. In particular, businesses have invested in sponsoring athletes, teams, sport programs, facilities and sport organisations, and they leverage their sponsorship of, and connection with, sport to engage sport consumers who they ultimately wish to secure as customers of their own businesses.

From an organisational perspective, the increasing investment in sport by both government and business has led to the need for sport organisations to professionalise. That is, they have been required to develop policy and governance practices that are formal and to structure themselves in ways that allow them to approach the development and delivery of their products and services in a business-like manner – regardless of whether their sport business is aimed at a local club or at a professional-level championship match or event. Further, they have had to engage with government and the corporate sector in ways that reflect professional practice.

From an occupational perspective, there is an increasing number of specialist roles required in the business of sport, including in sport development, upon which this textbook focuses. Later in this chapter, the reader can explore the different specialist roles that are available to individuals who choose a career in sport development.

Through this textbook, the reader will explore the impact that the professionalisation of sport is having on sport development at all levels of delivery – from grass roots to elite. For example, governments are increasingly realising that sport provides opportunities beyond winning gold medals and international success. Investing in sport can prove to be a wise investment in community because sport – if managed appropriately – has the ability to facilitate the achievement of many social and community goals that may have nothing to do with competition and winning. Sport development, as a field of endeavour and academic enquiry, challenges governments, businesses and sport organisations to define and value sport for a range of different outcomes beyond winning. The following section starts to unpack what sport development means and provides a platform for readers of this textbook to continue the journey of understanding sport development.

CONCEPTUALISING THE TWO ARMS OF SPORT DEVELOPMENT

Sport development, for the purposes of our textbook, includes both *development of sport* (SD), as well as *sport for development* (SFD). These two arms of sport development have much in common and they are certainly related; however, they are distinct in their specific purpose and focus. While SD aims to create pathways for professional participation and talent identification, SFD focuses on the role that sport can play in contributing to specific social outcomes and overall community well-being. In other words, SD aims at improving the sport-related skills of particular athletes, while SFD refers to improvement of sport and other skills achieved through sport participation. In SD, individuals and groups participate with the focus on achieving mastery and potentially excellence in the sport. In SFD, individuals and groups participate to achieve more than just physical outcomes: they also participate with aspirations to realise certain social, cultural, psychological, educational and/or economic goals.

Traditionally, the management and delivery of SD are the responsibilities of each individual sport organisation and are usually planned by a national sport organisation (NSO). That is, as readers will discover through this text, SD requires a range of elements from the macro to the micro level of organisation to be in place in order to provide appropriate SD. This includes the provision of appropriate facilities for individuals to have an opportunity to participate; programs that offer appropriate experiences depending on age, skill and other factors; pathways so that participants can transition to various programs at different levels to meet their needs; and personnel to facilitate the delivery of programs and the development of participants. Of course, all of these activities require financial investments and relevant budget appropriations. Traditionally, sport organisations have each developed their own facilities, programs, pathways and personnel in order to achieve SD, and hence have been internally focused on achieving this goal. However, as the reader will see in this textbook, sport organisations are sometimes turning to external organisations in order to successfully achieve SD outcomes.

The management and delivery of SFD can be a little more complex than that of SD, because SFD goes beyond sport per se, and instead links to the wider field of community development. The management and delivery of SFD focuses on using sport as a tool to achieve broader aims that are most often outside the scope of the sport itself. This might

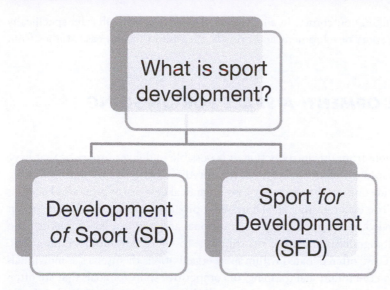

FIGURE 1.1 Defining sport development

include using participation in sport to achieve wide-ranging aims such as social development, local empowerment or peace objectives (Coalter 2010; Schulenkorf 2012; Sugden 2010). As such, the achievement of SFD outcomes often requires that managers take a much more externally focused view and develop partnerships with other organisations who might offer greater skills, experience and qualifications in the broader goals desired.

Although SD and SFD are different in the way that they are defined, as the reader will see from the information presented throughout this textbook, sport programs are not necessarily exclusively focused on either SD or SFD. It is true that while some programs are aimed specifically at SD and others may specifically be aimed at achieving SFD outcomes, others find a balance between SD and SFD. Case studies throughout this textbook allow the reader to explore a variety of different permutations of programs that deliver SD and/or SFD outcomes.

Overall, an easy and practical way of distinguishing whether a sport program focuses on SD or SFD, or is perhaps a combination of both, is by asking the following question:

> Are the intended outcomes of the sport program to develop participants' skills and athletic performance, or to develop participants beyond the sport itself?

The answer to this question will determine if the program is focused on SD or SFD, or perhaps a combination of both. For any SD program initiative, success is closely linked to outcomes that are related to the particular sport in question. For example, a program that is focused on specific training to develop skills, techniques and competition tactics related to winning is most likely an SD program. In contrast, in the case of any SFD program initiative, success is not linked to sport-related outcomes. For example, to achieve social inclusion outcomes for recently arrived immigrants, the type of sport played is less important than how the program is managed and delivered so that it provides opportunities for social interaction and the like. In some cases, programs are designed to deliver both SD and SFD outcomes. In all chapters of this book, we will refer specifically to the two arms of sport development and provide examples through case studies from the field.

SPORT DEVELOPMENT: A SPACE FOR ONGOING TENSIONS

As the reader will note from this introduction, it is possible to deliver programs that have SD and SFD outcomes simultaneously; however, for the most part, SD and SFD have not sat easily alongside one another. In many cases, practical delivery of programs becomes either SD *or* SFD. The different foci of SD and SFD programs often cause debate about what should be funded and supported by local, regional and national governments, who are often the most significant financial contributors to sport development programs. Further, SD and SFD are often debated within sport organisations themselves as individuals struggle to give up on the traditional trappings of competitive sport for goals that are often seen as more lofty and idealistic. As the reader will discover throughout this textbook, there are strong arguments to support both of the arms of sport development.

Often, due to limited funding and personnel available to them, sport organisations and policymakers need to make difficult decisions regarding resources that can be directed to SD and/or SFD initiatives. Ideally, both SD sport and SFD initiatives would be funded and supported to secure: (1) sustained international success for club and country; and (2) involvement of the community in regular physical activity and play. Unfortunately, the total amount of sport funding available rarely satisfies the demand for both arms of sport development, and hence political ideologies and strategies – as well as behind-the-scenes bargaining – tend to inform and influence the final sport development funding policies implemented.

SPORT DEVELOPMENT CAREERS

Sport development offers a range of employment opportunities and career paths for individuals who are looking for a career in the sport industry. Sport development is unique in that it can offer an individual the opportunity to work either on or off the field of play, or perhaps to combine both on- and off-field roles.

On the field, for example, sport coaches, fitness instructors, sport development officers and community workers contribute to the delivery of sport programs, and through their expertise at the coalface they can facilitate the development of participants in terms of sport and personal skills. Their work can be very hands-on with participants to achieve physical and/or emotional development.

Off the field, sport development officers and game coordinators, as well as school program managers and youth development staff, are involved in planning, managing and implementing sport programs, events and activities for teams and communities. These are only a handful of examples of roles in the sport development industry. Additional career opportunities and positions related to the field of sport development are listed below:

- sport development officer;
- sport program manager;
- international sport advisor;
- community development officer;
- sport policymaker;
- professional coach;
- junior coach;
- player development expert;
- school attendance officer;
- after-school program coordinator;
- sport science manager;
- exercise and health specialist;
- customer service manager;
- community safety and youth development coordinator;
- sport for development and peace coordinator;
- competition and scheduling manager;
- sport event manager;
- coach education officer/manager; and
- facility manager.

Almost all of the sport development positions listed above require jobseekers to hold a sport-related university degree and/or have significant work experience in the sector; moreover, professional management knowledge is needed to be competitive. Hence, this textbook is designed to equip readers with the theoretical and applied knowledge necessary to secure – and succeed in – their chosen careers.

ABOUT THIS TEXTBOOK

The textbook is comprised of 12 chapters that are subdivided into six separate but interdependent sections. First, the 'Introduction and theory' section – Chapters 1 and 2 – provides an understanding of the definition of sport development with its two arms: the development of sport (SD) and sport for development (SFD). In doing so, it explains the significance of the sport development field, its breadth, opportunities and tensions in both theory and practice. Second, the 'Policy and international differences' section – Chapters 3 and 4 – focuses on the roles and responsibilities of key players in sport development, including government, sporting bodies and relevant stakeholders. This section also compares different approaches and models of sport development in a global context, including the involvement and support of large international organisations such as the United Nations (UN), International Olympic Committee (IOC) and international sport federations.

Third, the 'High performance and community' section – Chapters 5 and 6 – provides an overview of the different institutions and organisations that manage and/or support elite and grass-roots sports. It covers a large spectrum of sport development providers and highlights the different goals and foci of professional and community sport. In doing so, the chapters highlight the different systems and pathways in high performance sport, as well as opportunities and tensions that arise as a result of the professionalisation of sport; for example, through special technology or the use of drugs. Also discussed are the ways in which sport and events can be best used to benefit the wider community, including disadvantaged populations. Fourth, the section on 'Support networks for sport development' – Chapters 7 and 8 – critically discusses partnerships with other organisations and institutions from within and beyond the sport arena. A focus is placed on the benefits and challenges of engaging with partners, as well as the importance of establishing and managing relations within SD and SFD. Here, special attention is given to the development and delivery of coaches, officials and change agents who engage directly with players, stakeholders and communities.

Fifth, the section titled 'Sport and social change' comprises Chapters 9, 10 and 11. These chapters focus on specific social development outcomes that can be intentionally achieved through sport. In particular, the link between sport and health promotion in both western societies and developing nations will be analysed in Chapter 9, while opportunities for sport and social inclusion – particularly for disadvantaged and at-risk communities – will be discussed in Chapter 10. Building on this, Chapter 11 is titled 'Sport for conflict resolution and peace building', and looks at opportunities and limitations of improving intergroup relations through sport – a challenging idea that has become rather popular over the past decade. Finally, Section 6 reflects on the previous 11 chapters and asks the question, 'How do we know that we have been successful?' In other words, the final chapter looks at the different approaches to evaluating sport development. It provides an overview of different evaluation and measurement options, and uses two case studies, for which evaluation was conducted, to reflect on the tension between people's expectations and actual sport development outcomes.

SUMMARY

Sport development is an exciting, fresh and important element of sport management. In this first chapter, we have provided our rationale for compiling a textbook on managing sport development. We have briefly reviewed the history and evolution of sport development over time and have discussed our conceptualisation of the two arms of sport development, namely the development *of* sport (SD) and the development *through* sport, or sport for development (SFD). We have pinpointed key opportunities and tensions for the sport development field, both in terms of theory and praxis. Finally, we have established how this textbook – and its constituent sections and chapters – proposes to discuss the different aspects of sport development and their application to theory and practice.

We are confident that by using this textbook, readers will explore, learn and discuss the latest concepts and trends in managing sport development. We also believe that they will subsequently be equipped with the necessary knowledge to appropriately conceive and manage sport development assignments that can make a significant difference for elite athletes, as well as grass-roots clubs and local communities.

REFERENCES

Chandler, T. J. L. (1991) 'Games at Oxbridge and the public schools, 1830–80: the diffusion of an innovation', *International Journal of the History of Sport*, 8(2): 171–204.

Coalter, F. (2010) 'The politics of sport-for-development: limited focus programmes and broad gauge problems?', *International Review for the Sociology of Sport*, 45(3): 295–314.

Dowling, M., Edwards, J. and Washington, M. (2014) 'Understanding the concept of professionalisation in sport management research', *Sport Management Review*, 17(4): 520–29.

Holt, R. (1990) *Sport and the British: A Modern History*, Oxford: Oxford University Press.

Jobling, I. (2000) 'In pursuit of status, respectability and idealism: pioneers of the Olympic movement in Australasia', *The International Journal of the History of Sport*, 17(2–3): 142–63.

Obel, C. (2005) 'Amateur rugby's spectator success: cultivating inter-provincial publics in New Zealand (1902–1995)', *Sporting Traditions*, 21(2): 97–118.

Owen, P. D. and Weatherston, C. R. (2002) 'Professionalization of New Zealand rugby union: historical background, structural changes and competitive balance', *Economics Discussion Paper*, Otago, New Zealand: University of Otago.

Schulenkorf, N. (2012) 'Sustainable community development through sport and events: a conceptual framework for sport-for-development projects', *Sport Management Review*, 15(1): 1–12.

Schulenkorf, N. and Adair, D. (2012) 'Sport development', in S. Leberman, C. Collins and L. Trenberth (eds), *Sport Business Management in New Zealand and Australia*, 3rd edn, South Melbourne: Cengage, pp. 284–98.

Seynard, J. (2002) 'From gentleman to the manly: a large step for the amateur', *Sporting Traditions*, 18(2): 1–14.

Shilbury, D., Sotiriadou, K. and Green, C. B. (2008) 'Sport development. Systems, policies and pathways: an introduction to the special issue', *Sport Management Review*, 11(3): 217–23.

Sugden, J. (2010) 'Critical left-realism and sport interventions in divided societies', *International Review for the Sociology of Sport*, 45(3): 258–72.

CHAPTER 2

Theory of development *of* and *through* sport

Matthew T. Bowers and B. Christine Green

INTRODUCTION

The previous chapter introduced us to some of the basic aspects of sport development by providing an overview of how we define the field and how it has evolved. The present chapter aims to build upon that basic understanding of sport development and to extend it into the realm of praxis: the application of theory to practice. This chapter focuses on describing the development of academic models, approaches and frameworks of development *of* and *through* sport.

OUTLINE OF THE CHAPTER

A brief audit about what we know – and a bit about what we do not – with respect to theories of SD and SFD will be presented. The remainder of the chapter will emphasise how theories function in a more practical sense. Specifically, the *raison d'être* of this chapter and its placement at the end of the introductory section of this textbook is to facilitate an understanding of the broader tensions within sport development that will be discussed briefly here and then revisited throughout the textbook. Drawing upon examples from the US, the tension between theory and practice is considered, as is the tension between SD and SFD.

After completing this chapter, you should be able to:

* articulate an understanding of different models of sport development;
* compare and contrast academic models of sport development;
* identify and work through practical examples of how different sports put sport development into practice;
* recognise the tension between academic theory and practical implementation; and
* appreciate how national context impacts sport development approaches.

WHAT DOES THE THEORY TELL US?

Theories and frameworks for sport development are, like the field itself, differentiated based on the outcomes they seek to explain. Some seek to explain the ways in which we develop the sport. These focus on the athletes, coaches, support services, administration and systems that provide opportunities to participate in sport at all levels. These are theories for the development of sport (SD). Others seek to understand and optimise the ways in which we use sport for the purpose of developing individuals, groups, communities and society as a whole. These are theories of sport for development (SFD). In the following section, discussion will first turn to SD.

There are numerous frameworks that attempt to describe the process of SD. While they vary in significant ways, nearly every framework has, at its core, a focus on sport pathways. One of the oldest analogies for sport development is that it is like a pyramid structure wherein the base of the pyramid represents the entry level of the sport and consists of a large group of participants at a recreational level. As one moves up through the pyramid, the number of participants narrows and the skill and competitive levels increase. The pathway to excellence, then, begins at the base of the pyramid and advances upward through increasingly competitive sport settings (see Green 2005). Successful development of the sport is thus a function of athlete development and consists of three critical tasks: (1) recruiting players into the sport; (2) keeping them involved in the sport and increasing their commitment to the sport; and (3) assisting the top players at each level to successfully transition to the next level of competition. There are at least two major flaws in the pyramid analogy. The first is that it is an *up or out* model. That is, it assumes that athletes move systematically from the bottom to the top of the pyramid; when they don't move up, they drop out. The second is that it has only one entry point: the bottom. Neither of these conditions holds true in practice.

There have been other models based on these same principles. Perhaps the most famous is Balyi's (2001) long-term athlete development model (LTAD). Essentially, the LTAD model uses sport science to specify four (for early specialisation sports) or five (for late specialisation sports) necessary training stages that an athlete must master to reach elite levels. The model breaks down these stages according to age and gender in order to consider the athlete's readiness to move to the next level. Côté and Hay (2002) also outlined stages of athlete development based on principles of child development and determined their stages based on age, assuming that athlete pathways begin with the youngest of children. More recently, Gulbin *et al.* (2013) developed the FTEM (Foundations, Talent, Elite, Mastery) framework for athlete development. Their model expands the stages to 10, with seven of the 10 aspects of the sport excellence section of the model. Although the actual stages are not dissimilar to the aforementioned models, the FTEM does not classify stages by age or gender. Each of these models is based in the sport sciences and each is a micro-level framework in that they focus on the individual athlete.

Green's (2005) theory is also a micro-level theory. However, it is based in the social sciences and provides insight regarding potential strategies for recruitment, retention and transition of athletes. Similarly, Sotiriadou *et al.* (2008) identify processes of sport development: attraction, retention/transition and nurturing. Each of these frameworks also considers the meso-level processes that are necessary to develop individual athletes and, consequently, increase participation levels in the sport, as well as enhance the performance levels of athletes within the sport.

The final frameworks concerned with developing sport take a macro-view and focus on sport policies at the national level. The framework developed by Green and Houlihan (2008) suggested that nations' SD policies were becoming more homogeneous due to globalisation, commercialisation and what they term *governmentalisation*. In short, they argue that sport systems are becoming more alike because: there is more sharing and comparing due to globalisation; transnational corporations have an increasing stake in high performance sport; and governments have taken on a more central role in sport. Green and Houlihan's work has been built upon by numerous researchers. In fact, De Bosscher *et al.* (2009) compared elite sport systems and policies across six countries. Not only did they examine policies, but they also related the policy and systems elements to success in international competitions. Nine pillars were associated with sporting success: financial support, organisation and structure of sport policies, foundation and participation, talent identification and development system, athletic and post-career support, training facilities, coaching, (inter)national competition and scientific research.

In summary, frameworks for SD occur at the micro, meso, and macro levels of analysis. They provide some direction for the design of programs, systems and policies to enable sport success and, perhaps to a lesser degree, recommendations for increasing participation. However, their primary focus is on skill and performance outcomes only. SFD is rarely a consideration in these frameworks; it is discussed next.

Theories of SFD are very much concerned with the ways in which sport can create change – in individuals, groups, communities, nations and even society as a whole. It is important to note that programs vary considerably in their focus on sport (SD) or social development (SFD). Sport plus programs are sport-focused programs that may also provide other development opportunities. Other programs are more focused on development, and have very little interest or investment in developing sport skills or elite athletes. These have been characterised as plus sport. Both consider sport to be an effective setting for the delivery of other benefits. Coalter (2007) provides the following classification system based upon the relative emphasis to sport and/or its objectives:

- traditional forms of *sport*, with an implicit assumption or explicit affirmation that such sport has inherent developmental properties for participants;
- *sport plus*, in which sports are adapted and often augmented with parallel programs in order to maximise their potential to achieve developmental objectives; and
- *plus sport*, in which sport's popularity is used to attract young people to programs of education and training, with the systematic development of sport rarely a strategic aim.

Green (2008) includes three categories within her framework: (1) sport for social inclusion; (2) sport as a diversion; and (3) sport as a hook. Sport for social inclusion is based on the premise that sport participation of any kind provides participants with critical development benefits. Thus, it would be important to find ways to provide sport to underserved populations. A plethora of SFD programs have been created to provide sport to minority groups and underserved populations. However, the outcomes of these programs are mixed (Long *et al.* 2009; Maxwell *et al.* 2013). One could argue that sport for social inclusion programs are clearly *sport plus*, while sport as a hook would predictably be *plus sport*. Sport as a hook initiatives use sport merely as a recruiting tool and a site for the delivery of other services and benefits (Green 2008; Olushola *et al.* 2013). Sport as a diversion initiatives could be either *sport plus* or *plus sport* – or perhaps both – as these are programs – such as midnight basketball – that use sport to keep participants away from antisocial activities and petty crimes; although it should be noted that the more effective programs also incorporate significant social welfare programs for participants (Hartmann and Depro 2006). No single program type seems to be more effective than the others; instead, the specific components and the delivery of the program are key. Patriksson (1995: 128) puts it this way: 'sport, like most activities, is not a priori good or bad, but has the potential of producing both positive and negative outcomes'.

At this point, the field lacks strong, evidence-based theory that provides an understanding of the specific program elements, under what conditions, lead to which outcomes, for what groups. Lyras and Welty Peachey (2011) have provided an initial theoretical framework, sport-for-development theory (SFDT), to identify the necessary components for a successful program. Their theory identifies five components: impacts assessment, organisational components, sport components, educational components and cultural enrichment. Schulenkorf (2012) has also developed a framework for using events in SFD. Like Lyras and Welty Peachey's (2011) framework, Schulenkorf (2012) provides specific areas of attention for positive development through sport events: sport event management, direct social impacts and long-term social outcomes. These theoretical frameworks begin to address the need for strong theoretical foundations in the SFD community. Yet, these theories fail to consider potential points of integration or leverage with theories of SD; these points are now considered.

We continue to distinguish between the two types of sport development as if one has no bearing on the other. Yet, there is no inherent reason that development cannot occur *in* and *through* sport synergistically. This is particularly, but not exclusively, the case for youth sport. Why wouldn't you want to develop children's sport skills and abilities *while at the same time* developing their social and interpersonal skills? Vice versa, if you were to participate in a sport-for-development program that included sport activities, is there any reason that you would not want to enhance your sport skills and abilities? Too often, programs fail to consider the full development of the participant and the potential development benefits that can accrue to the community and groups within the community. This would require dual goals and close attention to the design and implementation of programs. As we see in the case studies later in this chapter, this rarely occurs.

IMPLICATIONS OF THEORY FOR PRACTICE

Academic models of development – both *of* and *through* sport – have been met with varying degrees of support and adoption within practical settings. In some parts of the world, the development of theory has coincided with and informed practical models in a type of recursive symbiosis wherein the practical side informs the theoretical side, and vice versa. When considering the contextual factors that enable or inhibit such synergies, it is perhaps simplest to zoom out and to frame the issue in terms of national approaches to development. We must bear in mind, though, that examining the context from a national level perspective is somewhat heavy-handed as it unavoidably blurs important within nation variation; it is, however, a useful preliminary approach. In countries where the practical and theoretical development of the field has occurred more or less concomitantly, two preconditions have tended to exist that support and facilitate the interweaving of these two branches: SD is largely managed through a centralised governance structure, and government sponsors sport science research. It is no surprise, then, that the countries that are on the vanguard of praxis (that is, synergising the practical and theoretical models of sport development) are countries that have garnered considerable respect on the international stage for their sport development approaches; for example, Australia and Germany.

One of the other primary challenges of studying or working in the field comes from the disconnect between the efforts of those who are working to develop high performance athletes in elite settings (SD) versus those who work to utilise sport as a context to achieve some non-sport developmental outcome (SFD). In theory, there need not be a distinction between these two goals, but in practice considerable psychological and structural barriers to coordinating these efforts have been shown to exist; in fact, in many cases, initiatives are characterised by distinct policies and programs that often target distinct populations. Moreover, SFD programs tend to be treated as stand-alone or spin-off programs that fail to include pathways to transition program participants into – or out of – an SD program. The major professional leagues in the US offer poignant examples of how the challenge of connecting SD with SFD is often conceptualised as one of mutual exclusivity: the professional leagues have an existing SD model from which they reap the rewards of other organisations' work developing elite athletes, while SFD initiatives are often managed by public relations and community outreach divisions within the league offices whose goals serve marketing, not sport development, ends.

While there have been a number of in-depth texts, articles and chapters written about the various national approaches to the SD – fewer on SFD – that highlight the successful areas of implementation of sport development theoretical principles in a practical setting, it may be instructive to an international readership to learn about these topics through a less successful national context: the US. Sport development scholars in the US are often faced with the odd challenge of explaining how the US has been able to achieve considerable success as a sporting nation virtually *in spite of* its approach to both SD and SFD. In the US, there is no centralised governance, no efficacious guiding sport policies, and in many sports little coordination of athlete recruitment, retention and transition beyond what the free market provides. Further, SFD programs tend to function as fractured, ad hoc efforts that integrate little understanding of theories of development, thus tending to produce only accidental or incidental developmental outcomes for participants that are difficult to replicate on a programmatic level.

When non-Americans examine SD in the US, there are often a number of misconceptions about how the system functions relative to other SD systems around the world. In reality, the very use of the term *system* creates somewhat of a misnomer, as the systems employed by many other countries are characterised by far more centralisation and coordination than exists for most sports in the US. The sustained success of the US on the elite international stage has only cloaked this lack of coordination in Olympic medals and a multibillion-dollar professional sports industry, but the fact remains: the US sport development paradigm (SD and SFD) operates as an inefficient, fractured and largely unregulated field. Moreover, from a policy standpoint, the structure and governance of American sport creates a development landscape in which the organisation and management of sport is qualitatively different than is found elsewhere around the world

(Chalip *et al.* 1996). Thus, those looking on the US from outside the system often draw conclusions in which overall effectiveness in high-profile sport contests is conflated with a finely tuned and well-coordinated development system. Outsiders, however, are not the only ones to mistake relative effectiveness with systemic efficiency. As Bowers *et al.* (2011a: 254) describe:

> Americans themselves rarely have much understanding of the structure and governance of American sport, even if they work in sport, because the United States does not have an integrated system for sport or for the development of athletes (Sparvero *et al.* 2008). American sport policies are few, and are generally designed to enable free and unencumbered functioning of American sport markets. Further, since American popular media work hand-in-hand with the entertainment side of the American sport industry, Americans are typically exposed to a simplistic and mythologized [*sic*] version of American sporting culture (Koppett 1994). Consequently, Americans who have never worked in American sport misunderstand it, and those who do work in American sport typically understand only the particular realm in which they work. Those who seek to learn about American sport by interviewing sports executives or through content analysis of American media actually learn only about isolated corners of American sport, or about the popular mythologies that masquerade as fact throughout American sport.

Although the US is often looked toward as a model for other countries seeking to develop their domestic and international sports agendas, the unique lack of governance structure and policy orientation of the US sport system can present difficulties with respect to translating best practices to a different national context. Distilled down to its most essential premises, sport in the US is left largely ungoverned because of the country's history of avowedly capitalistic, market-driven, politico-economic philosophy and a cultural resistance to any type of government imposition within these free markets. Basically, the more general tenets of American free-market capitalism pervade even the sporting landscape, as stakeholders at virtually all levels – often, even policymakers – subscribe to the American ethos that the individual actors operating within the free market will determine the optimal solution to any challenges; to encourage government intervention would represent an affront to the core beliefs of the stakeholders. These philosophical incompatibilities, in turn, render a sport governance system that avoids policy-driven solutions and, when forced to develop policy, often undermines its legitimacy by failing to provide any mechanisms for implementation or enforcement within the policy.

In the place of a centralised, top-down approach to sport development, the market-driven model tends to promote a reversal of power and autonomy in the system: actors take ownership over their own development and the pathways to elite development are paved with individual choices within a localised market comprised of often nebulous inter-organisational linkages. Rather than national governing bodies (NGBs) of sports driving broad development policies to which member institutions adhere, the more common development approach of most sports in the US emerges from the aggregation of local actors participating in sports through local sport providers that themselves are in competition with other local providers of the same sport. This local-centric development paradigm makes it difficult to generate praxis, as the local, private sector SD actors tend to be entrepreneurial in nature with little formal sport development training; moreover, the SFD stakeholders are often either under-resourced or lacking in the incentives to properly leverage and resource their programs.

Further, the sport provider marketplace is diverse, competitive and marked by both public and private investment. A major portion of the relatively meagre public sport provision is delivered through local recreation departments, which are typically funded through tax revenues and participation fees (Bowers *et al.* 2011b). The remaining public expenditure on sport comes from school-based sports offered at the middle school, high school and university levels – there is little to no federal funding of any kind for sport. There are private clubs that offer increasingly professionalised sports training beginning at an early age that require a significant financial investment by the individual. Additionally, there are service organisations, along with church-based organisations, that include sport programming as a component of their offerings and endeavour to blend SD and SFD goals, with varying degrees of success. Within this marketplace, there exists no central registry of sport organisations and no mechanism to coordinate delivery of sport programming. As a result, sport organisations often offer redundant and cannibalistic programming and tend to operate with little connection to one another, even within the same community or the same sport. Consequently, there are often multiple avenues for sport participation with no single pathway for athlete development (Sparvero *et al.* 2008).

Despite the uniqueness of the US system, there are lessons that can be drawn from it. If care is taken to understand the antecedents and by-products of the traditional approach to sport development in the US, readers can take away a nuanced appreciation for the particular ways in which it may serve as a model for what – or what *not* – to do in other national contexts. The next section examines how the tensions identified in this section – between theory and practice of SD and SFD – are manifested in specific cases within the US.

APPLICATION OF THEORY TO PRACTICE: TENSIONS IN THE US

SD and SFD in the US have been described as disparate from other nations, and further, SD and SFD can be nearly as disparate across sports within the country. For example, basketball and football (soccer) are two of the most popular sports in the US. Both share fundamental contextual constraints by operating within a market-driven, policy-free, national governance structure, yet the manner in which an athlete progresses through elite pathways is fundamentally different at all levels of each sport. For basketball, a chaotic travel club/school sport amalgam funnels elite athletes almost exclusively through the collegiate sport pathway. For football, a similar development landscape exists, but it has been overlaid with clearer pathways, such as the Olympic Development Program and new US Soccer Development Academy (USSDA) model. As market-driven as it remains, football in the US looks almost communist in its efforts to centralise and coordinate through the USSDA, compared with the surface-level, public relations style coordination in basketball. Despite this, compared with other high-income countries (HICs), football development in the US likely appears as unregulated as the fabled Wild West of the American frontier.

The US is one of the most successful sporting nations in global history, but the encroaching competition from nations all across the world in a multitude of sports offers an opportunity for the US to critically examine its practices in order to pursue a sustainable competitive advantage. As Bowers *et al.* (2011b: 181) conclude, however:

> Challenges to the status quo are likely to be met with intense ideological resistance and major structural impediments. The ramifications of decades-long systemic disorganization [*sic*] are beginning to become apparent in terms of decrements in both elite international performance (Wu *et al.* 2009) and domestic mass participation (Johnston *et al.* 2007). Moving forward, the challenge is to forge a means (be it through federal legislation or not) of integrating the national, regional, and local resources into a more synergistic, sustainable system of youth sport development based on complementary rather than competing sectors.

The challenge for US sport policymakers is to decide whether market competition allows for coordination in any form. Can a system be devised that preserves the fundamental bases of the federalist/capitalist paradigm while also promoting greater degrees of systemic integration and a more managed athlete development model? The two cases included below help the reader to consider these issues.

SD Case: USA Hockey and the American Development Model

Matthew T. Bowers and B. Christine Green

The relative advantages and disadvantages of the market-driven approach to SD and SFD in the US alluded to in the preceding sections have been articulated in a number of publications (for example, Bowers *et al.* 2011a, 2011b; Green *et al.* 2013), but for the sake of this particular case – in which the tensions between the theoretical concepts and practical implementation are explored – the US can serve as perhaps the most salient, high-profile example of the disconnect that can occur at the national level between theory and practice.

In 2009, USA Hockey, the NSO responsible for ice hockey in the US, became the first national governing body under the US Olympic Committee umbrella to develop and deploy a fully integrated, research-based development model (Thompson 2009). Termed the American Development Model (ADM), this approach borrowed heavily – and explicitly – in its design from the Long-Term Athlete Development (LTAD) model developed in the Canadian context (Balyi *et al.* 2013). The ADM website notes that 'LTAD principles are being utilized [*sic*] by over 100 different sport federations and government health ministries from countries around the globe and LTAD principles have been used in successful hockey playing nations like Sweden, Finland and the Czech Republic with very positive results' (ADM 2015). Given the widespread adoption of the LTAD and its research-based principles of development, it is not surprising that the model was adopted in other national contexts; however, the pervasiveness of the pro-market, anti-intervention approach to sport development in the US means that the ADM represents a monumental step towards linking theory and practice.

Even though the ADM has been in use by the US for over five years at the time of this writing, there has been shockingly little scholarly attention to its design, implementation or evaluation. Other than a few passing references in other sport development texts, a brief paper on how the ADM improves physical activity rates during practices (Kanters *et al.* 2014) and a recent article written by the lead designer of the ADM, Ken Martel (2015), the vast majority of the information on the ADM comes from USA Hockey itself. As a result, most of the information describing the program can be accessed from the website provided in the further resources listed below. The ADM website offers a broad range of information for youth, parents, coaches and administrators, and contains detailed practice plans, explanations of athlete progression through the system and answers to virtually any question that someone might have about how the model operates. As laudable as the program is, the purpose of focusing on the ADM in this particular case is narrower than a simple explanation of how *or* why it works; instead, our focus is on understanding the intersection between how (practice) *and* why (theory) it works.

According to Martel (2015), USA Hockey began its efforts to overhaul the development system by starting with research and determining how the theoretical understanding of development could inform the design of their new program. Specifically, Martel elected to ground the emerging framework in two models that both aim to promote the SD in a manner that also serves athletes' positive, healthy development *through* sport (SFD): the LTAD (Balyi *et al.* 2013); and the Developmental Model of Sport Participation (Côté and Lidor 2013). In particular, the LTAD provided much of the backbone of the ADM programming, as USA Hockey (2014: 7) notes that 'The ADM, through the utilization [*sic*] of LTAD principles, allows us to integrate training, competition and recovery programming with relation to biological development so that we can fully get at a kid's potential'. In delving into the research that undergirds the LTAD, USA Hockey found that the adult-driven rhetoric surrounding the importance of elite competitions beginning at very young ages – such a prevalent feature of youth sport in the US – is misguided and often overemphasises the value of formal games (cf. Bowers and Green 2013). As the organisation notes:

> One of the first things that USA Hockey did when beginning this project was to look closely at the statistics related to player development – specifically, the skill development time each player has when in both a practice setting and a game setting. When viewed from the perspective of how kids learn the number of repetitions of specific skills and situations that occur in practice versus a game, we quickly learned where players have a chance to develop the most: practice. So a model was created

that valued practice and proper training above all else. This isn't to say that the ADM is about taking the fun out of hockey, quite the contrary. Practices can and should be fun, especially if the kids are all playing together and having a blast with a game that they love. The more they play it, the better chance that they'll love it. And when you combine a passion for the game with increased puck time, kids will start to excel at it. Play, love, excel. That's the ADM.

(ADM 2015: 6)

While USA Hockey distilling the ADM down to 'play, love, excel' offers a nice, succinct marketing tag line, 'play, love, excel' actually offers far more than just a catchy phrase. In fact, this tag line represents exactly what lies at the essence of this chapter: praxis. 'Play, love, excel' is decades of research into both child development and sport development being converted into a practical approach to sell this new vision for sport to an always sceptical American sport consumer. If children are robbed of the opportunity to enjoy the sport at a young age ('play'), they will struggle to develop long-term commitment ('love') and will be less likely to reach their potential as athletes ('excel'). Although that may seem like a conclusion so intuitive that it should not require research to reach it, the frustrating reality is that very few sports in the US – for the reasons described in the preceding section – adhere to even these basic principles (Bowers and Hunt 2011). In many ways, USA Hockey is serving as a true test case in the US: if the ADM can prove successful for this sport, the likelihood of it being adopted by other sports increases dramatically. At stake is not only the future of sport for generations of young athletes, but also the future willingness of a system that resists coordination to utilise theories of development to inform the design of its sports policies and programs.

Further resources

USA Hockey American Development Model website: www.admkids.com

Case study extension activities

1 Explore the USA American Development Model website as noted above. Draw up three columns with headings Play, Love and Excel. From the resources presented on the website, provide examples of how each is delivered and record them in the table that you have developed.
2 Choose an SD development program that you are familiar with in your own country. Does it include elements that can be categorised as play, love and excel? Compare and contrast your program to the USA Hockey program.

SFD Case: Major League Baseball's RBI program

Matthew T. Bowers and B. Christine Green

Major League Baseball (MLB) governs the highest level of professional baseball in the US and also operates multiple not-for-profit, SFD programs. The league's most prominent SFD initiative is called the Reviving Baseball in Inner Cities (RBI) program. The mission of the RBI program is 'to use baseball and softball and the power of teams to provide inner city youth with opportunities to play, learn, and grow, inspiring them to recognize their potential and realize their dreams [*sic*]' (Berlin *et al.* 2007: 86). In essence, it is a longitudinal program that aims to provide academic and athletic support to children growing up in economically disadvantaged inner-city areas. What makes the RBI program unique among peer programs (for example, the National Football League's Play 60 program and the NBA's Read to Achieve program, see the glossary in this book) is that the league's SFD ambitions actually align quite strategically with its SD needs.

While ice hockey in the US undergoes a massive, theory-driven overhaul to its entire development system, baseball has been less willing to embrace changes and adapt its approach. Consequently, although pronouncements of baseball's demise are generally overstated, its popularity has stagnated and is beginning to trend downward (Fisher 2015). Its historical place in the pantheon of iconographic American culture is one of the sport's most important strengths from a sport development standpoint; however, the 'tether of tradition' (cf. Chalip and Scott 2005: 61) has also made it difficult for baseball to evolve at the same rate that other sports have evolved. This lack of evolution – or the more rapid evolution of other sports – has contributed to disparities in participation rates between different populations. Perhaps most prominently, Major League Baseball has faced declining participation numbers among African-American athletes since a high of 19 per cent of the league's total players in 1986; in fact, only 8.3 per cent of players on Opening Day rosters in 2014 were African American (Kepner 2014).

Naturally, then, it behoves MLB to develop stronger inroads to the African-American athlete population, so a program such as RBI would seem an apt mechanism to be able to leverage an SFD initiative towards SD gain. What is perhaps most fascinating about this situation, however, is how laissez-faire MLB's approach to managing the sport development aspect of this program has been. In the US, coordination of athlete development pathways has historically been left to the market to manage, with the consequence in this instance of leaving a program such as RBI on a proverbial island and relegated to serving public relations needs over those of SD. MLB has identified a need to increase baseball participation rates among African-Americans and has developed a program aimed at supporting inner-city youth, yet the problem and the solution have been organisationally disconnected from one another to the point where SD and SFD are functioning in a mutually independent way with little to no coordination of efforts. Even decades into the program, there were only mere trickles of athletes who participated in the RBI program being drafted into the league (Czerwinski 2007). That is not to say that there has not been impact; only that the impact, in true American fashion, was left to occur naturally rather than in a systematic, coordinated sport development approach.

The RBI program continues to make substantial contributions to improving the lives of inner-city youth (Platt 2008). For example, in 2007, Richard Berlin, the Executive Director of the Harlem (NY) chapter of RBI, boasted:

> Now fifteen years old and with an annual budget exceeding $2.7 million, a well-functioning board of directors, and an experienced, professional staff, Harlem RBI is poised for future success. Its model youth development programs garner much support from a growing number of institutional and individual supporters who believe in the program model and understand that while baseball and softball are powerful hooks, the real game is about learning and growing.
>
> (Berlin *et al.* 2007: 87)

For an SFD program that operates under the umbrella of a major professional sports league, the language used by Berlin to describe the program is particularly stark. While the Harlem RBI program utilises the MLB brand, its funding structure – as is common in the US – requires that each chapter raise its own funds to support programming (Berlin *et al.* 2007). In turn, this creates disconnect between the local actors, who exist as much in competition with one another as in coordination, and it certainly reinforces the disconnect between the league office and individual chapters of the program.

This is not the end of the story, however, and there is an interesting sport development twist. In 2009, Major League Baseball (2015) launched the Urban Youth Academy (UYA) initiative, a program that sounds quite similar to the ongoing RBI program: 'As a not-for-profit organization [*sic*], the UYA aims to set the standard for baseball and softball instruction, teach and educate in Urban America, and enhance the quality of life in the surrounding communities' (MLB 2015). The difference, however, appears to be in the fact that the function of the program is not simply to promote the SFD goals like RBI, but primarily to improve the on-field performance of urban youth: 'Our coaching staff consists of highly experienced baseball and softball personnel. We specialize [*sic*] in fundamental instruction by way of open workouts. Our workouts give members practical and theoretical training on the fundamentals of the game' (MLB 2015). In essence, it would seem that MLB understood that the structure and function of the RBI program was not adequately addressing the SD issues of the organisation, and rather than reboot an otherwise reasonably successful SFD program, MLB decided to create a complementary SD program, albeit in a format that remains confusingly similar to RBI.

From an SD standpoint, the early returns from the UYA seem to be demonstrating that the closer connection to the actual development pathways of the sport is paying dividends. As Fordin (2013) notes, 'The Urban Youth Academy has already made a huge impact on the draft, with hundreds of players with ties to one of the four facilities being selected over the last eight years. Carlos Correa, the top player taken in last year's draft, came from the Urban Youth Academy in Puerto Rico'. Although less aggressive than the systemic overhaul of USA Hockey's ADM, the pivoting of MLB to tacitly acknowledge the importance of creating clearer pathways between SD and SFD programs represents another enormous shift for sport development in the US. If one of the major professional leagues is identifying an issue with athlete recruitment, retention and transition within a participant population – in this case, African-Americans – and taking organisational steps to leverage SFD programming to achieve SD ends, then that bodes well for the future of sport development in the US – in spite of all the cultural and structural impediments to coordination.

Further resources

MLB Urban Youth Academy: http://mlb.mlb.com/community/uya.jsp
MLB Reviving Baseball in Inner Cities:
http://web.mlbcommunity.org/index.jsp?content=programs&program=rbi

Case study extension activities

1 What are the advantages of linking SD and SFD programs for MLB?
2 Choose a sport that you are familiar with. What programs does this sport offer that can contribute to both SD and SFD for the sport? What opportunities does this sport have to create synergies between SD and SFD efforts?

SUMMARY

This chapter has introduced the reader to a discussion of the role that theory can – and should – play in sport development. It began with a brief introduction to major theories informing SD and SFD before transitioning into a more nuanced interpretation of the tensions surrounding these dual aims. The US was used as a contextual frame for understanding the tensions complicating the use of theory to inform practice – or praxis, as we have come to know it – and the tensions inhibiting the interconnectedness between programs designed to promote SD and SFD. Although the US is a unique context in that it has traditionally eschewed sport development as it is theorised and practiced around the globe, the example cases discussed – USA Hockey's ADM and MLB's transition from the RBI program to the UYA – both represent remarkable steps in the advancement of sport development, both in the US and around the world. The tensions and barriers to praxis are real and manifest themselves differently depending on the national context, but the research into sport development continues to expand and the results are already being implemented at the highest levels.

DISCUSSION QUESTIONS

1 Can you provide examples where theory has informed SD and/or SFD practices in your country or local context?

2 Can you provide examples where theory has not been used to inform SD and/or SFD practices in your country or local context?

3 This chapter has explored the tensions that create barriers for the implementation of SD and SFD practices and programming in the US. What tensions exist in the implementation of SD and/or SFD practices and programming in your country or local context?

REFERENCES

ADM (2015) 'Frequently asked questions', *American Development Model USA Hockey*, available at: www.admkids.com/page/show/910847-frequently-asked-questions (accessed July 2015).

Balyi, I. (2001) *Sport System Building and Long-Term Athlete Development in British Columbia*, Canada: SportsMed BC.

Balyi, I., Way, R. and Higgs, C. (2013) *Long-Term Athlete Development*, Champaign, IL: Human Kinetics.

Berlin, R. A., Dworkin, A., Eames, N., Menconi, A. and Perkins, D. F. (2007) 'Examples of sport-based youth development programs', *New Directions for Youth Development*, 115: 85–106.

Bowers, M. T. and Green, B. C. (2013) 'Reconstructing the youth sport experience: how children derive meaning from unstructured and organized settings', *Journal of Sport Management*, 27(6): 422–38.

Bowers, M. T. and Hunt, T. M. (2011) 'The President's Council on Physical Fitness and the systematization of children's play in America', *International Journal of the History of Sport*, 28(11): 1496–511.

Bowers, M. T., Chalip, L. and Green, B. C. (2011a) 'Sport participation under laissez-faire policy: the case of the United States', in M. Nicholson, R. Hoye and B. Houlihan (eds), *Participation in Sport: International Policy Perspectives*, Oxford: Routledge, pp. 254–67.

Bowers, M. T., Chalip, L. and Green, B. C. (2011b) 'Beyond the façade: youth sport development in the United States and the illusion of synergy', in B. Houlihan and M. Green (eds), *Routledge Handbook of Sports Development*, London: Routledge, pp. 173–83.

Chalip, L. and Scott, E. P. (2005) 'Centrifugal social forces in a youth sport league', *Sport Management Review*, 8(1): 43–67.

Chalip, L., Johnson, A. and Stachura, L. (1996) *National Sports Policies: An International Handbook*, Westport, CT: Greenwood Press.

Coalter, F. (2007) *A Wider Social Role for Sport: Who's Keeping the Score?* London: Routledge.

Côté, J. and Hay, J. (2002) 'Children's involvement in sport: a developmental perspective', in J. M. Silva and D. E. Stevens (eds), *Psychological Foundations of Sport*, Berkeley, CA: Allyn & Bacon, pp. 485–502.

Côté, J. and Lidor, R. (2013) *Conditions of Children's Talent Development in Sport*, Morgantown, WV: FIT Publishing.

Czerwinski, K. T. (2007) 'RBI program again impacts MLB Draft', *MLB*, available at: http://m.mlb.com/news/article/2019555/ (accessed June 2015).

De Bosscher, V., De Knop, P., van Bottenburg, M., Shibli, S. and Bingham, J. (2009) 'Explaining international sporting success: an international comparison of elite sport systems and policies in six countries', *Sport Management Review*, 12(3): 113–36.

Fisher, M. (2015) 'Baseball is struggling to hook kids – and risks losing fans to other sports', *Washington Post Online*, 5 April 2015, available at: www.washingtonpost.com/sports/nationals/baseballs-trouble-with-the-youth-curve-and-what-that-means-for-the-game/2015/04/05/2da36dca-d7e8-11e4-8103-fa84725dbf9d_story.html (accessed June 2015).

Fordin, S. (2013) 'UYA, RBI programs' impact on Draft continues', *MLB*, available at: http://m.mlb.com/news/article/49669746/ (accessed June 2015).

Green, B. C. (2005) 'Building sport programs to optimize athlete recruitment, retention, and transition: toward a normative theory of sport development', *Journal of Sport Management*, 19(3): 233–53.

Green, B. C. (2008) 'Sport as an agent for social and personal change', in V. Girginov (ed.), *Management of Sports Development*, Oxford: Taylor & Francis, pp. 129–45.

Green, B. C., Chalip, L. and Bowers, M. T. (2013) 'United States of America', in I. O'Boyle and T. Bradbury (eds), *Sport Governance: International Case Studies*, London: Routledge, pp. 20–36.

Green, M. and Houlihan, B. (2008) 'Conclusion', in B. Houlihan and M. Green (eds), *Comparative Elite Sport Development*, Oxford: Butterworth-Heineman, pp. 272–94.

Gulbin, J. P., Croser, M. J., Morley, E. J. and Weissensteiner, J. R. (2013) 'An integrated framework for the optimisation of sport and athlete development', *Journal of Sports Sciences*, 31(12): 1319–31.

Hartmann, D. and Depro, B. (2006) 'Rethinking sports-based community crime prevention: a preliminary analysis of the relationship between midnight basketball and urban crime rates', *Journal of Sport and Social Issues*, 30(2): 180–96.

Johnston, L., Delva, J. and O'Malley, P. (2007) 'Sports participation and physical education in American secondary schools: current levels and racial/ethnic and socioeconomic disparities', *American Journal of Preventive Medicine*, 33(4): S195–S208.

Kanters, M., McKenzie, T., Edwards, M., Bocarro, J., Mahar, M. and Hidge, C. (2014) 'Youth sport practice model gets more kids active with more time practicing skills', *Active Living Research*, 3: 1–4, available at: http://activelivingresearch.org/sites/default/files/Kanters_Brief_PhysicalActivityDuringSportPractice.pdf (accessed June 2015).

Kepner, T. (2014) 'MLB report highlights sobering number of black players', *New York Times*, 9 April 2014, available at: www.nytimes.com/2014/04/10/sports/baseball/mlb-report-highlights-sobering-number-of-black-players.html?_r=0 (accessed June 2015).

Koppett, L. (1994) *Sports Illusion, Sports Reality: A Reporter's View of Sports, Journalism, and Society*, Urbana, IL: University of Illinois Press.

Long, J., Hylton, K., Spracklen, K., Ratna, A. and Bailey, S. (2009) *Systematic Review of the Literature on Black and Minority Ethnic Communities in Sport and Physical Recreation*, Leeds: Carnegie Research Institute, Leeds Metropolitan University.

Lyras, A. and Welty Peachey, J. (2011) 'Integrating sport-for-development theory and praxis', *Sport Management Review*, 14(4): 311–26.

Major League Baseball (MLB) (2015) 'MLB Urban Youth Academy: about us', *MLB*, available at: http://mlb.mlb.com/community/uya.jsp?id=about (accessed June 2015).

Martel, K. (2015) 'USA Hockey's American Development Model: changing the coaching and player development paradigm', *International Sport Coaching Journal*, 2(1): 39–49.

Maxwell, H., Foley, C., Taylor, T. and Burton, C. (2013) 'Social inclusion in community sport: a case study of Muslim women in Australia', *Journal of Sport Management*, 27(6): 467–81.

Olushola, J., Jones, D. F., Dixon, M. and Green, B. C. (2013) 'More than basketball: determining the sport components that lead to long-term benefits for African-American girls', *Sport Management Review*, 16(2): 211–25.

Patriksson, M. (1995) 'Scientific review part 2', in *The Significance of Sport for Society – Health, Socialisation, Economy: A Scientific Review*, prepared for the 8th Conference of European Ministers Responsible for Sport, Lisbon, 17–18 May, Council of Europe Press, Strasburg.

Platt, B. (2008) 'MLB's RBI program enters 20th year', *MLB*, available at: http://m.mlb.com/news/article/2387908/ (accessed June 2015).

Schulenkorf, N. (2012) 'Sustainable community development through sport and events: a conceptual framework for sport-for-development projects', *Sport Management Review*, 15(1): 1–12.

Sotiriadou, K., Shilbury, D. and Quick, S. (2008) 'The attraction, retention/transition, and nurturing process of sport development: some Australian evidence', *Journal of Sport Management*, 22(3): 247–72.

Sparvero, E., Chalip, L. and Green, B. C. (2008) 'United States', in B. Houlihan and M. Green (eds), *Comparative Elite Sport Development*, Oxford: Butterworth-Heinemann, pp. 242–71.

Thompson, H. (2009) 'American Development Model: high performance, high ideals', *USA Hockey Magazine*, available at: www.usahockeymagazine.com/article/2009-02/american-development-model-high-performance-high-ideals (accessed June 2015).

USA Hockey (2014) 'American Development Model guide', *ADM Website*, available at: http://assets.ngin.com/attachments/document/0042/7978/USA100001-NewspaperRev3_2013.pdf (accessed June 2015).

Wu, J., Liang, L. and Yang, F. (2009) 'Achievement and benchmarking of countries at the Summer Olympics using cross efficiency evaluation method', *European Journal of Operational Research*, 197(2): 722–30.

SECTION 2

Policy and international differences

CHAPTER 3

International sport development

Laura Misener and Kylie Wasser

INTRODUCTION

With the rise of the SFD sector, international sport organisations have increasingly become part of setting the agenda for the international SFD movement. These organisations, which have typically focused on the agenda of traditional sport development (moving up the ladder of participation to high performance, see Chapter 5), have reoriented their internal agendas towards an emphasis on the outcomes and possibilities of involvement in sport. In particular, international governing organisations (IGOs), such as the International Olympic Committee (IOC), that were once reluctant to be part of the agenda have now taken on influential roles with increased ties to the UN and have become a strong voice in setting the agenda for international SFD (Darnell 2012; Hayhurst 2009). This change in focus by international governing bodies has resulted in a number of concerns about the nature of this involvement and the control that such organisations take in guiding a sector that has largely flourished as a result of locally based development activities. There are tensions between global forces, pushing particular ideologies of sport and development, and local understandings of issues and concepts; there are instances where sport is used by international organisations to further assert global dominance, sometimes contrary to the interests of those at the local level. For example, international organisations' strategic foci may differ markedly from those of local organisations and communities, but their greater organisational power and resources can serve to eclipse local-level understandings, focus and desired outcomes. The power held by these international organisations to force their way into local development activities demonstrates the processes and outcomes of globalisation.

In this chapter, we focus on the theoretical notion of globalisation and the global-local nexus to demonstrate how international governing bodies are increasingly becoming involved in local development-related activities, further exacerbating the power differentials inherent in globalisation. It is through this lens that we interrogate the international development agenda that is focused often on macro-level outcomes at the expense of locally based social change. This, we argue, results in problems about ownership, sustainability and relevance.

However, we also demonstrate the possibility of using sport to achieve broader social change by examining examples of a number of international governing organisations that have long been involved in the development agenda – before the term sport for development was coined.

OUTLINE OF THE CHAPTER

We begin our chapter by focusing on the concept of globalisation, and more specifically the global-local nexus. In recent years, we have noted profound changes in international development that have seen the focus move away from local community well-being and community development issues, towards a focus on accumulating resources and capital for the purposes of competition. This perspective will ground our discussion about the ways in which global forces inhere power struggles in the sport development sector. We use two examples of international sport governing bodies' agendas for sport for development to demonstrate how this shift towards competition and resource accumulation has yielded particularly narrow understandings of the outcomes of success.

After completing this chapter, you should be able to:

- define globalisation and the global-local nexus as it applies to sport development;
- differentiate between SD and SFD in global and local contexts;
- understand the interplay between transnational organisations and localities;
- critically examine the influence of organisations such as the UN and IOC on SFD policies and regulations; and
- interrogate the pro-Olympic agenda in tensions of the sport and development movement.

THE GLOBAL-LOCAL NEXUS AND ITS IMPACT ON SOCIETY

The modern sport landscape is bound up in an interconnected network of inter-dependencies with multiple dimensions and is continuously shaping and being shaped by our changing global environment (Maguire 2011). With rapidly changing communication and transportation technologies, a shrinking of both time and space has occurred to connect people, places, cultures and economies around the world. Individuals' beliefs, knowledge, identities and actions have become intertwined, intersecting across countries and continents rapidly, if not immediately (Maguire 1994).

Globalisation is frequently used to describe these interconnected processes, and its definition has been debated and contested across various academic disciplines. The definition most appropriate for our understanding describes globalisation as a set of interrelated processes occurring on a global scale where actions in one part of the world can have distinct and immediate consequences in another part of the world (Appadurai 2000; Kellner 2002). These processes connect the multidirectional movements of people, practices, customs, money and ideas, and involve a series of power balances involving class, gender and ethnic relationships and a complex interweaving of interdependencies between them.

Important in understanding globalisation and the impacts are the moderators of *scope* and *intensity* (Sassen 1998). Scope refers to the range of globalisation effects on a worldwide scale, while intensity refers to the rate at which global processes are becoming dominant. Certainly, these impacts differ on a number of variables such as culture, locality and so on. Also related to globalisation are the terms *internationalisation* and *transnationalisation,* jargon previously used that attempted to encapsulate the complexity of globalisation at the time. Internationalisation is the process that took place during the 1960s and 1970s whereby companies that were originally situated in one location expanded globally (for example, NFL International, Super Rugby); as a result, international economies have become increasingly interwoven through international trade. Transnationalisation refers to the process by which companies subvert, and ultimately contribute to the deconstruction of, the nation state as a result of their cross-border operations; transnational companies own and control international stock and resources, and are sometimes referred to as stateless companies (for example, Nike, Starbucks, Coca-Cola). While these terms can assist in dissecting the different factors crucial to the understanding of globalisation and related processes of the dominance of particular corporate ideologies, they do not accurately depict the *intensification* of worldwide relations at the very core of globalisation.

Another way of understanding globalisation is to view the linkages and interconnections between states and societies as factors that significantly impact events, decisions and activities in quite distant parts of the globe. While these factors affect individuals and communities at the local level, they also have serious implications for regional, national and global communities. The interconnected relationship between the global, local and those in between is referred to as the *global-local nexus* (illustrated in Figure 3.1): the intersection of processes that affects and is affected at all levels. The relationships between the intersections become increasingly crucial to comprehend as global processes dramatically shape the local processes. Consider, for example, the proliferation of multinational corporations such as Starbucks, Nike or Coca-Cola that have influence and often crowd out small, locally based companies.

Important to note is that individuals within the local level still have the power to resist notions of global influence on local processes, particularly as related to development. This

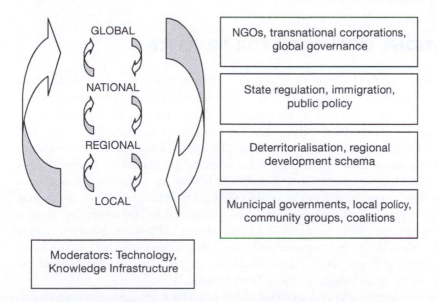

FIGURE 3.1 The global-local nexus

ability to act on our own power is often referred to as *agency*; all individuals have agency, within their own abilities, to make free choices (Giddens 1984). However, societal structures exist that regulate both who is able to negotiate their power and how they are able to do so. This negotiation is increasingly complex in the context of global processes. Marginalised individuals all have power, but they must negotiate the complexity of structures in order to access their agency. When local individuals exhibit their agency by thwarting global influence on local processes such as policy, they are said to demonstrate resistance. This is particularly salient for SFD-related activities, which are typically focused on socially excluded or disadvantaged members of society who lack the skills, knowledge and resources to access these structures.

The impacts of globalisation on the local become increasingly alarming when examining notions of identity, as individuals become bound up by global projects (for example, Right to Play), which influence locally based identities and ideologies. Although individuals do not have one fixed, unchanging identity, the dynamic interweaving of levels of the global-local nexus results in multiple identities along the lines of class, gender and ethnic dimensions (Maguire 1994). Swyngedouw (2000) has introduced the concept of the *glocal* to represent the unique interplay that is being created through the influence of globalisation on local processes. The concepts of the global-local nexus and glocal relate to the notion that local communities are increasingly competing in a neocapitalist environment on global scale. As a result, there have been some profound changes in local development where the focus has moved away from concerns surrounding local community well-being and community development issues to a focus on accumulating resources and capital for the purposes of competition and the promotion of global harmonious development. The globalisation process – in and of itself – causes diverse, fluid and unpredictable global flows or consequences, and in our modern society it is further evident that HIC perceptions, ideologies and conduct have influenced the shaping of many aspects of international cultures, including sport (Maguire 1994).

IMPLICATIONS OF THEORY FOR PRACTICE

We now turn to the SFD sector to examine the contrasting concepts of both sport development and sport for development. As indicated in Chapter 1, sport development (SD) refers to the improvement of programs for those involved in organised sport, including physical infrastructure such as facilities and institutions for athletes, coaches, officials and administrators alike (Green 2005). The very purpose of SD is to enhance both sport participation and performance; it has been led internationally in recent years by the IOC's Olympic Solidarity Commission, which reinvests broadcast revenues into sport development programs across the world (Kidd 2008). Primary foci for these sport development programs include coaching education, equipment and infrastructure. In comparison, SFD programs aim to fulfil non-sport-related social objectives, most commonly pursuing the UN's Millennium Development Goals (UN Inter-Agency Taskforce on Sport for Development and Peace 2003). These broad overarching goals provide most of the rationale driving the organisations in the SFD movement.

In their various forms, SFD organisations and policies have brought benefits to numerous children and youth, regardless of how underfunded, uncoordinated or unregulated these efforts may have been at times. These organisations and policies can be classified into four categories (Guillanoti 2014):

- governmental organisations – for example, the UN Inter-Agency Taskforce on Sport for Development and Peace;
- non-governmental, not-for-profit organisations – for example, international- and national-level NGOs involved with SFD projects such as Right to Play;
- private sector institutions and private donors – for example, large organisations that fund SFD activity such as Coca-Cola or Nike; and
- campaign groups and social movements – for example, some sport-focused NGOs or campaigning movements such as the Clean Clothes Campaign or Football Against Racism in Europe (FARE).

Against this background, it is noted that the future of the SFD sector will be largely determined by the interrelationships and further development of the aforementioned categories and their unique priorities and agendas. Government organisations, including intergovernmental agencies, national governments or ministries of sport, as well as local government at state, county or regional levels, must be noted for facilitating and overseeing the majority of sport for development projects, as they have evident power, resources and often long-term goals (Dudfield 2014). The varying levels of government intervention and interaction are reflective of the global-local nexus, and highlight the complexity represented by the presence of various levels of power and influence. Clearly, the intentions and outcomes of projects developed by governments at different levels are influenced by scope and scale in terms of their reach and effectiveness.

Theories of globalisation are wide-ranging in their definitions and beliefs, but for the most part the focus lies in the narrowing of global corporate strategies increasing the flow of information and resources across nations (Brysk and Shafir 2004); a similar narrowing of focus has been noted in sport for development as a result of transnational processes that serve to prioritise specific strategies and outcomes, not necessarily aligned with those that are the most locally relevant. The UN has already been mentioned for its notable influence and authority within the SFD sector, but the IOC has furthered its influence by obtaining official UN General Assembly's (UNGA) recognition in 2014 (IOC 2014a). This is particularly alarming with regards to our previous discussion about power in the context of globalisation, and demonstrates the blurring of conventional understandings of nation, rights and citizens belonging to a nation state. With transnational organisations such as the IOC gaining increased control and influence over international policies, local governments may have decreased control over SFD initiatives occurring within their limits. Accordingly, transnationalism – referring to 'the horizontal and relational nature of contemporary economic, social, and cultural processes that stream across spaces' (Ong 1999: 4) – means that organisations such as the IOC, with significant amounts of structural power and the ability to exercise that power, will increasingly have influence over SFD-related processes across the globe. The nature of this influence generates an asymmetrical social process, providing reason for the diminishing contrasts among SFD programs in their design and functioning. The result of these processes is that SFD programs tend to become *top-down* in nature as they are designed, administered and executed by government officials, promote the same value structures and fail to adequately account for local culture and context.

APPLICATION OF THEORY TO PRACTICE

The realms of SD and SFD are evidently not without their own individual complexities, but what is the overlap between the two concepts? More specifically, how do they intertwine in the global-local nexus? The following case studies further outline and discuss the relationship between SD and SFD and the globalised agenda influencing both.

Case Study 1: the International Paralympic Committee (IPC)

Laura Misener and Kylie Wasser

The formal governing body of what could be considered the *Paralympic Movement* is the International Paralympic Committee (IPC). Founded in 1989, the IPC's vision is broadly to 'enable Paralympic athletes to achieve sporting excellence and inspire and excite the world' (IPC 2014a). While it is typically understood that the IPC is under the overarching influence of the Olympic umbrella, the IPC has taken a different approach as an international sporting body in its structures, programs and development processes.

Prior to the establishment of the IPC, sport for individuals with a disability was mainly a means of rehabilitation organised by able-bodied individuals. Highlighting that organisers were able-bodied is crucial in this circumstance in order to recognise that able-bodied individuals' understanding of disability is likely to greatly differ from those of the athletes they represent. It is this *ableist* mindset that has driven the direction of parasport towards the able-bodied marker of success: high performance sport. In the past few decades, the IPC has utilised its position and influence as an international governing body of sport for persons with a disability to promote a particular ideology surrounding disability sport that moves away from the medical model of disability, which emphasises physiological impairment, towards one of empowerment for athletes that views the physical impairment as occurring within a constraining social context.

The IPC has thus been credited with shaping the discourse surrounding parasport towards a more inclusive model of impairment that recognises the structural constraints that serve to disempower and exclude people with a disability. As evidence, the IPC's 2011–2014 Strategic Plan outlined an increased commitment to influencing change regarding disability related policies and aspirations to 'build a bridge which links sport with social awareness thus contributing to the development of a more equitable society with respect and equal opportunities for all individuals' (IPC, cited in Blauwet and Iezzoni 2014). The Agitos Foundation was created by the IPC in 2012, and is located in Germany within the IPC offices (IPC 2014b). The foundation's purpose is to assist in the development and promotion of physical activity and sport programs, parasport, for those with a physical disability, while also focusing on the Paralympic Movement's primary global objective of moving towards a more inclusive society (IPC 2014b). This is accomplished mainly through the Agitos Foundation's Grant Support program, which funds and assists many international parasport projects.

Each year, the Agitos Foundation forms partnerships with organisations across the world to implement and grow sport for people with a disability. While this is seen as an SFD program, the focus of the programs offered is on continuing to strengthen parasport development and build capacity for parasport internationally. Eligible applicants include National Paralympic Committees (NPCs), and regional sport organisations or international federations (IF). The programs selected are based upon qualifying criteria and a given focus area each year, typically emphasising parasport development. Projects are encouraged to involve multiple countries and are assessed based on the relevance of the project to the Paralympic Movement, the quality of project design and implementation and possible impact and dissemination of results.

We now bring our discussion back to the global-local nexus, whereby we can consider the impacts of the IPC and Agitos Foundation at both the local and international levels. Offering support to NPCs and regional sport organisations represents the IPC's commitment to local development, as these organisations have increased understanding of local communities' needs and resources. The IPC's history is rich in examples of local development, as understanding and knowledge of parasport differs across countries, regions and communities. As a result, there is much more interplay between levels of the nexus, as the local and regional context can influence the national and international domain of parasport. Many more interdependencies exist between levels, in essence demonstrating the need for local and regional levels held by global organisations such as the IPC to dictate and drive the Paralympic agenda. The global Paralympic field can thus be recognised as a non-rigid, horizontal spanning of organisations varying in their level of authority to focus on sport development processes.

The IPC and the Agitos Foundation hope to increase and strengthen sport for individuals across the world through their sport development efforts. Through locally developed ideas, the IPC has successfully shaped the global field of sport for individuals with a disability, hopefully demonstrating the benefits of interplay of the global-local nexus to other domain of sports. One particularly salient example is the Paralympic Games themselves. This is a showcase of elite-level athletes promoting an ideology of empowerment through sport. While the narrative of empowerment evoked in the Paralympic Games has been heavily criticised for its distancing from the everyday realities of persons with impairments, it is one of the only global opportunities to showcase disability sport and promote the identities and possibilities for persons with disabilities in a highly recognisable arena. The Games can have a significant impact on local understandings of disability, attitudes towards persons with disability, and locally developed programming for the promotion of parasport (IPC 2013).

Further resources

The Agitos Foundation: www.paralympic.org/agitos-foundation
Team Canada Parasport: www.paralympic.ca

Case study extension activities

1 You are writing a letter to your local government official to promote a parasport development initiative in your home town. Examine several sport-for-development initiatives/organisations in your local, regional or national neighbourhood that focus on disability. Present an argument for why your parasport project should be prioritised above others and why it will benefit the community. Use the following questions to guide the development of your argument:
   • What is the emphasis of these programs? Sport development or sport for other outcomes?
   • What is the relevance of these programs for the local community?
   • What are their differences at the organisational, financial and program level?
   • What are the benefits associated with the similarities and/or differences of the initiatives or programs?
   • Which of the initiatives has the best possibility for influencing policy regarding health, physical education or disability?
2 Compare two SD or SFD initiatives that have been implemented in your city, region or country. Choose one that has been successfully implemented and another that was not successful. Consider the following questions:
   • What infrastructure, people, systems or organisations were in place for either of these organisations?
   • In your opinion, what led to the success or unsuccessfulness of the initiatives?

Case Study 2: the International Olympic Committee (IOC)

Laura Misener and Kylie Wasser

The International Olympic Committee (IOC) is arguably one of the most recognisable, influential and powerful sporting organisations in the world. While the IOC has worked to establish and promote Olympic values through its charity work, it only became officially involved in SFD matters in the early 2000s.

The IOC first ventured into SFD with Olympic Aid in 1992 – a charity conceived by the Lillehammer Olympic Organising Committee to provide assistance to war-torn countries. In 2002, Olympic Aid was renamed Right to Play, with the specific focus of children's development programs, advocacy for children's rights and the promotion of a child's right to play and physical activity. Right to Play has since moved away from its association with the IOC and is no longer restricted to assisting with Olympic-associated countries; nowadays, programming is focused on developing countries across the world. Without Right to Play, the IOC lacked SFD presence and looked for new ways to remain globally influential in the SFD sector. More recently, the IOC has become involved in the SFD movement with programs such as the Olympism for Humanity Alliance associated with its International Olympic Academy programming (Olympism4Humanity 2015).

The IOC's International Relations Committee (IRC) was formed to facilitate and promote relationships between IOC and benefitting organisations such as NOCs, governments and public authorities (IOC 2014b). Together, the IRC and its partners 'develop and implement a range of projects using sport as a tool for development' (IOC 2014c) for projects aimed at SFD outcomes, such as local socio-economic development and humanitarian assistance. The IOC Director of International Cooperation and Development oversees the IRC, who then assists in overseeing the strengthening of existing dialogue and cooperation between all development partners (IOC 2014b). Relationships are crucial, but they only represent a fraction of the IRC's responsibilities, as the broader focus is to ensure long-term development of sport globally, while utilising the aforementioned partnerships to assist in international humanitarian efforts (IOC 2014c). These efforts include HIV/AIDS prevention, healthy lifestyle promotion and, perhaps most prominently, collaboration with UN agencies to further their sport for development and peace initiatives (IOC 2014c). The IOC has retained Observer Status with the UN since 2009 and, while it lacks the ability to vote or propose resolutions, it is recognised as a sovereign entity with a powerful position at the table (IOC 2014a).

The IOC's development arm was created and organised by individuals in high-income countries (HICs) for those considered less fortunate in low-income countries (LICs) and lower middle-income countries (LMICs), in much the same way that Right to Play has evolved (Darnell 2007). What emerges as a consequence is several privileged nations dictating the direction of various SFD programs, usually focusing on national priorities (that is: high performance sport). Referring to the global-local nexus described above, we see little interplay between the various levels and more of a top-down approach from the global powers of the IOC to local organisations and communities receiving aid. Such a scenario can be problematic, as without input from local communities, 'sport-led efforts to pursue international development do not necessarily promote or recognise the agency of marginalised people and may actually perpetuate geopolitical flows of capital and resources to rich countries and away from the poor' (Darnell 2013: 1003). In other words, countries are externally positioned as being in need of SFD efforts that have become a donation rather than being an avenue for participation for local community members. This can diminish intended positive impacts, most notably the empowerment associated with participation in community matters (Schulenkorf 2012). In addition, the promotion of Olympic values can act as a form of neocolonialism in promoting foreign culture and values without recognising, appreciating or encouraging local culture and uniqueness. These negative effects on host nations for development efforts are rarely portrayed in depictions of SFD initiatives, with the focus often remaining on the beneficial charitable outreach of the organisation.

In April 2014, the IOC and the UN officially united under a memorandum of understanding (MOU), to use the power of sport to promote peace and economic development (IOC 2014a). Both leaders of each organisation agreed that 'Olympic principles are United Nations principles' (IOC 2014a), a questionable quote considering the abundance of scandals and investigations surrounding the IOC (for example, Salt Lake City 2002; Sochi 2014). In addition, November 2014 saw the UN officially recognise the independence and autonomy of sport through the support of the IOC's mission of leading the Olympic Movement (IOC 2014c). These monumental events have assisted in galvanising the relationship of the UN and IOC, so that the IOC has become the most recognised global sport organisation in the world, wielding significant levels of power. These two events – the IOC-UN signing of an official MOU and the UN's official recognition of the independence and autonomy of sport – have further increased the legitimacy and authority of the IOC on all sporting matters internationally, as well as within the UN's own senate. Holding increased influence – comparable to a sovereign nation – the IOC has the power to influence and drive SFD agendas around the world. Since the IOC and UN have closely aligned SFD goals, the IOC can influence the direction, policies, delivery and the overall future of SFD projects, without the disclosure of hidden motives or agenda. Although the IOC has not been granted a seat at the UNGA for voting purposes, the abundant resources of the IOC make it an increasingly attractive partner for the UN moving forward.

The increase of authority and legitimacy given to the IOC further intensifies the power of the organisation in sovereign nation states involved in the Olympic bidding and hosting process. While the IOC does not currently have a mandate affecting sovereign states outside its own fields (IOC 2014a), the increased control of a transcontinental organisation is significant when considering the influences of globalisation. As discussed, global organisations are increasingly dictating priorities for local communities. In this case, the superlative influence of the IOC sets the agenda for SFD efforts around the globe, not only perpetuating the IOC's intentions, but also possibly delivering more harm than good in its top-down design as a result of failure to acknowledge, appreciate and prioritise local culture and capacity. The IOC and its SFD efforts can therefore be recognised as a form of neocolonialism, including their promotion of culturally situated and informed correct values and understandings originating in HICs (Darnell 2012). In short, the path set by IOC in LICs and LMICs increasingly influences and directs these countries' national priorities at the expense of the localised understanding of context and bottom-up development efforts that empower local people and are founded on internal cultural and regional understandings. Frankly, we argue that the IOC is dictating the path of global flows and interdependencies by becoming interwoven throughout the global level of the broader sporting global-local nexus, thereby increasing IOC influence over multiple levels and domains, leaving little opportunity for local communities to have a meaningful voice in their own matters.

Further resources

United Nations: www.un.org/sport
Olympic Movement: www.olympic.org

Case study extension activities

1 What international sport organisations are involved with your city? How have they influenced sport locally and globally?
2 Discuss the implications of the IOC and UN partnership for your country, region or city's policies regarding sport.
3 Examine the partnerships existing between your branch of local, regional and federal government and international sport organisations. Are the organisations considered transnational? What impacts have these organisations had on the respective community(ies)?

SUPPLEMENTARY EXERCISE

Examine an SFD initiative from the IPC or IOC (for example, Olympism4Humanity) and discuss its challenges and opportunities, taking into account the global-local nexus perspective.

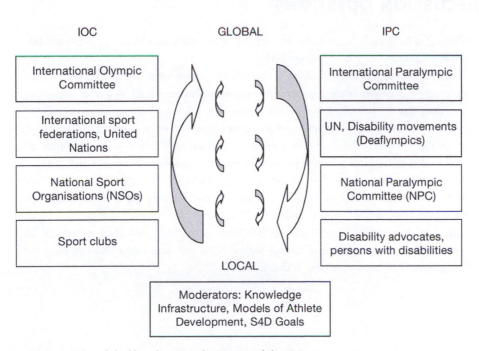

FIGURE 3.2 The global-local nexus, the IOC and the IPC

SUMMARY

This chapter has demonstrated how international non-governmental organisations (INGOs) and international governing bodies (IGOs) are influencing the direction and appearance of sport development and SFD, furthering the concept of how global influences are impacting local communities and issues.

For illustrative purposes, in Figure 3.2 we have placed the two cases in the context of the global-local nexus, as discussed throughout this chapter. The emphasis here in each of the cases is demonstrative of the differing influences of the global on the local, and vice versa. In the case of the IPC, the movement has been fuelled by local and differing understandings of disability, alongside a global agenda for increasing participation opportunities. The way in which the Agitos Foundation has offered grants at the national level has meant that the state agenda and the local context of disability are regarded as significant, which is argued to be critical for the development and local contextualisation of parasport within the local sport development agenda. On the other hand, the increasing might of the IOC, evidenced by its positioning within the UN, provides a demonstration of the way that power at the global level can be exercised, risking a failure to take into account local forces – resistance or otherwise – as a result of differing ideologies around sport development.

DISCUSSION QUESTIONS

1 Utilising a bottom-up approach, which type of initiative would be more beneficial/ appropriate to your city – SFD or SD?
2 Select an SFD organisation/initiative/project and position it on the global-local nexus. Indicate the multiple levels of influence from the global, national, regional and local, and describe the interplay that occurs within.
3 Examine the global-local interplay between the organisations of a sport of your choice, including the hierarchy and influence of organisations, any resultant impacts on local/regional/federal government and the overall impacts on local and global sport.
4 Discuss the implications of the UN recognising additional international organisations in the future. What impact could this have on your federal/regional/local government and their respective policies?
5 How has your view of sport, SD or SFD been previously limited or narrowed by organisations or transnational corporations? How can you assist in increasing the transparency of organisations' SFD agendas?

REFERENCES

Appadurai, A. (2000) 'Grassroots globalization and the research imagination', *Public Culture*, 12(1): 1–19.

Blauwet, C. A. and Iezzoni, L. I. (2014) 'From the Paralympics to public health: increasing physical activity through legislative and policy initiatives', *PM & R: The Journal of Injury, Function, and Rehabilitation*, 6(8): S4–S10.

Brysk, A. and Shafir, G. (eds) (2004) *People Out of Place: Globalization, Human Rights and the Citizenship Gap*, London: Routledge.

Darnell, S. C. (2007) 'Playing with race: Right to Play and the production of whiteness in "Development through Sport"', *Sport in Society*, 10(4): 560–79.

Darnell, S. C. (2012) 'Olympism in action, Olympic hosting and the politics of "sport for development and peace": investigating the development discourses of Rio 2016', *Sport in Society*, 15(6): 869–87.

Darnell, S. C. (2013) 'Orientalism through sport: towards a Said-ian analysis of imperialism and "sport for development and peace"', *Sport in Society*, 17(8): 1000–14.

Dudfield, O. (2014) *Strengthening Sport for Development and Peace National Policies and Strategies*, London: Commonwealth Secretariat.

Giddens, A. (1984) *The Constitution of Society*, Cambridge: Polity Press.

Green, B. C. (2005) 'Building sport programs to optimize athlete recruitment, retention, and transition: toward a normative theory of sport development', *Journal of Sport Management*, 19(3): 233–53.

Guillanoti, R. (2014) 'Sport for development and peace policy options in the Commonwealth', *Strengthening Sport for Development and Peace National Policies and Strategies*, London: Commonwealth Secretariat.

Hayhurst, L. M. C. (2009) 'The power to shape policy: charting sport for development and peace policy discourses', *International Journal of Sport Policy and Politics*, 1(2): 203–27.

International Olympic Committee (IOC) (2014a) 'IOC and UN Secretariat agree historic deal to work together to use sport to build a better world', *Olympic.org*, available at: www.olympic.org/news/ioc-and-un-secretariat-agree-historic-deal/230542 (accessed June 2015).

International Olympic Committee (IOC) (2014b) 'International Relations Commission', *Olympic.org*, available at: www.olympic.org/international-relations-commission (accessed June 2015).

International Olympic Committee (IOC) (2014c) 'Historic milestone: United Nations recognises autonomy of sport', *Olympic.org*, available at: www.olympic.org/news/historic-milestone-united-nations-recognises-autonomy-of-sport/240276 (accessed June 2015).

International Paralympic Committee (IPC) (2013) 'Agitos Foundation 2013 Grant Support Programme projects', *IPC*, available at: www.paralympic.org/sites/default/files/document/131205163439717_2013+agitos+foundation_gsp+projects.pdf (accessed June 2015).

International Paralympic Committee (IPC) (2014a) 'Agitos Foundation – who we are', *IPC*, available at: www.paralympic.org/agitos-foundation/who-we-are (accessed June 2015).

International Paralympic Committee (IPC) (2014b) 'Agitos Foundation – what we do', *IPC*, available at: www.paralympic.org/agitos-foundation/what-we-do (accessed June 2015).

Kellner, D. (2002) 'Theorizing globalization', *Sociological Theory*, 20(3): 285–305.

Kidd, B. (2008) 'A new social movement: sport for development and peace', *Sport in Society*, 11(4): 370–80.

Maguire, J. (1994) 'Preliminary observations on globalisation and the migration of sport labour', *The Sociological Review*, 42(3): 452–80.

Maguire, J. (2011) 'Sport and globalisation', *Swiss Academy for Development*, available at: http://assets.sportanddev.org/downloads/81__sport_and_globalisation.pdf (accessed May 2015).

Olympism4Humanity (2015) 'About us', *Olympism4Humanity*, available at: http://olympism4humanity. com (accessed May 2015).

Ong, A. (1999) *Flexible Citizenship: The Cultural Logics of Transnationality*, Durham, NC: Duke University Press.

Sassen, S. (1998) *Globalization and Its Discontents: Essays on the New Mobility of People and Money*, New York: The New Press.

Schulenkorf, N. (2012) 'Sustainable community development through sport and events: a conceptual framework for sport-for-development project', *Sport Management Review*, 15(1): 1–12.

Swyngedouw, E. (2000) 'Elite power, global forces, and the political economy of "glocal" development', in G. L. Clark, M. P. Feldman and M. S. Gertler (eds), *The Oxford Handbook of Economic Geography*, Oxford: Oxford University Press, pp. 541–58.

UN Inter-Agency Taskforce on Sport for Development and Peace (2003) *Sport for Development and Peace: Towards Achieving the Millennium Development Goals*, available at: www.un.org/wcm/ webdav/site/sport/shared/sport/pdfs/Reports/2003_interagency_report_ENGLISH.pdf (accessed July 2015).

CHAPTER 4

Sport development policy

Iain Lindsey, Ruth Jeanes and Henry Lihaya

INTRODUCTION

Sport development has, in its relatively short history, shared a strong association with sport policy in both practical and academic domains. In terms of practice, sport development (SD and SFD) can be considered as (one component of) the operationalisation or implementation of sport policy. Many important features of what is known as the policy process are considered significant to the practice of sport development; for example, decisions regarding the distribution of resources, partnership working and evaluation. On the other hand, the academic study of sport development (SD and SFD) has commonly been underpinned – both explicitly and implicitly – by theories, concepts and frameworks drawn from the interrelated disciplines of policy and political analysis.

OUTLINE OF THE CHAPTER

Our purpose in this chapter is to examine policy as it relates to sport development in different international contexts. In particular, we investigate the focus of sport policies and the factors affecting their formulation. There has been a considerable expansion in such studies of sport policy since Houlihan decried the lack of academic interest in the field in 2005. While a significant proportion of studies are focused on single countries or specific geographic areas, there has also been an increased interest in international comparison of sport policies (for example, Bergsgard *et al.* 2007; Green and Collins 2008; Nicholson *et al.* 2010).

International studies of sport policy are important for – at least – two reasons. First, as Houlihan (1997: 3) indicates, international comparison provides 'an opportunity to avoid the policy mistakes of other countries and an opportunity to identify potentially successful policies which may be imported'. Especially in elite SD, and in elements of SFD, such policy transfer and learning has become commonplace. Second, examining the similarities and differences in sport policies in different countries helps to identify the factors that are important in shaping such policies. We hope that this chapter will indicate something of the value of international comparison by offering case studies of sport policy in England, Australia and Tanzania.

After completing this chapter, you should be able to:

- recognise the value of theory in guiding the analysis of sport policy;
- consider the value of international comparison in analysing sport policy and development;
- identify reasons why sport may or may not be accorded policy priority in different contexts; and
- understand how the context of sport policy influences different aspects of SD and SFD.

THEORIES AND FRAMEWORKS FOR POLICY ANALYSIS

Analysis of sport policy, as it relates to SD and SFD, commonly utilises what are termed as meso-level frameworks. Compared to macro-level theories, which largely concern broader distributions of power in society, meso-level frameworks lend themselves to analysis of the policy process in particular sectors, such as sport. There are numerous meso-level frameworks that may be suitable for the analysis of sport policy. Common examples include the advocacy coalition framework (ACF), multiple streams framework, path dependency and punctuated equilibrium. Considering the application of such frameworks to sport policy enables the identification of important aspects of the process of making sport policy, and consequently the implementation of SD and SFD. It is not our purpose here to review or apply specific meso-level frameworks; those seeking fuller explanations of these would be advised to read Paul Cairney's (2015) excellent 1,000-word introductions or Houlihan (2005) for assessment of the value of four such frameworks to analysing sport policy. In the remainder of this section, drawing on contributions from different meso-level frameworks, our focus will be on identifying how and why there may be policy change and continuity, and also considering the influence of institutions and individuals on the process of policymaking.

Change and continuity in policy

In line with authors from mainstream policy analysis, Houlihan and Lindsey (2013) indicate that it is necessary to analyse policy over a timescale of at least ten years in order to be able to appropriately identify the extent of change or continuity. The balance between emphasising policy continuity or change differs across different meso-level frameworks. For example, continuity in policy is a feature of literature on path dependency, whereas the multiple streams framework emphasises the potential volatility in policymaking. The punctuated equilibrium framework suggests that periods of relative continuity in policy are punctuated by dramatic changes at particular times.

Meso-level frameworks also vary according to the extent that they suggest that policymaking is a result of (reasonably) rational decisions or a consequence of alignment of (somewhat) random occurrences (Hill 2005). While frameworks that suggest that policymaking is an entirely rational process now have little support, others suggest that policymakers may have a bounded rationality based on a necessarily incomplete level of knowledge and understanding (Parsons 1995). For example, the ACF suggests that learning from existing policy will contribute to the development of subsequent policies over the medium term. Similarly, frameworks that could be more broadly classified as emphasising incremental policy change emphasise how ongoing and relatively minor alterations are made based on analysis of policy approaches and impacts. In contrast, the multiple streams framework suggests a greater degree of randomness with the acceptance of new policies based on a potentially coincidental alignment of factors across three streams of problem recognition, suggested policy solutions and politics. In examining policy in sectors such as sport, therefore, an awareness of the potentially different ways in which policies come to be developed is necessary.

The preceding debates about the likelihood of policy change and extent to which it may be (ir)rationally oriented are underpinned by the identification of different influences on the policy process in various meso-level frameworks. The punctuated equilibrium and multiple streams frameworks, among others, emphasise that major policy change may occur as a result of events; for example, changes of government or particular crises – including, potentially, moral panics. That such events may not be specific to a particular policy area, such as sport, indicates the importance of *spillover* between different policy areas. Other than as a result of events, policies that spill over may be ones – such as privatisation – that are based on broader governmental agendas or may involve the more specific adoption of particular approaches from other areas; for example, the use of types of public information campaigns in public health. These different types of policy spillover suggest the alternative influences of governmental ideologies or policy evidence. This recognition brings us back to the fundamental importance – identified to various degrees in almost all meso-level frameworks – of the potentially differential impact of knowledge, ideas, values, beliefs and interests on policymaking. All of these different elements may originate independently from – or through interaction between – different institutions and individuals, and it is to the influence of such *policy actors* that we now turn.

The influence of institutions and individuals in policymaking

Much policy analysis starts from a position that identifies government as central to the policymaking process. Beyond such a relatively simplistic assertion, it remains important to analyse the extent of government involvement – as well as its degree of influence – in particular policy areas. Moreover, in line with relatively recent, broader debates about governance (see Bevir 2011), some meso-level frameworks are particularly useful in examining the ways in which particular branches of (central and local) government interact with other organisations and institutions from both the voluntary and private sectors in the policy process. The ACF suggests that groups of such policy actors form different *advocacy coalitions* that align around particular interests and it is the interaction – and potential primacy – of these coalitions that is important in determining policy. The Policy Networks Framework suggests that policymaking in a particular area may be characterised by loose and diverse issue networks or tighter and more exclusionary policy communities (Marsh and Rhodes 1992). Although the division between issue networks and policy communities may not be as clear-cut in reality, the consequences may be that the latter results in more stable policy than the former (Marsh 1998).

Policy actors are not limited to institutions and organisations and the influence of particular individuals is recognised in some meso-level frameworks. While some individuals may have importance due to their status or position, others may utilise particular skills to a greater extent within the policy process. The multiple streams framework highlights the potential of *policy entrepreneurs* to bring about policy change through efforts to align each of the three streams of problems, policy and politics. Similarly, *policy brokers* can play a role in mediating between different advocacy coalitions in a particular policy area.

IMPLICATIONS OF THEORY FOR PRACTICE

These theoretical considerations can – and have – been used to identify and illuminate important aspects of sport policy. Generally, it can be suggested that sport has gained increasing importance both for institutions of global governance (for example, the UN) and across different countries (Nicholson *et al.* 2010). In large part, this increasing salience has been on account of the view that sport can contribute to broader objectives of government. Such a generalisation indicates that sport policy is not made in a vacuum, but influenced by spillover from policies and concerns in other areas of government. Nevertheless, in terms of sport policy, it remains vital to specifically distinguish the level of salience of sport across different countries, the particular aspects of sport that are promoted in policy and the factors that have been influential in such trends. For example, elite sport development has often been promoted across different nations on account of politicians' desires to promote national identity at home and abroad (Nicholson *et al.* 2010). On the other hand, the policy priority given to youth and grass-roots sport development has been more variable both over time and across countries, and has been aligned with a greater range of issues, such as health, crime and education, that may be more locally oriented and dependent.

Many of the factors that are theoretically identified as influencing policy can similarly be readily identified as important in sport development, both SD and SFD. For example, there has been increasing examination of sporting mega-events (SMEs), not only in terms of the systems of elite sport development designed to bring national success (SD), but also in the way such events may be leveraged to produce other sport development legacies (SFD) (for example, Gratton and Preuss 2008). Globally, the influence of particularly prominent individuals on sport policy, for example Sepp Blatter of FIFA, has often been debated (for a further and recent examination of this organisation and individual, see Pielke 2013). Across various aspects of sport policy, there have also been increasing calls for – but also critiques of – the use of evidence to underpin the development of sport policy. Fred Coalter has been a particularly strong voice in such debates and has provided comprehensive reviews of evidence (for example, in Coalter 2007), while also being critical of sport policy made on the basis of poorly informed beliefs (Coalter 2013).

Institutions and organisations are also particularly important to both the making and implementation of sport policy. Like other policy sectors, there is typically a wide array of institutions engaged across the different dimensions of sport development. As each institution comes with its own interests and resources, examination of their different influences on sport policy and its implementation is necessary. Beyond the governments of different countries, institutions such as national sports councils and national governing bodies of particular sports may both be influential in – and affected by – sport policies. The existence, extent and arrangement of an array of more local bodies – including regional and local tiers of government, private and voluntary clubs and schools – can also be influential on the scope and orientation of sport policy. As a result, alongside the consideration of sport policies in different countries, our analysis of the following case studies will focus in significant part on how sport policy takes into account various factors, including the interaction between different institutions.

Case Study 1: England

Iain Lindsey, Ruth Jeanes and Henry Lihaya

The year 1990, which saw John Major installed as British Prime Minister, has been commonly cited as a significant turning point in sport policy in England (Houlihan and Lindsey 2013). Before this point – certainly under the previous premiership of Margaret Thatcher – sport had largely been neglected by government. Initially, it was mainly John Major's personal interest in sport and prime ministerial intervention that led to sport gaining in importance as a policy concern for government, and this salience has continued across subsequent Labour (1997–2010) and Coalition (2010–2015) governments. However, this overall trend masks variation in the extent to which different aspects of sport development have been prioritised and also the more nuanced shifts in approaches to achieving policy objectives, as well as the reasons for these variations.

Elite SD has been a consistent policy priority across the period since 1990. Perhaps John Major's single most long-standing achievement as Prime Minister was the instigation of a National Lottery, from which a significant proportion of funds has been used to develop an elite sport development system and support individual athletes towards success in the Olympic Games and other international events. The approach to elite sport development has been based, initially, on policy transfer from other successful countries and, more recently, on an increasingly evidence-based approach to both prioritisation of sports and preparation of athletes. In line with the path dependency framework discussed above, the prioritisation of elite sport can be seen as continually self-reinforcing. As funding has led to success, this has not only strengthened the position of those policy actors lobbying for elite sport, but has also made it harder for politicians to remove or reduce support for elite sport. As an example, even in a time of wider governmental austerity, budgets for elite sport were increased after the success of British athletes at the London Olympic Games in 2012. More generally, support for elite sport development has been further fortified by Britain hosting a number of other high-profile international events, despite weak evidence pointing to the wider benefits of this hosting policy when first instigated in the Labour government's Game Plan policy document (Department of Culture Media and Sport/Strategy Unit 2002).

Alongside elite sport, youth sport development has become an increasingly prominent aspect of policy. Green (2007) argued that the focus on young people could be regarded as a social investment in terms of addressing long-term policy concerns such as: rising obesity across the population; addressing crime and antisocial behaviour; and improving educational attainment. In this regard, Baronness Sue Campbell, then Chief Executive of the Youth Sport Trust, was very influential as a *policy entrepreneur* in convincing government ministers of the potential benefits of using sport to address these wider agendas (Houlihan and Green 2006). As a result, the Labour government began investment of substantial funds into school and youth sport, although there were some continued debates and variations in implementation as to the use of funds to support physical education (PE), competitive sport or physical activity, respectively. Initially, the advent of the Coalition government in 2010 appeared to signal a change in policy, with the Education Minister, at first, unilaterally removing previous Labour government funding. However, the increasing strength of a network of youth sport advocates – including high-profile elite athletes – led to the reinstatement of funding, albeit through a new system of distribution. As with elite sport, this development indicates the importance of considering factors – such as public opinion and advocacy – that can constrain any attempts at significant policy change.

In contrast to elite and youth sport development, (adult) community sport has been at best an inconsistent aspect of policy, if not one treated with a degree of indifference. One reason put forward for this lack of policy priority has been the absence of a single organisation or collective lobbying to promote grass-roots sport agendas (Houlihan and Lindsey 2013). While National Lottery and government funding have been made available through Sport England, there have been relatively frequent changes of strategy, both in terms of the types of organisations in which funding has been invested and also in terms of the extent to which strategy has been focused on increasing participation in competitive sport and/or other forms of physical activity. That increases in levels of participation have been marginal at best could be suggested to be both a factor and a consequence of this inconsistent policy. In this regard, grass-roots sport policy can be seen as the opposite side of the coin from the continuity associated with elite sport success.

In terms of institutions and organisations involved in sport policy, there has long been a recognition of the inefficiencies resulting from the fragmented nature of the English sport system (Roche 1993). Linked with its broader modernisation agenda that affected many different policy sectors, the previous Labour (1997–2010) government made substantial efforts at reform of the sport system. As a result, a process of modernisation was enforced on the national sport agencies – Sport England and UK Sport – that resulted in a weakening of their earlier independence from government. In turn, NGBs have been increasingly subject to direction from both national sport agencies, although for particular NGBs this has been accompanied by greater funding. By contrast, local government has become increasingly marginalised both in policy and in terms of receiving funding and, as a result, its position as a key provider of local sporting provision may well be dissipating (King 2014). In a further example of inconsistency in approaches to achieve policy objectives, the Labour government's attempts to overcome fragmentation in school and youth sport by instigating local partnerships across England was subsequently undermined when the incoming Coalition government reoriented funding directly to individual primary schools.

Further resources

Sport England: www.sportengland.org/
UK Sport: www.uksport.gov.uk/
Youth Sport Trust: www.youthsporttrust.org/

Case study extension activities

1 What are some of the implications for sport program participants as a result of the changes in strategy; for example, from the abandonment of the partnership model in favour of funding directly to primary schools?

2 What do you think of the policy of funding SD and SFD sport development programming via a national lottery? Present an argument for funding sport via tax revenue; relate your argument to the ways in which the funding affects policy.

3 Consider the role of policy entrepreneurs, policy advocates and policy brokers. What are the strengths and weaknesses inherent in the system?

Case Study 2: Australia

Iain Lindsey, Ruth Jeanes and Henry Lihaya

Australia is frequently described as a sporting nation (Hoye and Nicholson 2010), but this perception of a fanatical sporting country has not necessarily translated into coherent sport development policies. The Australian Sports Commission (ASC) provides the federal lead for sport development and performs this role predominantly in conjunction with National (NSA) and State Sporting Associations (SSA), as well as local government. The challenges of this structure will be discussed further in the case study.

The election of Gough Whitlam's Labor party in 1972 marked a significant development for sport policy in Australia (Hoye and Nicholson 2009). Until that point, the government had provided limited intervention in sport beyond federal government funding for Olympic participation; at the state level, governments supported life-saving and water associations, and local government financed sports grounds and facilities (Cashman 1995). Whitlam's election saw the introduction of a tourism and recreation portfolio that provided grants for community sports and for the improvement of recreational facilities. In 1973, the Australian Federal Government commissioned the Bloomfield Report on community recreation and, then, in 1975, the Coles Report, which investigated Australia's declining performance at elite tournaments. This period marked an important milestone: for the 'first time in the history of Australia, sport was politically recognised as an integral part of Australians' lives and received federal government attention' (Sotiriadou 2009: 854).

The 1980s saw the introduction by federal government of two key national sports governance bodies, the Australian Institute of Sport (AIS) in 1981 – whose remit was to develop high performance sport – and the ASC in 1985, which performed a wider mandate, ranging from providing ministerial advice on overall sport development to consulting with federal and state authorities. In 1989, the two organisations were merged, with the ASC as the overseeing body. The ASC, to the current day, is 'charged with achieving two outcomes: an effective national sport system that offers improved participation in quality sports activities by Australians and excellence in sports performances by Australians' (Hoye and Nicholson 2009: 235). However, Magdalinski (2000) argued that the establishment of these bodies mainly demonstrated federal government's priority on restoring Australian performance in elite sport. Right up until the present day, whenever policy documents have featured links between elite and grassroots participation, the priority has repeatedly been given to elite development over grass roots (Green and Collins 2008).

Rhetorically, national sport policies have also focused on mass participation, SFD programs and increasing participation within particular target groups; for example, women, culturally and linguistically diverse communities, indigenous people and people with a disability. However, such policies have received a fraction of the funding awarded to elite SD, making the translation of policy rhetoric into SFD practice difficult in reality (Hogan and Norton 2000). While during the 1980s and 1990s federal assistance led to the 'emergence of a systematic, planned and increasingly scientific approach to developing the countries' elite athletes' (Green and Collins 2008: 232), the development of community sport was significantly more ad hoc. Consequently, there has been limited change in levels of sports participation over the previous three decades (Stewart *et al.* 2004). During the 2000s, increasing levels of obesity and declining levels of physical activity led to greater connections between health and sport development policy, particularly focusing on children and young people. The Active After-School Communities program, funded by federal government, was developed in 2005 with the aim of increasing participation among primary school children; research suggests that it has not led to a significant 'long term shift in the prioritisation of grassroots sports as an area of sport policy development' (Green and Collins 2008: 235). The program has evolved to become Sporting Schools; according to the ASC, the revised program 'forms an important part of the ASC's future participation strategy with a focus on kids and young adults and improving the capacity of NSOs to develop and grow' (AIS 2014). Its impact on grass-roots policy development is yet to be determined.

A further potentially significant turning point for sport development policy arose with the change of government in 2007. The incoming Labor government commissioned an independent report of sport development and policy that was eventually released in 2009 and is known as the Crawford Report. The report was critical of the ongoing focus on elite sport; it outlined the need for more coherent national sport development participation policies, greater investment in grass-roots sport and a broadening of understanding of what constitutes sporting success in sport development policy. In other words, it called for increased investment in SFD, as opposed to SD. For a period of time, it appeared as though fundamental shifts in Australian sport policy would arise from the report, in particular a rebalancing of the elite/grass-roots focus. However, the perception that Australia performed poorly at the 2012 Olympics has resulted in a retreat by federal government to traditional approaches, with continued heavy investment and priority placed on elite sport development, as the latest national strategy, 'Australia's winning edge 2012–2022', (ASC 2012) demonstrates.

While within this brief overview we have focused on sport development policy and direction at the national, federal level, it is important to acknowledge that Australia's sports governance system is complex and there can be significant deviation among states and sporting codes as to how policy is developed. Each state has a sport and recreation division within state government and, while this department receives federal funding via the ASC, the state government may also decide to invest further funding, potentially leading to greater investment in sport development in some states compared to others. Additionally, each sport has its own national and state association, with links between the two varying across states. Although national organisations provide funding for state bodies, the latter still have a reasonable amount of autonomy to develop their own sport development policies and priorities. It is not unusual for state sporting associations (SSAs) to lead in the development of policies and approaches, which are then adopted at national level (Magee *et al.* 2013). At the very local level, minimal funding is provided for voluntary sports clubs and as a result these tend to operate independently. Although frequently charged with the task of operationalising SFD policy, there are limited structures in place for the various sports governance agencies to support clubs, which, again, reduces capacity to achieve broader policy goals for grass-roots participation in sport. As illustrated previously, the elite system has far greater connections and cohesion between the main stakeholders of NSAs, the ASC and the AIS.

Further resources

Australian Sports Commission: www.ausport.gov.au/
Australian Institute of Sport: www.ausport.gov.au/ais

Case study extension activities

1 Examine the current funding on offer in your country to support sport development. How does the level of funding on offer for elite sport (SD) compare with that on offer for participation? What are the implications of this funding arrangement?
2 Why do you think the Australian government prioritises sport policy?
3 Do you think that funding and policy should be directed towards SD or SFD, or can you conceive of a funding arrangement and policy setting that addresses all kinds of sport development?
4 Examine the ASC's funding strategy for 2015–2016 (ASC 2015). What do you note about how funding will be allocated to minority sports? What impact might this have on the development of these sports? Present an argument in favour of or against the funding decision.

Case Study 3: Tanzania

Iain Lindsey, Ruth Jeanes and Henry Lihaya

As in the other two case studies, the wider context of the east African country of Tanzania is significantly influential on the country's sport policy. In global comparison – and in contrast to the case studies from England and Australia – Tanzania suffers from significant poverty, being placed 196th of 213 countries in terms of GNI (World Bank 2015) and 159th of 187 countries according to the broader Human Development Index (UNDP 2014). The difficulties facing Tanzania frame the country's key policy priorities, namely: developing infrastructure; agriculture; industry; human capital; and tourism, trade and financial services (United Republic of Tanzania 2011). Next to the scale of these significant policy issues and priorities, it is unsurprising that sport policy has received extremely limited attention or resources in Tanzania. Reflecting this, Tanzania's sole documented sport policy was published in 1995; prior to this, and subsequently, overarching aspirations that sport organisations may work towards have been lacking.

This is not to say that policy decisions that affect sport have not been made, but the following examples of particular decisions are both a representation and a consequence of the lack of policy value attached to sport. First, responsibility for sport has been passed between various ministries within the Tanzanian Government. At various times since the 1960s, sport has been associated with, for example, Ministries of National Culture and Youth (1961), the Prime Minister's Office (1984), the Ministry of Education and Culture (1990) and the Ministry of Labour, Employment, Youth and Sports (1995) before being currently situated in the Ministry of Information, Youth, Culture and Sport. With different ministries have come different priorities for sport, resulting in a lack of continuity in policy for sport. Second, from 2000 to 2008, national governmental policy precluded the practice of sport in Tanzanian schools in order to prioritise subjects viewed as having greater academic importance. The Tanzanian parliament's assent demonstrates national politicians' collective view that sport is a relatively inconsequential leisure activity. As we will see, the consequences of this policy on school sport continue to affect the development of sport to this day.

The key state agency associated with all aspects of policy and development is the National Sports Council (NSC), which was established by statute in 1967. The stated vision of the NSC is 'to lead Tanzanians towards healthy, active lifestyles and sporting excellence for community development, unity and identity' (NSC 2013). This vision indicates both an aspiration for sport to contribute to wider development and a commitment to a holistic and integrated approach to the development of different aspects of sport. In practice, both challenges to, and consequences of, this holistic vision can be identified.

Within Tanzania, elite sport development receives the greatest share of financial resources. The meagre allocation of governmental budgetary funds for sport is primarily allocated to competing internationally in a small number of sports, such as football, athletics, boxing, netball and Paralympic sport, chosen respectively for their popularity, historical international success and equity reasons. Moreover, the existing profile of, and commercial sponsorship available to, national-level football has the potential to skew overall priorities to a particular aspect of this single sport within Tanzania. Such a distribution of financial resources is common across other African countries (Akindes and Kirwan 2009), as is the use of funds to hire foreign coaches in football and other sports. International influence and elite prioritisation can also be identified in the construction of the first, modern national sport stadium in 2007, catering for football and athletics. Funding for the stadium came equally from the Tanzanian and Chinese governments, as part of growing cooperation between the two countries.

However, in contrast to the other two case studies presented in this chapter, Tanzania has not been successful in international elite sport: the country has not won an Olympic medal since 1980 and, in men's football, has never qualified for the FIFA World Cup Finals. In terms of Tanzanian elite sport policy and development, some specific difficulties can be identified as important. For example, the geographic size of the country, being the 21st largest land mass in the world, presents particular challenges for talent identification. More generally, Tanzania has insufficient resources to support its athletes, develop elite sport expertise or build an elite sport development system to achieve success in an increasingly competitive international context.

Beyond elite sport, the NSC's work to develop participation in sport is predicated on, and subject to, varied rationales and influences. Prioritisation of young people is justified both in terms of talent identification and as a social investment in addressing health. If the latter is an example of spillover from other governmental priorities that would have resonance in other national contexts (Houlihan and Green 2006), there are also examples of alternative influences on priorities in Tanzanian sport. Increasingly, emphasis has been drawn towards encouraging participation among females and people with a disability, both as a result of their wider political importance and as a result of the advocacy, influence and significance of both international and indigenous non-governmental organisations within Tanzania. As a result of the resources that can be garnered internationally by some of these organisations, they have also become increasingly important in the development and delivery of community-based sport programs. Even if some financial support can be secured through international project funding, there remain significant problems in the implementation of sustainable grass-roots sport development.

Concerning implementation, the economic context of Tanzania means that sport infrastructure, in terms of school and community facilities and equipment, is commonly limited. Neither has the sport policy context been supportive of grass-roots sport development: the previous policy precluding sport in schools resulted in an ongoing lack of teachers with expertise in sport or PE, despite the instigation of a National Sports College and the University of Dar es Salaam's degree program in Physical Education and Sport Sciences. Combined with the limited policy support, the limitations of financial, human and infrastructure resources continue to present significant challenges for sustainable sport development in Tanzania.

Further resources

National Sports Council of Tanzania (NSC): http://nationalsportscouncil.go.tz/en/

Case study extension activities

1 What are the possible implications of international investment in SFD projects in Tanzania?
2 How do you think Tanzania's lack of international success has impacted the development of sport policy?
3 What are the long-term implications for sport development in the light of funding allocation based on the popularity of a particular sport?
4 Examine an SFD program in Tanzania; for example, Camps International (2015). What do you note about the way the program is described to potential volunteers? What are the implications of this way of describing the program?

SUMMARY AND CONCLUSIONS

An underpinning understanding of the salience, or importance, of a particular issue is common to most policy analysis. The three case studies in this chapter demonstrate the importance of placing analysis of the policy salience of sport in the broader context of other governmental interests and constraints. In Tanzania, for example, the low salience of sport as a policy issue can significantly be accounted for in terms of the prioritisation of other areas of governmental activity considered more fundamental to the country's development. Nevertheless, notable across all three countries is a degree of continuity over extended periods of time in the overall level of policy priority accorded to sport. This continuity points to a lack of significant overall difference across the political spectrum – but not necessarily among individual politicians – regarding the importance of sport.

This is not to say that there have not been different political and governmental influences on specific aspects of sport policy. Notably, the implications of the switching of responsibility for sport among different government ministries in Tanzania is resonant of similar effects previously recognised by authors who have undertaken more in-depth analysis of sport policy in both England and Australia (Houlihan and Lindsey 2013). A further, significant aspect indicated by our comparative and historical analysis is the shifting agendas and prioritisation in respect of particular dimensions of sport development. In all three countries, a rhetorical commitment to both SFD and SD has been countered by the greater commitment of resources to elite sport development. While generalisations should not be drawn from three case studies, it is possible to identify the relevance of particular factors, including those identified from theory at the start of the chapter, in influencing different aspects of sport policy.

Perceptions of policymakers may align with a *virtuous cycle* (cf. Grix and Carmichael 2012), which has contributed to greater continuity in elite sport development policy in Australia and England especially. In such a virtuous cycle, the input of resources in support of policy may help generate levels of success, which is then presented as necessitating the allocation of further resources to continue such success. Even in the case of Australia, which has lately seen a decline in rates of success, the weight of public opinion and the influence of international competition have contributed to the continued prioritisation of elite sport. The international dimension of elite sport has further implications as comparison between countries in practice – including in England and Australia – has generated knowledge regarding the most effective SD policy and developmental approaches (Houlihan 2009). Implementing such approaches is, however, dependent on resources of a scale that are beyond countries such as Tanzania, which, in comparison, has struggled to compete internationally in the context of the SD undertaken in other, more affluent countries.

The need to consider sport policy developments over a period of time is also demonstrated with regard to grass-roots sport. It can be identified from the case studies that past policy decisions condition and constrain future possibilities. A prime example can be found in the Tanzanian decision in the early part of this century to preclude sport within schools, with this decision continuing to affect capacity for sport development years after a change of policy. Similarly, in England, ongoing changes in the particular policy approaches to grass-roots sport have contributed to a lack of success in increasing sport participation and also, in a potentially *vicious cycle*, a continued lack of enthusiasm among policymakers to provide the drive and stability required for improvements in participation. Examining grass-roots sport policy also helps to identify the importance of advocacy undertaken by different agencies in affecting sport policy decisions. Such advocacy limited potential change in youth sport policy in England. In Tanzania, the advocacy for gender and disability equity in sport development has come, in part, from international and issue-specific, non-governmental organisations, which is representative of the greater influence of such organisations to generate policy spillover in a country such as Tanzania.

In conclusion, the various influences on – and distinctions within – sport policy that have been identified throughout the chapter have important implications for the possibilities of sport development, both SD and SFD, in particular contexts. As well as being demonstrated in other chapters in this book, the influence of policy on sport development is also indicated in literature cited throughout the chapter. Such literature demonstrates the value of meso-level theories and frameworks, as well as international comparison in the analysis of sport policy. Hopefully, this chapter also demonstrates the value of these approaches in developing a more informed analysis of the development of sport policy.

DISCUSSION QUESTIONS

1 How does the overall policy importance/salience of sport vary across these case studies and other countries?
2 Why may different aspects of sport be prioritised differently in countries' sport policies?
3 What are the most important factors that influence the adoption of particular sport policy approaches?

4 How do national sport policies constrain or influence the practice of sport development?

5 How might opportunities for involvement in sport by under-represented groups (for example, people with a disability, females, ethnic minorities) be affected by the context of sport policy in each of the three case studies?

6 What effects do sport policies have on achieving positive outcomes in and through sport?

7 What further investigation and analysis may be valuable in order to answer these questions?

ACKNOWLEDGEMENT

The development of this chapter was supported by a Leverhulme Trust International Networks grant.

REFERENCES

Akindes, G. and Kirwan, M. (2009) 'Sport as international aid: assisting development or promoting under development in Sub-Saharan Africa?', in R. Levermore and A. Beacom (eds), *Sport and International Development*, Basingstoke: Palgrave Macmillan, pp. 219–45.

Australian Institute of Sport (AIS) (2014) 'Sporting schools', *Australian Institute of Sport*, available at: www.ausport.gov.au/participating/news/story_585663_sporting_schools (accessed July 2015).

Australian Sports Commission (ASC) (2012) 'Australia's winning edge', *Australian Sports Commission*, available at: www.ausport.gov.au/_data/assets/pdf_file/0011/509852/Australias_Winning_Edge.pdf (accessed March 2014).

Australian Sports Commission (ASC) (2015) 'Investment announcement 2015–2016', *Australian Sports Commission*, available at: www.ausport.gov.au/supporting/investment_announcement_2015-16 (accessed July 2015).

Bergsgard, N. A., Houlihan, B., Mangset, P., Nødland, S. I. and Rommetwedt, H. (2007) *Sport Policy: A Comparative Analysis of Stability and Change*, Oxford: Butterworth-Heinemann.

Bevir, M. (2011) 'Governance as theory, practice and dilemma', in M. Bevir (ed.), *The Sage Handbook of Governance*, London: Sage, pp. 1–16.

Cairney, P. (2015) '1000 words: key policy theories and concepts in 1000 words', *Paul Cairney: Politics & Public Policy*, available at: https://paulcairney.wordpress.com/1000-words/ (accessed July 2015).

Camps International (2015) 'Sports development in Tanzania', *Camps International*, available at: www.campsinternational.com.au/projects/sports-development-in-tanzania (accessed July 2015).

Cashman, R. I. (1995) *Paradise of Sport: The Rise of Organised Sport in Australia*, Oxford: Oxford University Press.

Coalter, F. (2007) *A Wider Social Role for Sport: Who's Keeping the Score?* London: Routledge.

Coalter, F. (2013) *Sport for Development: What Game Are We Playing?* London: Routledge.

Department of Culture Media and Sport/Strategy Unit (2002) *Game Plan: A Strategy for Delivering the Government's Sport and Physical Activity Objectives*, London: DCMS.

Gratton, C. and Preuss, H. (2008) 'Maximizing Olympic impacts by building up legacies', *The International Journal of the History of Sport*, 25(14): 1922–38.

Green, M. (2007) 'Olympic glory or grassroots development? Sport, policy priorities in Australia, Canada and the United Kingdom, 1960–2006', *The International Journal of History in Sport*, 24(7): 921–53.

Green, M. and Collins, S. (2008) 'Policy, politics and path dependency: sport development in Australia and Finland', *Sport Management Review*, 11(3): 225–51.

Grix, J. and Carmichael, F. (2012) 'Why do governments invest in elite sport? A polemic', *International Journal of Sport Policy and Politics*, 4(1): 73–90.

Hill, M. (2005) *The Public Policy Process*, 4th edn, London: Routledge.

Hogan, K. and Norton, K. (2000) 'The "price" of Olympic gold', *Journal of Science and Medicine in Sport*, 3(2): 203–18.

Houlihan, B. (1997) *Sport, Policy and Politics: A Comparative Analysis*, London: Routledge.

Houlihan, B. (2005) 'Public sector sport policy: developing a framework for analysis', *International Review for the Sociology of Sport*, 40(2): 163–85.

Houlihan, B. (2009) 'Mechanisms of international influence on domestic elite sport policy', *International Journal of Sport Policy*, 1(1): 51–69.

Houlihan, B. and Green, M. (2006) 'The changing status of school sport and physical education: explaining policy change', *Sport, Education and Society*, 11(1): 73–92.

Houlihan, B. and Lindsey, I. (2013) *Sport Policy in Britain*, London: Routledge.

Hoye, R. and Nicholson, M. (2009) 'Social capital and sport policies in Australia: policy transfer in action', *Public Management Review*, 11(4): 441–60.

Hoye, R. and Nicholson, M. (2010) 'Australia', in M. Nicholson, R. Hoye and B. Houlihan (eds), *Participation in Sport: International Policy Perspectives*, London: Routledge, pp. 223–37.

King, N. (2014) 'Local authority sport services under the UK coalition government: retention, revision or curtailment?', *International Journal of Sport Policy and Politics*, 6(3): 349–69.

Magdalinski, T. (2000) 'The reinvention of Australia for the Sydney 2000 Olympic Games', *The International Journal of the History of Sport*, 17(2–3): 305–22.

Magee, J., Jeanes, R., Spaaij, R., Farquharson, K., Gorman, S. and Lusher, D. (2013) '"It costs us to be a diverse sports club": junior sports clubs and provision for young disabled people', paper presented at *Understanding Leisure in a Complex World: Promoting a Critical Leisure Studies, 11th Biennial ANZALS Conference*, 4–6 December 2013, Monash University, Peninsula campus, Australia, unpublished.

Marsh, D. (1998) 'The development of the policy network approach', in D. Marsh (ed.), *Comparing Policy Networks*, Buckingham: Open University Press, pp. 3–20.

Marsh, D. and Rhodes, R. A. W. (1992) 'Policy communities and issue networks: beyond typology', in D. Marsh and R. A. W. Rhodes (eds), *Policy Networks in British Government*, Oxford: Oxford University Press, pp. 249–68.

National Sports Council of Tanzania (NSC) (2013) 'Strategic plan for the years 2013–2022', unpublished.

Nicholson, M., Hoye, R. and Houlihan, B. (2010) 'Introduction', in M. Nicholson, R. Hoye and B. Houlihan (eds), *Participation in Sport: International Policy Perspectives*, London: Routledge, pp. 1–9.

Parsons, D. W. (1995) *Public Policy: An Introduction to the Theory and Practice of Policy Analysis*, Aldershot: Edward Elgar.

Pielke, R. (2013) 'How can FIFA be held accountable?', *Sport Management Review*, 16(3): 255–67.

Roche, M. (1993) 'Sport and community: rhetoric and reality in the development of British sport policy', in J. C. Binfield and J. Stevenson (eds), *Sport, Culture and Politics*, Sheffield: Sheffield Academic Press, pp. 77–112.

Sotiriadou, K. (2009) 'The Australian sport system and its stakeholders: development of cooperative relationships', *Sport in Society*, 12(7): 842–60.

Stewart, B., Nicholson, M., Smith, A. and Westerbeck, H. (2004) *Australian Sport: Better by Design? The Evolution of Australian Sport Policy*, London: Routledge.

United Nations Development Programme (UNDP) (2014) *Human Development Report 2014: Tanzania*, available at: http://hdr.undp.org/sites/all/themes/hdr_theme/country-notes/TZA.pdf (accessed March 2015).

United Republic of Tanzania (2011) *The Tanzania Five Year Development Plan 2011/2012–2015/2016*, available at: www.tzdpg.or.tz/fileadmin/documents/external/national_development_frameworks/FYDP-2012-02-02.pdf (accessed March 2015).

World Bank (2015) 'GNI per capita ranking', *World Bank*, available at: http://data.worldbank.org/data-catalog/GNI-per-capita-Atlas-and-PPP-table (accessed March 2015).

SECTION 3

High performance and community

CHAPTER 5

High performance development pathways

Popi Sotiriadou, Jessie Brouwers and Veerle De Bosscher

INTRODUCTION

Elite or high performance sport development is important because it allows talented athletes to excel in their performances when representing their country at international and world-stage competitions. The sport development pyramid (Eady 1993), which implies that talent emerges from a large base of participants at the grass-roots level, has become inadequate in explaining the complexities of high performance development (Green 2005; Sotiriadou and Shilbury 2009; van Bottenburg 2003). The pyramid portrays sport development as a simple linear process where participants progress directly from one stage to another (Sotiriadou 2013). However, many people participate in a sport without any desire to progress to higher levels of performance (De Bosscher *et al.* 2013; Eichberg *et al.* 1998). Further, there are examples of sports that have high performance systems that do not rely on a broad participation base (De Bosscher and van Bottenburg 2011; van Bottenburg 2003).

Sotiriadou *et al.* (2008: 266) used a definition of sport development that captures its dynamic, convoluted and systematic nature: 'a dynamic process, in which sport development *stakeholder involvement* provides the necessary sport development *strategies* and *pathways* to facilitate the *attraction, retention/transition and nurturing* (ARTN) of sporting participants'. This definition places sport development within the context of systems theory (Midgley 2003) – that is: a process of input-throughput-output – and outlines sport development as a process that is inclusive of stakeholder involvement (input) who provide strategies or policies (throughput) for successful pathways (output). Successful pathways enable and facilitate the attraction, retention/transition and nurturing of participants or athletes within a sport system (Sotiriadou 2013).

Depending on the scope and capacity of a sport system to reach community participants or draw talent, sport development processes – attraction, retention, transition and nurturing – may be targeted towards mass participation or the development of elite athletes, respectively. As discussed in previous chapters, the distinction between mass participation and elite athlete development has led to the conception of the 'development *through* sport' (SFD) and the 'development *of* sport' (SD) to denote the different sport development purposes or desired outcomes (see Chapter 1). The focus in this chapter is on these systems and processes that offer the pathways for SD.

OUTLINE OF THE CHAPTER

This chapter outlines the complexities involved with designing and delivering pathways to elite or high performance. In doing so, the chapter discusses the input of various organisations and people who deliver athlete pathways. Last, comparisons and examples of different sports and practices show the diversity of elite pathways and the variety of policies, strategies and tactics used.

After completing this chapter, you should be able to:

• understand the dynamic nature of sport development that drives the systematic approach to developing athletes;
• recognise the need for diversity in elite pathways depending on sport- and country-related contexts;
• understand the non-linear nature of sport development that allows participants or athletes to enter, exit or re-enter a level of participation within the attraction, retention/transition and nurturing processes;
• understand pathway variations and their implication for elite development; and
• identify the services used to develop elite athletes and the roles of the stakeholders that initiate or implement them.

THE NEED FOR A SYSTEMATIC AND CONTEXT-SPECIFIC APPROACH TO DEVELOPING ELITE PATHWAYS

In most HICs, the processes of shaping and implementing the pathways for high performance athlete development follow a formalised set of steps. For instance, in Australia, the pathway for athlete development for elite swimmers in South Australia (at state level) forms part of Swimming Australia's Athlete Development Pathway (at the national level) and is specified within Swimming Australia's High Performance Strategic Plan submitted to the ASC. The formalisation of elite pathways is not simply required for organisational transparency and efficiency in order to achieve elite athlete success. Rather, it outlines the coordination of resources required to develop high performance athletes and implies the need for a sophisticated approach to developing and implementing high performance development pathways. This sophistication is highlighted through the emergence of professional, specialised staff (Emery *et al.* 2012) and targeted practices (Gould and Carson 2004) considered necessary for successful high performance development pathways. The rugby case study later in this chapter is an exemplar of evolving practice of high performance development, which represents a highly professionalised, competitive and sophisticated way of developing elite athletes.

The increased sophistication and professionalisation of high performance management have led to countries' successes at World Championships and Olympic Games. For example, Australia's success at the Sydney 2000 Olympic Games is the outcome of a systematic, professionalised and formalised, long-term and generously funded elite system that resulted in 58 medals, including 16 gold (Sotiriadou 2009). High performance sport systems of countries, such as Australia in the early 2000s and the UK more recently, have become the benchmark for other aspiring nations to duplicate (Böhlke and Robinson 2009). Such duplication of high performance managerial practices has led to the *homogenisation* of elite sport systems in the hope of emulating elite success (De Bosscher *et al.* 2009; Oakley and Green 2001). However, on many occasions, nations that applied other countries' benchmarks have not achieved the anticipated results. It has been found that a certain level of heterogeneity – variations in elite sport systems and delivery of services to athletes and coaches – is necessary to reflect country- and sport-specific contexts. For example, Sotiriadou *et al.* (2013) studied elite sprint canoe and kayak development pathways in Australia. That study demonstrated that canoeing in Australia has its own specific culture that relates to the talent transfer from surf life-saving to canoeing, driving Australian canoeists' pathways differently to those of European athletes. Although it might seem attractive for some sport managers to copy and adopt other high performance development systems and practices, research suggests that high performance systems and practices are only appropriate as a way of learning about and understanding elite sport pathways (for example, Andersen and Ronglan 2012; De Bosscher *et al.* 2006; Green and Houlihan 2005; Houlihan and Green 2008; Oakley and Green 2001), as best practice in one country may not correspond to best practice in another; simply reproducing benchmark practices is not appropriate (Böhlke and Robinson 2009).

THE NON-LINEAR NATURE OF SPORT DEVELOPMENT AND ELITE PATHWAYS

The development to high performance is far from a linear process (Sotiriadou *et al.* 2008). Participants, athletes and those who undertake other support roles – such as coaches, administrators and volunteers who are involved with sport in various capacities – can enter, exit and re-enter a sport at any development stage. This movement varies according to a number of factors. First, an individual's personal choice impacts the development pathway that they may take. For example, an individual may choose to retire as an athlete yet continue to be involved in the sport through a support role – such as coach, administrator or official. Moreover, an individual may discontinue with one sport in order to take up an alternative sport. Second, the skill level of an individual – that is: capacity to become an elite athlete – may impact the pathway taken. An individual may continue to be involved in the sport at a social or amateur level. Third, the pathway that an individual takes may also depend on the opportunities presented; for example, in terms of access to appropriate facilities and equipment, scholarships, quality coaching, sport science and level-specific training and competitions.

Figure 5.1 illustrates the non-linear nature of sport development pathways that allow participants to enter, exit or re-enter at various levels of participation. The numbers (1–7) in Figure 5.1 reflect these seven pathways of sport development. This non-linear approach to sport development recognises that many people practise a sport without any desire to ascend to a higher level (1). Others, though, given the opportunity and talent, may transition to higher levels of competition (2) and even become elite athletes who reach the top of their athletic career (3). At the end of their careers, some athletes choose to retire and leave the sport system (4). Others re-enter the system as an elite athlete in a different

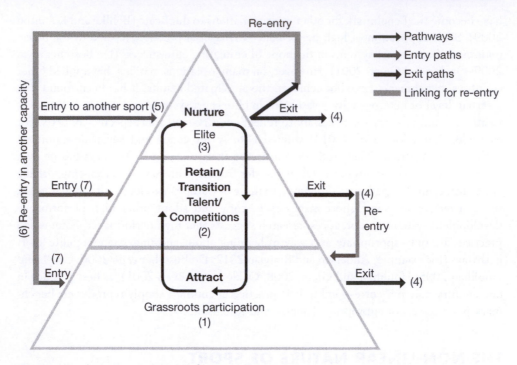

FIGURE 5.1 The seven pathways of sport development

sport (5). For instance, gymnasts can transition to diving, and surf life-savers can take up canoe or kayaking. This may also occur when athletes or participants stop their active participation to work in the system in another capacity, such as coaching, volunteer, media (6), or leave the elite levels of participation and play at grass-roots club or competitions levels (7). The following sections discuss these pathways, along with the stakeholders involved in delivering the pathways to elite success.

HIGH PERFORMANCE PATHWAYS, POLICIES AND PRACTICES

In their description of systems for managing excellence in sports performance, various researchers (for example, De Bosscher *et al.* 2006; Houlihan and Green 2008; Lyle 1997; Oakley and Green 2001) acknowledge the importance of sport development programs, facilities, competitions and other factors for the structural progression of athletes. While some research calls these factors delivery mechanisms (Lyle 1997) or elite development strategies and tactics (Sotiriadou *et al.* 2008), other studies refer to them as elite sport policies that lead to international success (De Bosscher *et al.* 2006). The intertwined nature of the terminology used to express the same phenomenon is grounded on the simple fact that policies give direction for strategies to be shaped and enacted. Sport development strategies are the delivery mechanisms and actions taken by the sport development stake-holders for successful elite pathways.

As Figure 5.2 outlines, there is a blend of services – strategies or tactics – that facilitate successful sport development processes and open up the pathways to elite success. These services – throughputs – include sport development or talent development programs tailored to specific sports and levels of participation within the ARTN. In addition, initiatives support athletes during their careers – scholarships and sport coaches – and after their careers – psychologists and tertiary education programs. Importantly, in addition, events – such as training camps – and competition structures – reflecting athletes' development levels – as well as facilities, technologies and equipment are required to train, compete and maintain the momentum of development and success.

Figure 5.2 also shows the various organisations and key people involved in the delivery of elite pathways. These organisations include governments, NOCs, NGBs, clubs and universities. People include coaches, volunteers, umpires, administrators, managers, high performance managers, sports scientists, sport medicine staff, family members and even friends. Part of a strategic approach to managing high performance sport is ensuring that the sport recruits, retains and supports staff, coaches and high performance managers capable of delivering the outlined throughputs and the sport's or the athlete's key

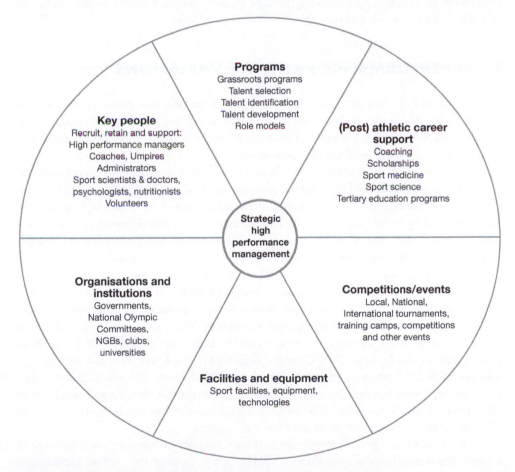

FIGURE 5.2 HP services – strategies, policies and people – for success

performance indicators (KPIs). Protecting athlete welfare and team cohesiveness becomes a priority and results in sports taking steps to protect the integrity of running a professional team. A case in point that attracted media attention was during the Glasgow 2014 Commonwealth Games when Athletics Australia suspended the team's head coach Eric Hollingsworth in a unanimous decision over his criticism of sprinter Sally Pearson. The decision was made in order to protect the integrity of the athlete and the sport and spare the team from unnecessary distractions during competition. Empowered by the decision and support, Pearson ended the week with a gold medal in the 100 m hurdles, publicly claiming that the suspension of the national head coach made the team happier (Gleeson 2014).

Noticeably, as Figure 5.2 shows, at the heart of the successful delivery of throughputs and practices is a strategic approach to managing high performance sport (Sotiriadou 2013; Sotiriadou and De Bosscher 2013). Indeed, after comparing the elite sport systems of nine countries, Houlihan and Green (2008: 276) concluded that 'the manifestation of business like values is evident in the establishment of performance targets, strategic planning, selectivity (of athletes and sports targeted for funding usually focused on the best medal prospects) and a growing trend of funding decisions based on the likelihood of achieving a return on investment'.

HIGH PERFORMANCE PATHWAY VARIATIONS

Several factors influence elite pathways and result in pathway variations. As this section outlines, when these variations are explored from a macro level, we see differences in the ways nations develop elite pathways. However, when we explore elite pathway variations at a micro level, sport-specific differences emerge.

At a macro level, the Olympic success of athletes or teams depends increasingly on the performance capacity of the national system and its effectiveness in 'using all relevant resources for the benefit of elite sport. Some nations do not have this option, as they are compelled by more basic needs, and others simply establish different priorities' (De Bosscher *et al.* 2006: 186). Consequently, many countries with sport systems in the nascent stages of system development – for example, Malaysia, Iraq and Bosnia and Herzegovina – cannot invest in sport policies to improve their high performance sport development pathways (Robinson 2013). Robinson and Minikin's (2011, 2012) research on elite sport systems in LICs and LMICs shows that most national federations in these countries are unable to support high performance sport development. The implications of such inability are demonstrated in Olympic Games representation. For example, 205 countries participated in the London 2012 Olympic Games, 41 sent fewer than five athletes, 95 sent fewer than 10 athletes, 85 won a medal and 120 did not. The research and policy focus on improving the performance capacity of national sport systems and processes of HICs has clear implications for LICs and LMICs with less-developed sport systems in terms of their capacity to compete in an international context.

High performance sport development pathways may vary depending on the nature of a sport. For instance, early specialisation sports such as gymnastics – whose participants start at a very young age – need to modify their policies, programs and subsequent pathways to meet the changing needs of athletes as they move towards high performance. In comparison, diving is typified by low grass-roots participation with little requirement for early specialisation; gymnasts and divers, then, require different high performance management, as a result of their age differences, which must be taken into account when designing elite pathways.

High performance sport development pathway variations are also evident depending on a sport's professionalised status. Golf and tennis, for instance, are professional sports that operate in a system where private coaches and/or academies offer alternatives to the publicly provided athlete development pathways. The case study on elite development pathways in tennis later in this chapter is a reminder of the complexities of elite pathways.

THE INTEGRATED NETWORK OF HIGH PERFORMANCE PARTNERS

The success of elite athletes is a result of a variety of factors, including talent, dedication to training and competition, as well as the coordinated efforts of various stakeholders who support athletes during their journey to high performance (Sotiriadou *et al.* 2008). As Figure 5.3 illustrates, government bodies, public and private sport and non-sport organisations and a host of individuals or groups of people are involved in a network of partnerships that facilitates elite pathways. Despite some variation across countries, in general, the key partners in elite pathways involve international, national, state, provincial and local sport organisations.

At an international level, the IGO of a sport is comprised of NGBs and is responsible for their governance. NGBs promote their sport nationally at every level, from grass roots to high performance; they are also responsible for the identification and development of talent and the coordination of elite development pathways. In addition to these predominantly publicly resourced organisations, private academies and private coaching centres are making a strong mark in highly professionalised and commercialised sport, such as tennis, golf and cycling.

In countries with a federal system – such as Canada, Spain and Australia – individual states or regions have a degree of political autonomy. In those circumstances, NSAs focus on the nurturing of their existing elite athletes and the responsibility of attracting and retaining new talent to SSAs at a state/provincial level. Within their states, SSAs are committed to supporting the development of a system that: (a) encourages participation; (b) develops talent; and (c) contributes to the health and well-being of individuals and groups. In their efforts to deliver development *of* and *through* sport to the communities they serve, state or regional sporting associations work closely with provincial or state departments of sport and recreation. These departments are the lead agencies responsible for the implementation of government policy and initiatives in sport and recreation.

This inter-organisational collaboration and the filtering of roles and responsibilities is equally present in other contexts, including between the IOC and NOCs, between schools, tertiary institutions or colleges that offer opportunities for participants to play sport, train, excel and be selected to participate at higher-level competitions. It is also evident within other regulatory bodies. For instance, the World Anti-Doping Agency

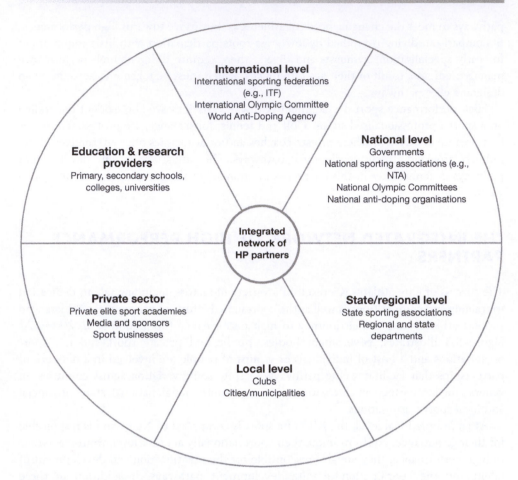

FIGURE 5.3 Integrated network of high performance partners

(WADA) is the international body that monitors and regulates the fight against doping in elite sport. The Australian Sports Anti-Doping Agency (ASADA), the United States Anti-Doping Agency (USADA) and the Autoridade Brasileira de Controle de Dopagem (ABCD) in Brazil are examples of the 133 National Anti-Doping Organisations (NADOs) that are responsible for testing national and visiting athletes in and out of competition.

All in all, stakeholders can vary in the role they play in facilitating high performance sport development pathways and enacting strategies, tactics and programs. It is also important to note that the same cluster of stakeholders – for example, coaches – may play a very different role depending on the level of their involvement in any, or all, of the ARTN phases. Collectively, the stakeholders shape an elite sport partner network that should allow for partnerships, integration and the sharing of knowledge and resources for best results.

Case Study 1: elite pathways in Australian tennis

Jessie Brouwers

This chapter illustrates the need for a sophisticated sport-specific and context-specific approach when examining elite pathways. This tennis-specific case study illustrates the complicated format of elite tennis pathways in Australia. Tennis Australia (TA) has fine-tuned its athlete development pathways over the past 10 years and is still continuing to do so by launching new programs and expanding them to all the states and territories. Even though TA sets out the overarching athlete development pathway, each state is responsible for implementing its own programs that contribute to the TA pathway. Consequently, state and territory programs differ in shape and format. This case study is based on an analysis of the TA training and competition pathway to set players on the path to becoming a professional, and links these pathways to the ARTN framework (Sotiriadou *et al.* 2008).

The *attraction* of children to tennis takes place at the local level in tennis clubs and schools. Two TA programs exist at local level: Community Play and ANZ Tennis Hot Shots aimed at children aged 5–10. These are modified tennis programs using smaller courts, lighter rackets and low-compression balls to make tennis fun and easy. Children progress through three development stages according to their age and level. The programs are mostly organised by TA-qualified coaches in the local tennis clubs. TA has also created partnerships to engage schools in the Hot Shots programs, allowing thousands of children to get a quality first tennis experience guided by qualified coaches. To *retain* the attracted members, TA has modified team competition formats – Tennis Hot Shots Leagues and Super 10s – linked with the modified training programs.

Talented players can *transition* from local- to regional-, state- and national-level programs. Each state or territory tennis association has its own programs that contribute to the overarching programs of TA. The Project Talent program forms the base of the athlete development pathway and seeks to identify and develop the most promising U12 players in Australia. Tennis Queensland has two projects within the overarching Project Talent program: Talent Development Camps provide opportunities for Queensland players – by invitation only – to train with the state's best peers; and the Talent Development Coaches program recognises private coaches who are specialised in training U12 players.

Players aged 10–16 who fulfil certain entry criteria – rankings, results, participation and ambition to become professional tennis players – can apply for a scholarship to train at one of the seven national academies (NA), where athletes receive multi-dimensional support: coaching, education planning, strength and conditioning programs, medical support and tournament support. Players in these programs can participate in the Junior Tour, Australian Money Tournaments and the Junior Davis Cup and Junior Fed Cup, the boys' and girls' U16 international team competitions. Moreover, international tours are organised for the best junior players. These trips give junior players the opportunity to compete against the world's best athletes. The aim of the NA programs is to prepare the players for their transition into the AIS Pro Tour program (age 17–19), a full-time travelling program, designed to facilitate the transition from junior to senior level. Players in this program participate in the Australian Pro Tour – professional-level events that offer prize money and rankings points. These *nurturing* events are stepping stones for the ATP World Tour and WTA Tour, the highest level of competition. At the pinnacle of the TA development pathway are the Davis Cup and Fed Cup Squads from which players may be picked to represent Australia.

As mentioned earlier in the chapter, high performance sport development pathways also vary depending on a sport's professionalised status. In the highly professionalised sport of tennis, addition to the training pathways of TA players can choose to train in private high performance academies – for example, Pat Cash Tennis Academy and Peter Smith Tennis Academy; another alternative for players who are not selected for the AIS Pro Tour program is US College Tennis, which provides competitive opportunities in combination with a degree.

Further resources

Tennis Australia: www.tennis.com.au

Case study extension activities

1 Discuss the role of the different stakeholders (see Figure 5.3) during the different development stages.
2 Select a high-profile tennis player from your country and examine their elite development pathway. How does their pathway compare with the TA elite pathway in terms of the four stages (ATRN) discussed in this chapter?

Case Study 2: elite pathways in rugby – the USA model

Ben Corbett

Rugby sevens has been a niche sport in the US, with less than 0.1 per cent of the population playing the sport. Therefore, the typical high performance pathway system in the United States that centres on the National Collegiate Athletic Association (NCAA) has not significantly developed for rugby. Men's rugby sevens is considered a club sport and women's rugby sevens is now considered an emerging sport by the NCAA, which severely limits the funding for facilities, coaching and athletic scholarships at universities. This resource void causes elite athletes to choose other sports.

Player identification was primarily done at three to four national competitions hosted annually by the national sporting organisation, USA Rugby (USAR). Once a player was identified, they would be invited to a national training camp for one to two weeks prior to international competition. In many cases, rugby's amateur status in the US caused players to miss training camps due to work and family commitments. Furthermore, some players selected into the national team would meet their teammates and coaches for the first time at the airport, a situation that earned the moniker *airport meet-and-greet high performance system*. In 2009, the IOC announced that rugby sevens would join the Olympic program in 2016. This set USAR into a furious evolution of their high performance system. The United States Olympic Committee (USOC) offered to provide funding, facilities and expertise, persuading USAR to centralise the national team operations at the Olympic Training Centre (OTC) in Chula Vista, California, in 2012.

The centralised *residency high performance system* consists of a core team of rugby sevens specialists residing and training together on one-year living expense contracts. The core team of 12–15 athletes are accompanied by players on short-term contracts (1–6 months), allowing for 25–35 players in the OTC at any given time. Additional players, brought in for training camps before competition, are on trial for tournament selection and/or a residency contract. This system has several benefits, but also several limitations to elite player pathways:

Benefits	Limitations
• controlled environment for coaching system – reduced exposure to bad habits, unlearn-relearn system	• cost of facilities – initial and maintenance
• build teamwork	• relocation of athletes – short and long term
• injury monitoring, prevention and rehab	• reduced access to athletes in regional competitions
• continual and elite sport science access – strength and conditioning, analytics, video, nutrition	• potential reduced exposure of national team coaching in regional areas
• athletes get paid for living expenses and can focus on sport	• reduced flexibility in selecting and recruiting athletes outside of those contracted in residency – contract turnover rates

One identified significant limitation of this residency system was the growing disconnect of a large number of potential elite players and national team coaches from the OTC. Many players and coaches expressed that the initial residency athletes had a major advantage in national team selection at the expense of potentially better athletes that could not take up a residency contract in California. Another argument against residency was that the dilution of talent in local clubs from relocating the athletes reduced the competition level in those regions.

USAR, realising the limitations, have intensified discussions with the NCAA and its member universities to develop the NCAA pathway model for rugby sevens. However, this will be a time-consuming process and will consist of either redirecting funding from current Olympic sports or developing new funding – one university at a time. In the meantime, USAR devised a new player pathway model that incorporates both universities, as they shift from club sport to varsity sport status, and privatised Olympic

Development Academies (ODAs). The ODAs are autonomous, regional training bases. Each ODA has the ability to generate its own programming, identify and recruit elite athletes, and link with any other organisations – such as local universities, local rugby clubs and high schools. In return for establishing an ODA, USAR offers coaching and technical support, invites ODA athletes to training camps, monitors athletes in conjunction with the ODA monitoring system and hosts tournaments for the ODAs to compete against each other.

The evolution of USAR's elite pathway system will continue towards the NCAA model, but may also stand as an example for future niche sports striving to elevate to international competitiveness.

Further resources

USA Rugby: http://usarugby.org/
Example ODA: http://atavus.com/

Case study extension activities

1 What are some limitations of the airport meet-and-greet high performance system that USAR utilised prior to residency at the OTC?
2 How would you minimise the limitations that a centralised residency program places on elite player pathways? What are your opinions on USAR's actions to address identified limitations?

SUMMARY

The seven pathways of sport development in Figure 5.1 illustrate the non-linear nature of people's involvement with sport. This chapter explained that elite pathways are interrelated: participants enter, exit or re-enter the sport system in various roles and capacities. In addition, elite pathways are not isolated from each other as people can move up, down or out and back in to the sport system at various times. More importantly, elite pathways can vary depending on the sport – for example, rugby versus tennis pathways – or the country of reference – developed versus developing sport systems. Regardless of such variations, the high performance practices outlined in this chapter (see Figure 5.2) point towards the need for strategic high performance management that is reflected through the availability of professionals – such as coaches and high performance managers – and well-designed and -delivered services – competition structures and athlete career support – that facilitate the pathways to elite success. This systematic approach to elite pathways is ultimately facilitated through the integration of a network of high performance partners (see Figure 5.3). This network includes international and national federations and state and regional associations, as well as, in many cases, schools and local clubs. Collectively, carefully designed elite pathways are of paramount importance in delivering sustainably successful elite athletes.

DISCUSSION QUESTIONS

1 Using the information from the case study in tennis, discuss how athlete development pathways in other professional sports (for example, golf, cycling) are structured. Consider the potential implications of a highly professionalised elite pathway for athletes. What, if any, are the benefits in the commercialisation and professionalisation of elite pathways?

2 Unlike sport systems in HICs, many LICs and LMICs do not have the required input and throughput to produce effective elite pathways and athletes. Examine the elite sport pathways in Malaysia, Iraq or Bosnia and Herzegovina. What alternatives do these countries use and what strategies you would recommend be adopted, given their fiscal and resource-related scarcities, to produce elite pathways with minimal input?

3 Discuss examples of elite sport policies – for example, research and sport sciences, talent identification and development, coaches and coach education – and practices – for example, physiotherapy treatments for injury prevention and recovery, talent selection processes, coach development seminars – and consider how these policies and related practices facilitate successful elite pathways.

4 Discuss the reasons behind the evolution of elite pathways as non-linear, rather convoluted processes that involve various parties and require a formalised strategic approach in order to be effective.

5 Elite sport cannot be regarded as a simple extension of mass participation because it is possible to build high-level competition systems without relying on a broad participation base. Discuss a sport or a situation where elite pathways do not rely on a broad participation base and analyse how and why that is the case.

REFERENCES

Andersen, S. and Ronglan, L. T. (2012) *Nordic Elite Sport: Same Ambitions, Different Tracks*, Norway: AIT Otta AS.

Böhlke, N. and Robinson, L. (2009) 'Benchmarking of élite sport systems', *Management Decision*, 47(1): 67–84.

De Bosscher, V. and van Bottenburg, M. (2011) 'Elite for all, all for elite? An assessment of the impact of sport development on elite sport success', in B. Houlihan (ed.), *Handbook of Sport Development*, London: Routledge, pp. 575–95.

De Bosscher, V., De Knop, P. and van Bottenburg, M. (2009) 'An analysis of homogeneity and heterogeneity of elite sports systems in six nations', *International Journal of Sports Marketing & Sponsorship*, 10(2): 111–31.

De Bosscher, V., Sotiriadou, P. and van Bottenburg, M. (2013) 'Scrutinizing the sport pyramid metaphor: an examination of the relationship between elite success and mass participation in Flanders', *International Journal of Sport Policy and Politics*, 5(3): 319–39.

De Bosscher, V., De Knop, P., van Bottenburg, M. and Shibli, S. (2006) 'A conceptual framework for analysing sports policy factors leading to international sporting success', *European Sport Management Quarterly*, 6(2): 185–215.

Eady, J. (1993) *Practical Sports Development*, London: Pitman.

Eichberg, H., Bale, J., Philo, C. and Bronwell, S. (1998) *Body Cultures: Essays on Sport, Space and Identity*, London: Routledge.

Emery, P. R., Crabtree, R. M. and Kerr, A. K. (2012) 'The Australian sport management job market: an advertisement audit of employer need', *Annals of Leisure Research*, 15(4): 335–53.

Gleeson, M. (2014) 'Commonwealth Games Glasgow 2014: Sally Pearson's gold medal spray at Eric Hollingsworth', *The Age*, 4 August 2014, available at: www.theage.com.au/commonwealth-games-glasgow-2014/commonwealth-games-news/commonwealth-games-glasgow-2014-sally-pearsons-gold-medal-spray-at-eric-hollingsworth-20140802-zzpby.html (accessed August 2014).

Gould, D. and Carson, S. (2004) 'Fun and games? Myths surrounding the role of youth sports in developing Olympic champions', *Youth Studies Australia*, 23(1): 19–26.

Green, B. C. (2005) 'Building sport programs to optimize athlete recruitment, retention, and transition: toward a normative theory of sport development', *Journal of Sport Management*, 19(3): 233–54.

Green, M. and Houlihan, B. (2005) *Elite Sport Development: Policy Learning and Political Priorities*, London: Routledge.

Houlihan, B. and Green, M. (2008) 'Comparative elite sport development', in B. Houlihan and M. Green (eds), *Comparative Elite Sport Development: Systems, Structures and Public Policy*, London: Butterworth-Heineman, pp. 1–25.

Lyle, J. W. B. (1997) 'Managing excellence in sports performance', *Career Development International*, 2(7): 314–23.

Midgley, G. (2003) *Systems Thinking*, London: Sage.

Oakley, B. and Green, M. (2001) 'The production of Olympic champions: international perspectives on elite sport development system', *European Journal for Sport Management*, 8: 83–105.

Robinson, L. (2013) 'Elite sport systems in developing sport nations: more questions than answers', paper presented at *SPLISS Conference on Elite Sport Success: Society Boost or Not?* 13–14 November, Antwerp, Belgium.

Robinson, L. and Minikin, B. (2011) 'Developing strategic capacity in Olympic sport organisations', *Sport, Business and Management*, 1(3): 219–33.

Robinson, L. and Minikin, B. (2012) 'Understanding the competitive advantage of National Olympic Committees', *Managing Leisure*, 17(2–3): 139–54.

Sotiriadou, P. (2009) 'The Australian sport system and its stakeholders: development of cooperative relationships', *Sport in Society*, 12(7): 842–60.

Sotiriadou, P. (2013) 'Sport development planning: the Sunny Golf Club', *Sport Management Review*, 16(4): 514–23.

Sotiriadou, P. and De Bosscher, V. (2013) *Managing High Performance Sport*, London: Routledge.

Sotiriadou, P. and Shilbury, D. (2009) 'Australian elite athlete development: an organisational perspective', *Sport Management Review*, 12(3): 137–48.

Sotiriadou, P., Gowthorp, L. and De Bosscher, V. (2013) 'Elite sport culture and policy interrelationships: the case of Sprint Canoe in Australia', *Leisure Studies*, 33(6): 598–617.

Sotiriadou, P., Shilbury, D. and Quick, S. (2008) 'The attraction, retention/transition, and nurturing process of sport development: some Australian evidence', *Journal of Sport Management*, 22(3): 247–72.

Van Bottenburg, M. (2003) 'Top-en Breedtesport: een Siamese Tweeling?' [Elite sport and sport for all: a Siamese twin], in R. Breedveld (ed.), *Rapportage sport 2003*, Den Haag: Sociaal en cultureel planbureau, pp. 285–312.

CHAPTER 6

Community sport

Pamm Phillips and Stacy Warner

INTRODUCTION

Following on from the previous chapter, which examined elite sport development, this chapter focuses on the delivery of sport at the community level. As already noted in Chapter 1, community, or grass-roots, sport is crucial to both SD and SFD. Within community sport, there is a wide variety of facilities, public spaces, sport organisations, programming and personnel that exists to provide opportunities for individuals to experience organised sport. Community sport sets the stage for the future of sport participation for individuals; a positive initial sport experience and appropriate sport opportunities along a program pathway may provide the impetus for individuals to continue in a sport activity. On the other hand, a negative experience, or lack of appropriate programming to match the needs of individuals, may discourage any further sport participation.

The importance of community sport to SD and SFD cannot be overstated. Without community sport organisations, which bring people together to manage and deliver programming within community-based venues and facilities, opportunities for sport involvement and pathways to facilitate participation – which together form the fundamental basis for SD – would not exist. Consequently, without sport activities for participation, the capability to leverage sport for wider benefits to the community – therefore SFD – is lost.

OUTLINE OF THE CHAPTER

This chapter focuses specifically on delivery of community sport. It explores three crucial issues that have theoretical and practical significance in community sport: (1) infrastructure for community sport; (2) programming for community sport; and (3) management of community sport. The theoretical and practical significance of each of the issues will be discussed in the proceeding sections of this chapter, followed by two case studies that highlight how these issues are impacting real-life decision-making in sport organisations. A summary and questions for further consideration and analysis will also be presented.

After completing this chapter, you should be able to:

*   discuss the challenges of delivering sport for participation at the community level;
*   recognise how sport can be leveraged for wider community benefit;
*   appreciate how sport programs can be designed for specific populations in the community;
*   determine how organisations need to build their capacity to deliver to diverse groups; and
*   review the role of facilities and place in the delivery of community sport.

INFRASTRUCTURE FOR COMMUNITY SPORT

As the reader will have ascertained from previous chapters, sport development – whether one considers SD or SFD – is often determined by the requirement for appropriate facilities and spaces for sport activities to occur and programming to be delivered (Green 2005; Sotiriadou *et al.* 2008). However, until recently, at least in the area of sport management and sport development literature, there has been little research devoted to examining the impact that sport infrastructure may have on SD or SFD. This is somewhat surprising because, after all, the facilities provided – or not provided – at the community level of sport will impact what sport activities community members have the opportunity to participate in, and how they might participate. From a practical perspective, sport organisations deal with issues of facilities and space on a daily basis, and this section of the chapter on community sport will begin to examine this important area of SD and SFD.

Empirical research in sport management has noted that there is a clear link between the availability of sport infrastructure and participation in organised sport (Wicker *et al.* 2009, 2013). Wicker *et al.* (2009, 2013) have provided quantitative evidence to suggest that the types and availability of existing sport infrastructure communities in Munich, Germany, impact *who* participates, and seem to draw participants of a certain age, gender, education and family commitments. Further, the type of facilities available also impacts *how* individuals engage in activities in facilities. The research was clear in highlighting the way in which the need for sport infrastructure and facilities was dependent on the types and nature of sports that were favoured throughout the course of an individual's lifetime. It was suggested, for example, that a minimum supply of sport infrastructure that caters for team or intense sports is particularly important for younger age groups (3–35 years), compared with older age groups (above 65 years), who prefer more health-oriented sports. For the middle age groups, the opening hours of facilities – to fit around work hours – were important. The impact of facilities on SD and SFD, at least in Germany, is clearly illustrated through this research.

Wicker *et al.* (2009, 2013) also noted the important role that local government authorities (LGAs) play in the establishment of sporting infrastructure. Traditionally in Australia, LGAs have been the main providers of strategic planning for sport and recreation facilities for communities (Carroll 1995). LGAs have used a variety of planning methods to assist them in deciding what sporting infrastructure to include. LGAs first developed planning for the provision of sport and recreation facilities using an approach that merely calculated a ratio of sport and recreation facilities required per capita (Carroll 1995). This process also meant that LGAs provided sporting infrastructure in line with what they perceived to be the most popular sports at the time of the assessment.

From a practical perspective, this strategy resulted in many of the older suburban areas including facilities for more traditional sports, such as cricket and football fields, golf courses, tennis and netball courts, swimming pools, leisure centres, and open spaces, such as beaches and parks (Shilbury and Kellett 2011). In most cases, LGAs own and maintain these as city assets while sport organisations pay nominal fees to lease them for their use. Accordingly, those more traditional sports continue to enjoy higher participation rates than other sports – simply because the facilities exist for people to use. In this way, these sports enjoy greater opportunities for SD in areas where facilities exist, and therefore greater opportunities for SFD. This analysis is in line with the work of Wicker *et al.* (2009, 2013), but their findings also signal implications for LGAs. As population profiles change and become more multicultural, facilities need to adapt to cater for expanding needs and motives of a more diverse population that seeks more variety in sport and recreation activities. This is further addressed in the following section about community sport programming.

The importance of LGAs in providing infrastructure for community sport is also apparent when considering the impact of the natural environment on sport facilities. Phillips and Turner (2014) examined the outcomes of drought on sport and recreation in one community in Victoria, Australia. Drought caused the LGA to close down 105 of its 120 natural turf playing fields as they were deemed unfit for public use. Sport organisations had little influence on which playing fields remained available for use, or which sports could use them. Many sport communities ceased to exist, as they had no facility or venue available for their use (Phillips and Turner 2014), further highlighting the importance of facilities for SD and the central role that LGAs can play in their provision.

Thus far, much of the discussion has centred on SD. However, facilities are also crucial for SFD. Preliminary evidence suggests that the design of newer suburban communities is leading to increased obesity, as well as mental and physical illnesses (see, for example, Perkins 2012). Much of the issue is purported to be largely due to the lack of appropriate sport and recreation facilities, and spaces that invite and encourage residents to engage in physical activity and/or to connect with other people (Perkins 2012). The link between sport and health promotion is discussed in more detail later in this book (see Chapter 9); however, pertinent to our discussion here is that public health experts suggest that current urban planning is ensuring that new suburbs will be ghettos of ill health in two decades (Perkins 2012). Communities that have been developed with cul-de-sacs and looping or lollipop roads are designed to cater for maximal housing density; the net result is a dearth of few footpaths, bike lanes and useable open spaces. Although such master planning of communities has encouraged quiet residential areas, on a practical level the design may inadvertently discourage walking, cycling, casual recreation, engagement and socialisation – the very things that SFD programs seek to provide.

Case study 1 later in this chapter provides the reader with the opportunity to explore the importance of LGAs in facility provision, in particular in the sport of triathlon.

The reader is invited to consider the impact of an LGA on both SD and SFD in that sport. However, beyond facilities, another important issue in community sport is that of programs: what programs should be offered and how? The following section begins to address this issue.

PROGRAMMING FOR COMMUNITY SPORT

As noted earlier in this chapter, community sport typically provides individuals with their first sport experience. As Palm (1991) described, a beginner in a sport activity can encounter a disturbance as he or she grapples with not only the new skills of a sport activity, but also the social pressures of others who are already established in the group, and are more accomplished at the activity.

Therefore, attracting and involving people in a particular sport are fundamental steps in the process of both SD and SFD (Green 2005; Shilbury *et al.* 2008; Sotiriadou *et al.* 2008). A crucial part of attracting individuals to sport is providing the appropriate product offering to the target population (Sotiriadou *et al.* 2014). Not only does this include providing the appropriate facilities and spaces – as discussed in the previous section – but it also involves providing appropriate programming that the targeted participants will value.

MODIFIED RULES

One way in which programming is often adapted to suit target populations is to modify the rules. The concept of modified rules – in particular for children – has existed for over three decades; it emerged from an awareness that competitive match play, rules and structures – designed for adult sport settings – can reduce the enjoyment for children so much that it discourages continued participation (Kirk and Gorely 2000; Smith 2005). The introduction of modified rules has steadily increased across all sports since the 1980s, and modified rules for children are now widely accepted as more than just inferior forms of the adult version of sport (Shilbury and Kellett 2011); modified sport programs for children can lead to improved skill development and continued participation (Chalip and Green 1998; Houlihan and Green 2011; Kirk and Gorely 2000). Typical rule modifications in sport include reducing playing field dimensions, match and season duration, rule complexity, size of playing equipment, and de-emphasising winning (Stewart *et al.* 2004). Essentially, such modifications are designed to match the environment to a child's level of ability.

By modifying rules, sport managers recognise that children require different sport environments to adults (Chalip and Green 1998). This is also true for individuals with disabilities. Sport culture tends to exclusively cater to able-bodied individuals; however, there is a wide range of individuals with various physical and intellectual impairments who can benefit from participating in sport. Programs such as the Paralympics, Special Olympics and National Beep Baseball Association are all examples of programs that also utilise sport modifications that can be administrated at the community level. Ultimately, these programs serve as a strategic vehicle for creating positive social, cultural or educational outcomes (Sherry *et al.* 2014). For example, beep baseball uses baseballs and bases that produce buzzing or beeping sounds so that blind athletes can participate in the sport, while those individuals without visual impairments or with only partial impairment wear a blindfold. Through their promotion and participation in the sport, visually impaired athletes demonstrate their abilities while simultaneously creating a greater awareness of visual impairments.

From a practical perspective, modified sport programs have become a key area of business for NSOs as they are seen as a way in which they can compete to attract and retain children in their sports. In Australia, NSOs for most sports – including, but not limited to, netball, football, cricket, Australian Rules football, baseball, basketball, field hockey and tennis – have developed their own unique modified sport programs. NSOs compete not only with NSOs of other sports, but also with other leisure activities, to first attract participants in their sports, and then to retain them. As a result of the competitive environment, the development of modified sport programming has become increasingly sophisticated in NSOs. Often, NSOs invest heavily in modified sports for youth by ensuring highly skilled and qualified individuals design all aspects of modified programs. This is done to ensure that skill development occurs and is scaffolded in an age-appropriate manner through to maturity. Further, this approach often involves marketing campaigns that aim to increase awareness and encourage participation. This is a difficult task to accomplish, as a balance needs to be struck to position modified sports as different from the adult forms of the sport – although equally legitimate – and fun.

Some sports have consolidated modified programming into their structures and strategy, and provide comprehensive information to all of their key stakeholders. For example, the International Tennis Federation (ITF) has endorsed a modified program on a global scale for its sport. This program uses modified racquets, balls, nets and court size. The ITF have mandated that from 1 January 2012, all 10-and-under competitions must use modified rules (Tennis Australia 2013). Tennis Australia has adopted the modified program and developed a sophisticated and integrated approach to delivering a modified sport that is specific to the Australian context. Tennis Australia has ensured that the modified rules tennis program includes:

- an education program for teachers and partnership with the Australian Council for Health, Physical Education and Recreation (ACHPER) to ensure it can be incorporated into curriculum in schools across the country;
- an education and incentive program for professional coaches to deliver modified tennis at their clubs;
- a program to educate administrators at clubs to adopt the program;
- a partnership with Nickelodeon to integrate Disney characters into merchandise and to use characters as part of an entertaining package for participants;
- education programs for parents; and
- interactive online games, delivered through apps on iTunes, to enhance the experience for children beyond the court.

The sport of tennis has recognised that teachers, coaches, club administrators and parents are key to SD in the implementation of their modified sport program, and have developed information and education programs accordingly.

MANAGEMENT AND DELIVERY OF COMMUNITY SPORT

Despite the best efforts of NSOs to design effective modified sport programs, the grass-roots level of sport is where such programs are delivered. As such, most sports – with the exception of professionalised sports, such as tennis and golf, where paid professional coaches typically deliver sport – rely solely on volunteers – many of whom may have little knowledge of the sport itself, and even less knowledge of the intent and purpose of modified rules – to implement programming.

It is recognised that modified rules programs are not easy to implement and their success depends on the perceptions of the adults who assist in their implementation. Chalip and Green (1998) followed the introduction of a modified soccer program into a traditional soccer club. The modified rules program was instituted because the volunteer club administrator noted decreasing participation rates and increasing parental pressure. He believed a modified program would be more attractive to participants and parents alike, and therefore drive an increase in participation. Although the modified program was implemented, a range of social forces resulted in re-adopting some of the traditional structures and processes that it first rejected. Those social forces were linked to long-held beliefs about the way in which dominant, professional (adult) sport models are believed to be the right ways to play sport; more specifically, these were the perceptions held by the key adult stakeholders involved in the implementation of the modified program. In other words, the adults were not sure how to behave differently in order to facilitate a modified rules program that had a different philosophical starting point from that they were familiar with. Specifically, Chalip and Green (1998) describe the way in which the club administrators, parents and coaches each had their own perspectives about what a youth soccer program should provide and, at the end of the season, the most traditional perspectives won out. As a result, the youth soccer program once again looked more like the adult and traditional version of the game. Unfortunately, the modified games were not accepted, and little change occurred either in terms of the declining youth participation rates or the increasing parental pressure (Chalip and Green 1998).

APPLICATION OF THEORY TO PRACTICE

The following case studies provide examples of the ideas discussed in this chapter. The first study demonstrates the importance of LGAs in facility provision, while the second case study provides the reader with the opportunity to explore a modified rules program in action that was designed to meet SD goals for the organisation, but rather surprisingly also met SFD needs in that community organisation.

Case Study 1: using a sport to showcase local community – partnerships between triathlon event organisers and local municipal councils

Brianna Newland and Pamm Phillips

From the perspective of SD and SFD in community sport, triathlon is unique. Unlike many sports, triathlon is an event-based sport that intermittently requires the use of public spaces including roads, water reserves and public parks. Participants in triathlon events traverse through community spaces, so it is essential for the safety of all concerned that roads and other areas are closed for public access during event times, sometimes only a few hours. For example, the bike and run segments of triathlon events generally use public roads while the swim segments use pools, beaches or lakes. Further, transition and bike storage areas, which need to be centrally located, can take up large amounts of public park space.

In this way, the infrastructure required for triathlon is dependent on LGAs for permits and approval of use. Other sports also rely on the provision of facilities and public spaces that are often under the jurisdiction of LGAs; however, while much of the infrastructure for other sports is permanent and dedicated for use, triathlon is different. Phillips and Newland (2014) found that triathlon represented a new model of managing and delivery of SD and noted that in both Australia and the US LGAs – along with the event management companies who deliver triathlon events – have become essential to the delivery of triathlon. Event organising companies who manage and deliver triathlon events – rather than the governing body, as is the case in many other sports – recognise LGAs as key stakeholders in triathlon SD.

Also noted in this research was that LGAs are becoming more adept at leveraging triathlon events for their own outcomes, and they carefully choose the triathlon events that will best be staged to showcase their communities. Further, LGAs develop good working relationships with triathlon event managers in order to secure a voice in the management and delivery of the event to ensure it meets their strategic needs. Local councils make choices about triathlon in their local communities based on which events will best match the strategic outcomes that they desire. This case study outlines the choices made by one LGA in Melbourne, Australia, where triathlon events are leveraged for development in their community.

The City of Port Phillip is located within 5 km of Melbourne's city centre and is a picturesque bayside suburb. It has a vibrant events calendar and, due to its location and natural amenities, such as the bay and beaches, it is home to many triathlon, biathlon, running, swimming and ironman events during the year. The City of Port Phillip, although not in need of more events for its calendar, chooses to support a portfolio of triathlon events organised by event management companies that they can work with to ensure the city benefits from the triathlons. Some of the larger high-profile triathlon events that they choose to host are televised, which allows the City of Port Phillip to showcase the municipality. When cameras follow athletes on the street circuits during the bike and run legs, imagery of the local community is captured and beamed into people's lounge rooms. Swim segments are usually filmed in part from the air, thereby showing that the City of Port Phillip is a destination in close proximity to Melbourne's city centre.

Part of the triathlon event portfolio also includes low-profile events aimed at participation. It is recognised that events can draw up to 3,000 participants, with perhaps even more attending as supporters and spectators. The City of Port Phillip works with event organisers to ensure that they can leverage the event for economic benefit. For example, the LGA negotiates with event organisers to ensure that events finish in spaces that will draw participants and their supporters/spectators into local businesses; further, the LGA worked with local businesses to encourage them to provide incentives that enhance retail experiences.

The City of Port Phillip is also keen to leverage triathlon events for local social engagement. The LGA works with event organisers to activate the event finish line by including festival-like activities on the local foreshore, designed not only for event participants, but also for local community members to attend and enjoy. In this way, triathlon events contribute to the community and the liveability of the municipality.

Further resources

City of Port Phillip Events Schedule: www.portphillip.vic.gov.au/events-calendar-2014-2015.htm

Case study extension activities

1 Triathlon is unique in the way it relies on a local council for its delivery and ultimate success. What other sports rely on an outside organisation for SD? Is this an advantage or disadvantage for the sport?
2 What strategies could triathlon event directors use to further leverage the community assets beyond the event itself in order to solidify buy-in and support of the community and its leaders?
3 Think about an event in your local area (triathlon or other sport event). How is the LGA involved and what do they stand to gain from it? What strategies could the LGA employ to leverage this event further?

Case Study 2: the Australian Football League's Junior Modified Rules Match Guide: contributing to SD and SFD

Kylie Bellesini and Pamm Phillips

The Australian Football League (AFL) is the governing body for the largest football code in Australia (Australian Rules football). The AFL recorded over 6 million attendances during the 2013 professional championship season, which makes it the third highest attended sport worldwide. On the professional level, the championship season is played between 17 professional teams located around Australia. On a wider scale, the sport boasted over 900,000 participants across all of its programs – from beginner programs to amateur senior competitions – in 2013, and the governing body has invested heavily in community sport by developing a comprehensive pathway for participants with programming that contributes to both SD and SFD.

The AFL's SD pathway begins with a non-competitive introductory program (Auskick), where play is fundamental. Participants then move into a modified rules program for competitive match play upon which is the focus of this case study. In the AFL SD pathway, junior competitive match play is for 8–12-year-old boys and girls. Although not the focus of this case, it is worth noting that from this program, participants can move into competitive match play based on age groupings until 18 years of age, and then into senior competition. There are alternative pathways for elite performers, and programs for special populations. The reader can examine these from the AFL's website, as directed in further resources below.

The modified junior match play program for 8–12 year olds is delivered through local community clubs around Australia and is largely run by volunteers. There are approximately 150 leagues nationally, and the rules and philosophy of the program are set out in the AFL's publication, the AFL Junior Match Guide, for all leagues to follow. The philosophy that underpins the match play program rules for junior match play is 'This is Our Game'. It is intended that children will embrace the modified rules as their own, as opposed to adopting the rules that are played by adults along with all the associated trappings, such as an emphasis on competition.

The AFL Junior Match Guide notes that the rules are modified into three phases according to progressive age groups, to match skill development and maturity. The first phase (for U8 age group) is the *introductory* phase, where modified rules are designed to introduce participants to the skills, rules and structure of competitive play. The second phase (for U10 and U11 age groups) is the *development* phase, where rule modifications are designed to maximise skill development and execution during competitive play. The third phase (for U12 age group) is the *competition* phase, where the rules of competitive play more closely resemble those of the adult form of the sport. There are over 20 rule modifications, and the progressive changes through the three phases take into account: the context – such as size of playing field, number of players on the field, size of ball used, and length of matches; competitive elements – such as scoring, championship ladders and participant awards; and contact between players – such as tackling.

The intent of the AFL Junior Match Guide is that all clubs and leagues around the nation implement all of the rule modifications concurrently. However, the governance of the sport across Australia means that the AFL is unable to regulate how the policy is implemented at the local – community – level of the sport. That is, different leagues have chosen to deliver modified sport programs that consist of different permutations of the rules. For example, some leagues have chosen to implement all 26 of the AFL Junior Match Guide rule modifications across the age groups as appropriate, while others have chosen to implement only a few. The AFL recognises that this may have a profound impact on SD for the sport.

Research conducted by the authors of this case study examined the efficacy of the modified rules and found that when all rule modifications are delivered consistently with the AFL Junior Match Guide, participants have greater opportunities for involvement, skill development and execution (Phillips *et al.* 2013). In this way, the modified rules program, when it is fully implemented, is delivering the desired SD outcomes. On the other hand, when it is not implemented – by leagues that choose to run the adult form of the sport for their juniors – optimal skill development may be compromised.

Skill development was perhaps further compromised by the behaviour of adults in those settings where modified rules were not implemented. The study found that when junior sport leagues did not use any modified rules in junior match play, but instead children played the adult form of the sport, sport experiences within these leagues were characterised by: more frequent use of negative language in coaching instruction and feedback; parent/child interaction about sport performance; spectator behaviour that emphasised competition and winning; and frequent umpire abuse (Phillips *et al.* 2013). The resulting culture was one in which children were expected to perform at levels similar to what might be seen on television by professional athletes. In contrast, those leagues that implemented modified rules in junior match play were characterised by a largely social environment where there was an acceptance of play and participation rather than performance. Parents cheered good skill execution, regardless of team affiliation, and no instances of umpire abuse were observed. Perhaps more importantly, parents engaged in social conversation as they were less interested in the score and were confident that their children were in a setting where they were safe and learning. Parents mingled together, again regardless of team affiliations, as they found that they had many things in common, such as schools, workplaces and neighbourhoods. In many instances, social connections made at football led to social groups being formed beyond the junior football context (Phillips *et al.* 2013). Without the elements of competition that are central to the adult forms of sport, the modified rules program facilitated parents to use the time for engagement and building connections with others in their community, rather than focusing on winners and losers; in this way, the implementation of the modified rules program unexpectedly contributed to SFD outcomes as it had positive impacts on community engagement.

Further resources

AFL Junior Match Guide: http://aflcommunityclub.com.au/index.php?id=1833
AFL player pathways: http://aflcommunityclub.com.au/index.php?id=5

Case study extension activities

1 Outline the elements of modified rules in the AFL Junior match play that contributed to SD and SFD.
2 Choose a junior sport program that you are familiar with. Draw up two columns, one for SD and one for SFD. Analyse that program and record the elements that contribute to each accordingly.
3 Choose a junior sport program that you are familiar with. Suggest some modifications that might contribute to SD and SFD in that program.

SUPPLEMENTARY EXERCISES

1 To familiarise and engage students in the topic of community sport, get together in small groups to discuss and describe your own community sport experiences – both positive and negative.** Share information, such as what first attracted you to the sport, where your first sport experience of it occurred, why you continued, if you participated in a modified program, and to describe the sport development pathway. Also share negative sport experiences, such as a sport that you may have tried and discontinued. Come together as a larger group to share experiences with the class and collate the information for further facilitated discussion. What common themes about positive and negative experiences, pathways – or perhaps lack thereof – emerge? How do these relate to the managerial lessons discussed in this chapter?
2 Choose a sport that is a popular participation sport in your area and one with which you are familiar. Next, gather information about the sport and its sport development pathways online – through the NSO website, for example. You can then conduct an audit of SD and SFD programming that the sport offers and draft some recommendations using this audit for the sport to further improve its SD and SFD activities.

** If there is time, a fun way to deepen involvement in this activity is to bring a piece of memorabilia that represents or reminds you of your childhood sport experience that you can share with the class.

SUMMARY

In summation, it is vital to consider both SD and SFD at the community sport level. The infrastructure for community sport is key to achieving both SD and SFD outcomes. Specifically, the support of government authorities and the availability of facilities must be taken into account. Without government support or facilities, SD and SFD programs become less likely to recruit and retain participants and meet their programmatic goals. Along these same lines, the actual programming and management of community sports have great implications on whether or not sport participants are recruited and retained for sporting activities. Modified games continue to be an avenue through which many community sport programs have found success. With expert input and good planning, modified games are fundamental in community sport to both SD and SFD programs. If clear and multiple pathways are created for a diverse cohort of sport participants at the community sport level, increased sport participation should be available for SD and better outcomes should be achieved within SFD programs.

DISCUSSION QUESTIONS

1 What common challenges exist in the delivery sport at the community level?
2 Should government authorities provide facilities for SD at community sport level? What about for SDF at the community level?
3 What are the pros and cons of SD and SFD sport programs being delivered by volunteers?
4 How can SD and SFD sport programs be leveraged to demonstrate their value at the community level?
5 What are some modifications that could be made to the sport most popular in your city to increase participation for youth? What about for seniors?

REFERENCES

Carroll, J. (1995) *Local Government Sport and Recreation Provision in Australia*, Canberra: Confederation of Australian Sport.

Chalip, L. and Green, B. C. (1998) 'Establishing and maintaining a modified youth sport program: lessons from Hotelling's location game', *Sociology of Sport Journal*, 15(4): 326–42.

Green, B. C. (2005) 'Building sport programs to optimize athlete recruitment, retention, and transition: toward a normative theory of sport development', *Journal of Sport Management*, 19(3): 233–54.

Houlihan, B. and Green, M. (2011) *Routledge Handbook of Sports Development*, London: Routledge.

Kirk, D. and Gorely, T. (2000) 'Challenging thinking about the relationship between school physical education and sport performance', *European Physical Education Review*, 6(2): 119–34.

Palm, J. (1991) *Sport for All: Approaches from Utopia to Reality*, Schorndorf, Germany: Verlag Karl Hofmann.

Perkins, M. (2012) 'Sick suburbs', *The Age*, 5 March, p. 15.

Phillips, P. and Newland, B. (2014) 'Emergent models of sports development and delivery: the case of triathlon in Australia and the US', *Sport Management Review*, 17(2): 107–20.

Phillips, P. and Turner, P. (2014) 'Water management in sport', *Sport Management Review*, 17(3): 376–89.

Phillips, P., Wehner, K., Allan, M., Gastin, P., Spittle, M. and Dawson, A. (2013) *Examining the AFL Junior Match Policy for Recruitment and Retention*, Deakin University, School of Management and Marketing, Melbourne, Vic, available at: http://hdl.handle.net/10536/DRO/DU:30065110 (accessed July 2015).

Sherry, E., Schulenkorf, N. and Chalip, L. (2014) 'Managing sport for social change: the state of play', *Sport Management Review*, 18(1): 1–5.

Shilbury, D. and Kellett, P. (2011) *Sport Management in Australia: An Organisational Overview*, 4th edn, Crow's Nest, NSW: Allen & Unwin.

Shilbury, D., Sotiriadou, K. and Green, B. C. (2008) 'Sport development systems policies and pathways: an introduction to the special issue', *Sport Management Review*, 11(3): 217–23.

Smith, A. C. T. (2005) 'Junior sport participation programs in Australia', *Youth Studies Australia*, 24(1): 54–9.

Sotiriadou, P., Shilbury, D. and Quick, S. (2008) 'The attraction, retention/transition, and nurturing process of sport development: some Australian evidence', *Journal of Sport Management*, 22(3): 247–72.

Sotiriadou, P., Wicker, P. and Quick, S. (2014) 'Attracting and retaining club members in times of changing societies: the case of cycling in Australia', *Managing Leisure*, 19(5): 345–58.

Stewart, B., Nicholson, M., Smith, A. and Westerbeek, H. (2004) *Australian Sport Better by Design? The Evolution of Australian Sport Policy*, London: Routledge.

Tennis Australia (2013) '10U rule changes', *Tennis Australia*, available at: http://hotshots.tennis.com.au/what-is-hot-shots/10u-rule-change (accessed July 2015).

Wicker, P., Breuer, C. and Pawlowski, T. (2009) 'Promoting sport for all to age-specific target groups: the impact of sport infrastructure', *European Sport Management Quarterly*, 9(2): 103–18.

Wicker, P., Hallmann, K. and Breuer, C. (2013) 'Analyzing the impact of sport infrastructure on sport participation using geo-coded data: evidence from multi-level models', *Sport Management Review*, 16(1): 54–67.

Support networks for sport development

Inter-organisational relationships in sport development

Geoff Dickson and Emma Sherry

INTRODUCTION

It is said that no person is an island. The same can be said for organisations. Organisations depend on other organisations. Just as there is a division of labour within organisations that create specialist roles, organisations within an industry are also specialised. The net result is that specialised organisations exchange resources with each other. Within the broad context of sport, organisations from the public, not-for-profit and for-profit sectors are entering more frequently into relationships with other organisations. Inter-organisational relationships (IORs) are formal arrangements that bring together any combination of tangible and intangible assets of two or more legally independent organisations with the aim to create additional value. IORs are created because each organisation lacks the ability to go it alone. The organisation(s) in the relationship provide something that the rest of the other organisations lack. Though promising much, IORs are fraught with difficulties such as conflict, trust, opportunistic behaviour, control, autonomy, competition and goal incongruence.

IORs are essential for delivering both SD and SFD programs and initiatives. While at first glance a single organisation appears responsible for a program, the reality is that other organisations are nearly always involved. A consideration of IORs allows for a more detailed explanation of why some organisations perform better than others. Examining IORs is not just about considering how sport organisations interact with other sport organisations, but it is also about understanding how sport organisations interact with other firms in their environment.

OUTLINE OF THE CHAPTER

In this chapter, we will examine key principles and concepts relating to IORs and sport development. First, we examine the theory relating to IORs, using relevant sport examples to demonstrate the importance of IORs in SD and SFD. Then we present two case studies that further demonstrate the theory in application before summarising the key points.

After completing this chapter, you should be able to:

*   understand the key theoretical concepts of IORs and social network analysis;
*   understand why organisations form IORs;
*   identify different forms of IORs;
*   understand why IORs are essential for sport development delivery and outcomes; and
*   discuss the benefits and risks of developing IORs in SD and SFD programs and organisations.

WHAT DOES THE THEORY TELL US?

An IOR is a 'voluntary, close, long-term, planned strategic action between two or more organisations with the objective of serving mutually beneficial purposes in a problem domain' (Babiak 2007: 339). If only two organisations are involved, it is known as a partnership. An inter-organisational network is a group of at least three organisations that interact to facilitate the achievement of a common goal (Provan *et al.* 2007). Networks are essentially multilateral IORs.

Patterns of relationships

Within sport development, IORs take a number of forms. These forms reflect variation in the relationship strength or commitment between the organisations. Figure 7.1 presents these patterns of relationships on a continuum of integration.

Exchange relationships exist between buyers and sellers. These are typically short-term and somewhat adversarial, given that buyers seek a low price and sellers want a maximum price. *Partnerships* are more stable and enduring and offer more opportunity for inter-organisational integration. Partners will exhibit more loyalty and mutual understanding than can be expected in simple exchange relationships. Most sponsorships are partnerships. *Strategic alliances* provide further opportunities for integration. To guide their study of a strategic alliance between Australian Rugby Union and a sport tourism operator, Kennelly and Toohey (2014: 408) define a strategic alliance as 'collaborative efforts and the pooling of resources between organisations in an effort to achieve mutually compatible goals that they could not easily achieve alone'. Strategic alliances require each organisation to sacrifice an element of autonomy to access the advantages provided by the common efforts

FIGURE 7.1 Patterns of relationships

of both organisations. An *interlocking directorate* occurs when one person is a director of two organisations. Interlocks enable greater cohesion, communication and knowledge exchange, and opportunities for coordinated action. A *joint venture* occurs when two or more parent organisations create a third organisation (the child). Both parent organisations retain their own identity and the child reflects the distinctive competencies and interests of each parent organisation. For example, for the Rugby World Cup 2011, New Zealand Rugby Union (NZRU) and the New Zealand government established a joint venture company, Rugby New Zealand 2011. Rugby New Zealand 2011 had its own chief executive and board, appointed by both parent organisations. Rugby New Zealand 2011 was never budgeted to make a profit, but it was agreed that the government would underwrite two-thirds of the financial shortfall, which reportedly reached approximately NZ$38 million, with the NZRU contributing the remaining third. *Mergers and acquisitions* represent total integration of organisations. One organisation will likely experience a complete loss of identity. As part of a wide process of integrating national sport organisations representing the interests of men's and women's sport, the English Women's Cricket Association (WCA) merged with the men's organisation, the England and Wales Cricket Board (ECB). Research examining the merger concluded that women's cricket, especially at the elite level, benefitted by greater access to financial resources. However, there was less opportunity for women to influence the direction of the sport (Velija *et al.* 2014).

Social network analysis

A useful approach to understanding the structure of IORs is social network analysis (SNA). SNA is a wide-ranging combination of theories and methods that places emphasis on relationships rather than the characteristics of the actors involved (Wasserman and Faust 1994). With SNA, organisations are depicted in network diagrams as nodes (points) that are linked by ties (relationships). The two basic premises of network analysis are: (1) all organisations are embedded in multiple social relationships; and (2) relational context significantly influences their behaviour. Most contemporary network studies utilise network science, computer simulations and network analysis software to quantify key network concepts. The analysis is presented by displaying nodes and ties in varying layouts, colours and sizes (Quatman and Chelladurai 2008). Table 7.1 summarises a number of concepts that can be used to understand a single organisation within a network. Table 7.2 summarises a number of concepts that can be used to describe an entire network. Table 7.3 summarises a number of concepts that can be used to describe a relationship.

A highly centralised network will have one or more hubs within the network. In a decentralised network, all organisations are linked to each other. Weak ties remain useful because they can provide new ideas and opportunities. This is because organisations typically have different expertise and operate in different fields. Weak tie organisations can also bridge *structural holes*. In these circumstances, the organisation connects two parts of the network that would otherwise be unconnected. Density scores express the number of direct linkages as a proportion of the maximum number of possible linkages. Density reflects cohesion, and is also linked to cooperation and collaboration. In a study of density among Canadian community basketball organisations, research revealed that only 27 per

TABLE 7.1 Social network analysis: organisational attributes

Organisational attribute	Description
Degree	Number of direct links with other nodes
In-degree	Number of directional ties leading to the node from other nodes (incoming ties)
Out-degree	Number of directional ties coming from the node toward other node (outgoing ties)
Isolate	A node that has no links or relatively few links to other nodes
Closeness	Extent to which a node is close to or can reach all other nodes in the network
Betweenness	Extent to which a node serves as a mediator or a necessary connector between two other nodes
Star	A node that is highly central to other nodes, which in turn are not highly connected to each other
Peripheral actor	A node that is located on the outer parts of the network as compared to all other nodes
Central actor	A node that is located in the inner parts of the network as compared to all other nodes

TABLE 7.2 Social network analysis: network attributes

Network attribute	Description
Density	Ratio of the number of present ties to the number of possible ties in the network
Size	Number of actors in networks
Connectivity	The extent to which actors in the network are linked to one another by direct or indirect ties
Cohesion	The extent to which a network can remain connected even when various nodes are removed from the network
Centralisation	A measure of how central its most central node is in relation to how central all the other nodes are

TABLE 7.3 Social network analysis: relationship attributes

Relationship attribute	Description
Strength	The emotional intensity, the intimacy (mutual confiding), the reciprocal services and duration of the relationship
Multiplexity	The extent to which two actors are linked together by more than one relationship

cent of all possible linkages were active (MacLean *et al.* 2011). The authors described this network as 'fragmented . . . with few organisations exploring linkages with others in their network' (MacLean *et al.* 2011: 568).

COLLABORATION, COMPETITION AND 'COOPETITION'

Organisations were once faced with a simple option: kill or collaborate. In the modern world, it is a bit more complicated. *Collaboration* occurs 'when a group of autonomous stakeholders of a problem domain engage in an interactive process using shared rules, norms, and structures, to act or decide on issues related to that domain' (Wood and Gray 1991: 146). *Competition* is often conceived as being the opposite of collaboration and cooperation. Competition emerges when there is demand for limited resources by multiple organisations (Barman 2002). *Coopetition* combines two opposite logics: the competitive paradigm – competing interests – and the collaborative paradigm – common interests. A coopetitive relationship between organisations is characterised by simultaneous competition and cooperation. Coopetition is particularly evident in sports leagues – teams compete on the field, but also cooperate with each other on a large number of off-field matters (Robert *et al.* 2009).

Why do organisations establish IORs?

Academic theories conceptualise the reasons underpinning the establishment of IORs differently; for example, exchange theory argues that organisations must acquire resources from other organisations to survive. Both ecology theory and contingency theory share a premise about fit between the organisations' external context and internal arrangements: IORs are an adaptation to the demands of their environment and allow an organisation to fit, and therefore survive. Transaction cost theory suggests that IORs are formed to lower the costs of negotiating, retaining and monitoring inter-organisational agreements. Organisations are motivated to establish IORs for a variety of reasons (Babiak 2007).

Necessity: Organisations establish links with other organisations(s) to meet a mandate or requirement from a higher authority or governing body. Without the direction of the higher authority, the relationship/link would be non-existent.

Asymmetry: Organisations will establish an IOR to exert power or control over other firms or their resources. An example of this is when a corporation may form a director interlock with a financial institution to increase control over sources of capital and increase its power compared to other firms competing for financial resources in the same industry.

Reciprocity: Organisations may want to cooperate and collaborate in a coordinated and organised approach. Reciprocity is the opposite of asymmetry. The relationships feature equal exchange and mutual support rather than conflict and coercion. The reciprocity motive would be evident when two organisations create a joint venture to target new markets.

Efficiency: Organisations will seek to improve the input/output ratio. Establishing an enduring relationship will be more efficient than a series of one-off transactions with different organisations.

Stability: Managers dislike uncertainty. IORs are one way of reducing uncertainty and should create an orderly and predictable flow of resources. This allows managers to operate with more certainty and confidence.

Legitimacy: Organisations will link with organisations because there is an expectation that they should. For example, an event may seek an association with a social cause, not because they are genuinely committed to helping, but because all other comparable events have a social responsibility partner.

At a slightly different level of analysis, Kolb (2013) provides a framework of what she calls triggers for IORs. The likelihood of inter-organisational cooperation is increased when: (1) organisations share an interest in achieving a common goal; (2) organisational self-interest is low; (3) the complexity of joint action is low; (4) geographic proximity is high; and (5) socialisation (trust and similar values) between organisations is high. These factors are presented in Figure 7.2.

What characterises an effective IOR?

The resource-based view (RBV) of the firm argues that an organisation's sustainable competitive advantage is underpinned by possession of resources that are valuable, rare, imperfectly imitable and non-substitutable (Truyens *et al.* 2014). There is growing evidence that IORs also facilitate competitive advantage (Dyer and Singh 1998). Dyer and Singh (1998: 662) define a relational rent as 'a supernormal profit jointly generated

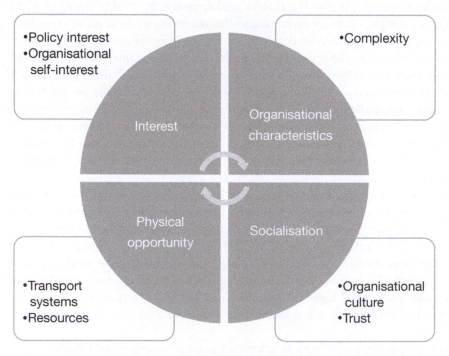

FIGURE 7.2 Factors facilitating inter-organisational relations

Source: Adapted from Kolb (2013)

in an exchange relationship that cannot be generated by either firm in isolation and can only be created through the joint idiosyncratic contributions of the specific alliance partners'. The ability to create and manage relationships more effectively than others can become a source of competitive advantage (Dyer *et al.* 2001). There are four potential sources of inter-organisational competitive advantage within a relationship.

Relationship-specific assets: Organisations invest in relationship-specific assets. These assets are specialised and have utility only if the relationship continues. The distinguishing feature of relationship-specific assets is that their value is greater within a relationship than outside it. Because the asset is relationship-specific, it is not easily acquired by other organisations.

Knowledge-sharing routines: While traditional approaches encouraged organisations to keep the cards close to their chests, IORs that are characterised by the free and open exchange of knowledge will likely outperform those that do not. The new knowledge leads to innovative ideas and new capabilities and technologies.

Complementary resources/capabilities: Each organisation brings a set of skills, resources, aspirations, expertise and knowledge to the relationship. The hope is that the combination of these resources is synergistic. In these circumstances, the combined resources are more valuable, rare and difficult to imitate and substitute than ever before. It is the metaphoric equivalent of $2 + 2 = 5$.

Effective governance: IORs need to be governed. Effective relationships do not just happen. It is important that transaction costs are minimised: time and energy devoted to managing the relationship is time and energy not directed at the relationship's outcomes. Management intensity is the extent to which partners are willing to intervene in the management of the relationship (Shaw and Allen 2006). There is an optimal level of intervention. If the relationship is hands-off, then confusion about partner responsibilities is likely. On the other hand, if a partner engages in micromanagement or over-management, then problems will also ensue. A balanced approach that reflects the nature of the relationship and the needs of partnering organisations is recommended. In addition to being low-maintenance, the governance of the relationship should also maximise value.

Communication is also key for both knowledge sharing and effective governance. Formal communication refers to written documents such as contracts and memoranda of understanding. These documents seek clarity, consistency and a common understanding, or what has been described as *joined-up thinking* (Shaw and Allen 2006). Formal communication can only do so much. Informal communication – interpersonal face-to-face, telephone and email communication – is essential to create understanding.

A study of the relationships between community sport clubs and various organisations in the community identified three critical relationship qualities: *engagement, reciprocity* and *trust* (Misener and Doherty 2012). Engagement is characterised by frequent and open communication – knowledge-sharing routines – and regular meetings – effective governance and management intensity. Reciprocity is the ability to give and take, or to scratch someone's back if they scratch yours. More technically, reciprocity is the process of responding favourably to another by returning benefits for benefits. In a study of event networks, research revealed a high reciprocity score for shared information, but not for shared resources, demonstrating different ways in which reciprocity can manifest (Ziakas and Costa 2010). Within IORs, reciprocity is associated with balance, harmony, equity and mutual support, and will likely limit coercion, conflict and domination (Oliver 1990).

Inter-organisational trust is the expectation between partners' intent to meet their obligations. Trust is both subjective and dynamic. Trust influences the nature of the relationship and the amount and quality of information and knowledge exchange. The extent to which values are shared will determine largely whether trust is absent, conditional or unconditional. Good partners are trustworthy partners.

Are there any problems with IORs?

Relationships offer many benefits, but they also come at a cost. Power is the ability of one organisation to negatively affect another organisation. Resource dependency theory recognises that organisations need the resources that are controlled by other organisations. This dependency exposes the organisation to the use of power by other organisations. The extent to which an organisation is dependent on another organisation for resources is largely determined by the extent to which the resource is important, and the availability of alternative sources from which the organisation can acquire the resources. According to Pfeffer and Salancik (1978: 16), 'The price of inclusion in any collective structure is the loss of discretion and control over one's own activities'. Organisations will tend to avoid inter-organisational linkages that significantly limit their autonomy.

IORs often require significant costs to negotiate, develop and monitor. Transaction costs include all costs associated with making an economic exchange. There are three categories of transaction costs: (1) search costs – the costs of locating information about opportunities for exchange; (2) negotiation costs – the costs of negotiating the terms of the exchange; and (3) enforcement costs – the costs of enforcing the contract. When applied to sport sponsorship, the three types of cost are: (1) planning and safeguarding; (2) adapting and servicing; and (3) monitoring and evaluating (Sam *et al.* 2005).

Opportunity costs are also relevant. Opportunity costs refer to the value of the next-highest-valued alternative use of that resource. The relationship opportunity costs are the benefits foregone from being constrained with specific partners. For example, when a government agency decides to invest $100,000 in an SFD program related to homelessness, they are unable to fund another program focusing on domestic violence.

Conflict occurs when one organisation perceives that another organisation has, or will, negatively affect them. This is underpinned by goal incongruence. Dysfunctional behaviour, in the form of withholding information or resources, will lead to further disagreement and frustration. Inter-organisational conflict can therefore compromise the relationship effectiveness.

IORs promise a lot in terms of cooperation and goodwill, but conflict and tension will always occur. Brinkerhoff (2002: 21) captures this sentiment: 'Partnership encompasses mutual influence, with a careful balance between synergy and respective autonomy, which incorporates mutual respect, equal participation in decision making, mutual accountability and transparency'.

Dissolution

IORs do not last forever. Some are purposefully timebound, but many do not last that long. A dissolved relationship occurs 'when all activity links are broken and no resource ties or actor bonds exist between the companies' (Halinen and Tahtinen 2002: 166).

Dissolution can be sudden but is normally preceded by relationship fading, the permanent or temporary weakening of a relationship. There are three groups of factors that underpin relationship dissolution: predisposing factors are those that were extant when the relationship was established; precipitating events can be either sudden or culminating; and attenuating factors reduce the effects of predisposing factors and precipitating events. Farrelly (2010) identified five reasons for sponsorship breakdowns: (1) strategic versus tactical intent; (2) failure to adapt to changing perceptions of value, opportunity and responsibility; (3) conflicting perceptions of contributions and the need to provide proof; (4) commitment asymmetry; and (5) capability gap.

IMPLICATIONS OF THEORY FOR PRACTICE

IORs are essential for delivering both SD and SFD programs and initiatives. IORs are evident within the three key areas of funding and infrastructure (for example, government, funders and sponsors), sport organisations (for example, pathways, participation and high performance institutes) and support agencies (for example, NGOs and government departments). While it may seem that a single organisation is responsible for delivering sport development pathways and programs, these are nearly always contingent upon the involvement of multiple organisations. Support agencies, institutes of sport, anti-doping authorities, sport facilities and sponsors must all work together with the sport club, team or governing body to achieve mutually desirable outcomes.

APPLICATION OF THEORY TO PRACTICE

IORs are of increased importance in the context of SFD because sport organisations rarely have the capacity and expertise to deliver on non-sport outcomes. This encourages sports organisations to bring in the necessary expertise to realise program goals. In turn, NGOs require the leverage and public profile of the sport to act as a hook or tool to engage the target populations. In some cases, a tripartite relationship can be developed between the sport organisation, an NGO and a funding body or sponsor, each with their own motives. Examples of these types of relationships are demonstrated in the two case studies provided below.

Case Study 1: making Australian Rules football a New Zealand game

Geoff Dickson and Emma Sherry

AFL New Zealand (AFLNZ) is recognised by both Sport New Zealand and the AFL as the governing body for Australian Rules football in New Zealand. The vision of AFLNZ is to make Australian Rules football a New Zealand game. This vision does not mean they expect Australian Rules football to become a dominant, significant national sport, or that New Zealand will supplant Australia as the home of Australian Rules football. Rather, AFLNZ seek to have Australian Rules football perceived as a natural part of the New Zealand sporting landscape. The aim is to eliminate the perception that it is just an Australian game.

AFLNZ receives annual funding from the AFL of approximately NZ$180,000. The AFL appoints four directors to the seven-person AFLNZ board. The remaining three directors are elected by AFLNZ's member organisations – the 16 NZ clubs and the Auckland AFL. AFLNZ directors have spoken openly of their desire to be treated the same as the AFL state affiliates (such as AFL Queensland and AFL Victoria). While the practice of AFL appointments may reduce the autonomy of AFLNZ, the resultant board considers 'being on the inside' of the AFL as offering significant opportunities.

Junior participation numbers have increased from zero in 2007 to nearly 40,000 in 2015. AFLNZ applies to Regional Sports Trusts and Gaming Machine Trusts for funding to its conduct in school, fundamental skills program. KiwiKick is an SD program for boys and girls aged 5–12 that mimics the Auskick program in Australia. The AFL has no concerns with AFLNZ using its intellectual property. The in-school program feeds into a 10-week, user-pays, after-school program. Organised lesson plans, volunteer retention initiatives, resource kits and coaching accreditation are all features of KiwiKick.

The secondary schools program is multifaceted. There are programs that develop skills, culminating in either intra-school (House Rules) or inter-school competitions (Hawks Cup). These competitions also include AFL 9s, which require only nine players and less space than the standard 18 players per team. AFLNZ is sanctioned by New Zealand Secondary School Sports Council (NZSSSC), and AFLNZ events appear in their calendar. The CEO of the NZSSSC is an appointed director of AFLNZ. The Leadership program trains students to manage a tournament within their own school or at local primary and intermediate schools. Sessions focus on game understanding, coaching, umpiring and event management. The Gateway program provides secondary school students with the opportunity to deliver the KiwiKick program. The Combine program provides participants with the opportunity to compete in a number of skills and athletic testing. Those who excel are directed towards New Zealand national teams and international scholarships with AFL clubs.

The High Performance program includes six men's teams, U15, 16, 17, 18 and the Hawks (open-age) and the women's national team, the Kahus. These teams play against touring teams from Australia – for example, the Victorian Amateur Football Association U18 representative team, the Australian Institute of Sport Level 1 team, the Australian Breeze (U18 women) and the Flying Boomerangs. Players in the Flying Boomerangs team are participants in the personal development and leadership program for Aboriginal and Torres Strait Islander young men aged 14–15 years. Depending on the age group, the New Zealand representative teams will also compete in tournaments against Pacific Island nations or Australian regional teams. The Hawks also participate in the International Cup. The International Cup is held every three years and is essentially the World Championships (without Australia). There is one other New Zealand team: the Heritage team, also known as the All New Zealand team, which consists of AFL players with New Zealand heritage.

AFLNZ has partnerships with two AFL clubs: Hawthorn and St Kilda. Both are keen to access talent (that is, players). St Kilda created history in 2013 when they played the Sydney Swans in Wellington – the first AFL fixture to be played outside of Australia. The event was facilitated by the AFL, in part to help AFLNZ increase junior participation rates.

The profile of AFL in New Zealand was greatly boosted in 2013 when Sommet TV began broadcasting AFL matches. Sommet TV is a free-to-air sports channel that is also included in the Sky Television package. There is no formal relationship between Sommet and AFLNZ; Sommet purchase the broadcast rights from the AFL. However, both organisations recognise that television viewers might be the next generation of players and that players are among those most likely to watch the AFL broadcasts. AFLNZ receive a share of all gambling revenue and profits from the New Zealand TAB. The New Zealand TAB is owned by the New Zealand Racing Board, which was established in 2003 under the Racing Act to administer all racing and sports wagering in New Zealand. AFLNZ revenues from betting increased significantly when Sommet began broadcasting; however, initially Sommet did not receive revenue from the New Zealand TAB, despite their direct role in increasing gambling turnover. The AFLNZ executive was instrumental in forging a formalised relationship between Sommet and the New Zealand TAB. It is now a case of a win-win-win situation.

This case study has shown how the growth of Australian Rules football in New Zealand was underpinned by a number of key relationships between a variety of organisations.

Further resources

AFLNZ: www.aflnz.co.nz
AFL: www.afl.com.au
AFL Europe: www.afleurope.org

Case study extension activities

1 Review the annual reports for the AFL and AFLNZ. Can you detect any changes to the way in which the AFL is developing football internationally? Can you detect any changes to the organisations that comprise AFLNZ's network?
2 Examine the AFL Europe website. How do the organisations in AFLNZ's network differ from those of AFL Europe?

Case Study 2: *The Big Issue* Community Street Soccer Program

Geoff Dickson and Emma Sherry

The Big Issue Community Street Soccer Program was founded in Melbourne in 2007. Its aim was to provide a sport and recreation program to the vendors of *The Big Issue* magazine, and to people living in supported housing nearby. From this small start, the program grew to over 30 sites across Australia, delivering regular football program activities to many thousands of disadvantaged and marginalised members of the community.

This success of the Community Street Soccer Program owes much to its successful relationships with local support agencies, including police, crisis housing services, community legal aid and food vans. Each program works in partnership with their local community service providers to deliver programs for the disadvantaged or at-risk members of their community. These combined efforts are greater than the sum of their parts.

At the national level, *The Big Issue* also developed strategic partnerships with government, health promotion agencies and corporate sponsors to fund the Community Street Soccer Program. In a unique tripartite arrangement, *The Big Issue* partnered with a professional football club (Melbourne Heart – A-League) and the public transport ticketing agency (Metlink) to provide tickets to the A-League games for Community Street Soccer participants. This initiative also allowed Metlink to educate the homeless and disadvantaged participants on the risks of fare evasion when travelling on public transport. Through this partnership, each organisation achieved its own unique aims: access to a target community; organisational corporate social responsibility programs and incentives; and education for program participants.

Further resources

The Big Issue: www.thebigissue.org.au/community-street-soccer/our-program/

Case study extension activities

Choose an SFD program in your area. How many organisations are involved in delivering this program? What other potential partnership opportunities could develop the program further?

SUPPLEMENTARY EXERCISES

1 For a sport organisation of your choosing, model their inter-organisational network. Ensure that your model categorises the organisation into similar groupings.
2 Using a social network approach and software of your choice, analyse your Facebook network data.
3 Choose a sport development or sport for development program. Use your understanding of IORs to identify three potential partners for the program, including the outcomes for each partner and the skills or expertise that each partner brings to the program.

SUMMARY

IORs are integral and essential components of sport development. IORs decrease environmental uncertainty and facilitate the acquisition of resources, which enables the provision of higher-quality sport experiences. Calls for a more efficient and effective sport system are essentially a call for improved IORs. A study of a sport organisation without any consideration to its embeddedness within its wider inter-organisational network will provide, at best, only half the story.

DISCUSSION QUESTIONS

1 In what ways are IORs analogous to interpersonal relationships, both intimate and professional?
2 What are the different outcomes typically sought by the following partners:
   (a) Government?
   (b) Sponsor?
   (c) National sport governing body?
   (d) Sport institute (high performance)?
   (e) Non-governmental organisation?
   (f) Charity?
   (g) Sport facility?
3 Thinking about the different partners identified above in question 2, what benefits does each partner bring to the relationship?
4 What are the risks associated with inter-organisational relationships in the SD sector?
5 What are the risks associated with inter-organisational relationships in the SFD sector?

REFERENCES

Babiak, K. (2007) 'Determinants of interorganisational relationships: the case of a Canadian nonprofit sport organization', *Journal of Sport Management*, 21(3): 338–76.

Barman, E. A. (2002) 'Asserting difference: the strategic response of nonprofit organizations to competition', *Social Forces*, 80(4): 1191–222.

Brinkerhoff, J. (2002) *Partnership for International Development: Rhetoric or Results?* Boulder, CO: Lynne Rienner Publishers.

Dyer, J. H. and Singh, H. (1998) 'The relational view: cooperative strategy and sources of interorganisational competitive advantage', *Academy of Management Review*, 23(4): 660–79.

Dyer, J. H., Kale, P. and Singh, H. (2001) 'How to make strategic alliances work', *MIT Sloan Management Review*, 42(4): 37–43.

Farrelly, F. (2010) 'Not playing the game: why sport sponsorship relationships break down', *Journal of Sport Management*, 24(3): 319–37.

Halinen, A. and Tahtinen, J. (2002) 'A process theory of relationship ending', *International Journal of Service Industry Management*, 13(2): 163–80.

Kennelly, M. and Toohey, K. (2014) 'Strategic alliances in sport tourism: national sport organisations and sport tour operators', *Sport Management Review*, 17(4): 407–18.

Kolb, M. (2013) *The European Union and the Council of Europe*, Hampshire: The European Union and the Council of Europe.

MacLean, J., Cousens, L. and Barnes, M. (2011) 'Look who's linked with whom: a case study of one community basketball network', *Journal of Sport Management*, 25(6): 562–75.

Misener, K. and Doherty, A. (2012) 'Connecting the community through sport club partnerships', *International Journal of Sport Policy and Politics*, 4(2): 243–56.

Oliver, C. (1990) 'Determinants of interorganisational relationships: integration and future directions', *Academy of Management Review*, 15(2): 241–65.

Pfeffer, J. and Salancik, G. (1978) *The External Control of Organizations: A Resource Dependence Perspective*, New York: Harper & Row.

Provan, K. G., Fish, A. and Sydow, J. (2007) 'Interorganisational networks at the network level: a review of the empirical literature on whole networks', *Journal of Management*, 33(3): 479–516.

Quatman, C. and Chelladurai, P. (2008) 'Social network theory and analysis: a complementary lens for inquiry', *Journal of Sport Management*, 22(3): 338–60.

Robert, F., Marques, P. and Le Roy, F. (2009) 'Coopetition between SMEs: an empirical study of French professional football', *International Journal of Entrepreneurship and Small Business*, 8(1): 23–43.

Sam, M. P., Batty, R. and Dean, R. G. K. (2005) 'A transaction cost approach to sport sponsorship', *Sport Management Review*, 8(1): 1–17.

Shaw, S. and Allen, J. B. (2006) ' "It basically is a fairly loose arrangement . . . and that works out fine, really": analysing the dynamics of an interorganisational partnership', *Sport Management Review*, 9(3): 203–28.

Truyens, J., De Bosscher, V., Heyndels, B. and Westerbeek, H. (2014) 'A resource-based perspective on countries' competitive advantage in elite athletics', *International Journal of Sport Policy*, 6(3): 459–89.

Velija, P., Ratna, A. and Flintoff, A. (2014) 'Exclusionary power in sports organisations: the merger between the Women's Cricket Association and the England and Wales Cricket Board', *International Review for the Sociology of Sport*, 49(2): 211–26.

Wasserman, S. and Faust, K. (1994) *Social Network Analysis: Methods and Applications*, New York: Cambridge University Press.

Wood, D. and Gray, B. (1991) 'Towards a comprehensive theory of collaboration', *Journal of Applied Behavioral Science*, 27(2): 139–62.

Ziakas, V. and Costa, C. (2010) 'Explicating inter-organizational linkages of a host community's events network', *International Journal of Event and Festival Management*, 1(2): 132–47.

CHAPTER 8

Coaches, officials and change agents in sport development

Pamm Phillips and Nico Schulenkorf

INTRODUCTION

Previous chapters in this book have discussed in detail models of sport development (SD) and sport for development (SFD). In particular, as the reader might have already gathered, coaches, officials and change agents have significant roles to play in facilitating SD for athletes, and for ensuring that programming is delivered appropriately so that SFD outcomes can be realised.

OUTLINE OF THE CHAPTER

This chapter highlights the roles and responsibilities of coaches and officials in SD, as well as highlighting the additional expectations and accountabilities of change agents working in SFD. Change agents can be described as facilitators or mediators that aim to support communities to achieve desired SFD outcomes – therefore, they are often involved both on and off the field of play. This chapter also examines the training and educational development of coaches, officials and change agents so that they can be most effective during their involvement in SD and SFD. We begin this chapter with a theoretical overview before providing a coaching case study from Australia and a study of change agents in an SFD program in Sri Lanka. The case studies will illustrate and further our theoretical arguments in an applied manner.

After completing this chapter, you should be able to:

- understand the roles and responsibilities of coaches, officials and change agents in the delivery of sport;
- understand the pathways for coach and official development for SD and SFD program delivery;
- articulate the differences and similarities between athlete development and coach/official development – systems and structures; and
- appreciate the important yet complex role of change agents within the community development process.

COACHING AND SD

In a sporting context, coaches can be one of the most positive influences on participants (USADA 2011). In Australia alone, almost 700,000 coaches are involved in sport at all levels, and each week touch the lives of almost seven million people (Dawson and Phillips 2013). Coaches can, and do, fulfil many roles in the lives of participants. Researchers have suggested that coaches can play the role of mentors, teachers (Banks 2006; Pyke 2001), managers and leaders (Gilbert and Trudel 2004; Kellett 1999), father figures (Tutko and Richards 1971) and moral educators (Bergmann Drewe 2000; Russell 2011). In other words, not only are coaches deemed responsible for the technical and skill development of athletes; they are also seen to be responsible for developing individuals beyond sport. In this way, it is implied that coaches have a role in SFD (Schulenkorf 2010), as well as in SD (Green 2005; Sotiriadou *et al.* 2008). However, the importance of their role is only beginning to be understood and articulated from a research perspective. Research that informs practice seems particularly important in this space because many coaches report that they are ill prepared for their roles (Wiersma and Sherman 2005). Overall, it seems that sport organisations have some ground to cover in order to devise programs and support for the development of their coaches.

The work of coaches is diverse and multifaceted. For example, Dawson and Phillips (2013) note that coaches work at various levels and in various capacities within a broad range of sport systems and settings. Coaches can be full- or part-time professionals who are employed by a sport organisation. Some coaches may also be employed in multiple sport organisations due to their expertise and transferability of skills across sports – such as a cycling coach who may train triathletes, or a baseball coach who may coach cricket players in pitching or throwing. Coaches may manage assistant coaches and support staff, or be self-employed. Coaches may also volunteer in the role. Such coaches work for minimal, or no, pay and may work anywhere in an SD system from community to elite levels. Across a coaching career, individuals may coach in any or all of these various capacities.

Of course, this makes for a diverse workforce, and understanding what to offer in training, education and accreditation for the large number of coaches, who work in very different capacities within sport, is difficult to do. It is well recognised internationally that a major problem in creating coach development resources is that a large proportion of the coaching workforce are volunteer coaches who may not have the willingness, nor the time, to devote to furthering their qualifications in what essentially might be a hobby or a position that they temporarily fulfil while their children participate (Lynn and Lyle 2010; Shilbury and Kellett 2011; Vargas-Tonsing 2007). Adding further complexity to the problem of creating resources for coach education and training is that individuals come to the coaching context at varying ages and from various backgrounds. Wehner and Dawson (2010) noted that some individuals may begin coaching as teenagers, while others begin the role as a parent. Not only do coach education resources need to consider the multitude of ways in which individuals may work in sport – and therefore consider the relevance of information to their role – they also need to consider the type of learner the individual may be. For example, a coach might come to the learning environment as an adult or as a youth. They may be a parent, with experience of working with children, or they may have no experience of working with children at all. Alternatively, they may be a manager, who works with people, or they may have no management experience at all.

There are a number of challenges to address in order to manage coaching workforces (Crawford 2009; Lynn and Lyle 2010). Governments in the UK and Canada have recognised the important contributions that coaches make across all levels of sport and athlete development, and have invested heavily in their development. For example, the UK government invested approximately £45 million into providing more support for coaching development and practice through the establishment of Sports Coach UK (DCMS 2002). The investment included providing dedicated personnel to work in schools (Timson-Katchis and North 2008), as well as developing an education system that provided extensive online development resources for coaches (DCMS 2002; Sports Coach UK 2008, 2012). In Australia, an independent review of the state of Australian sport suggested that although there are national coach accreditation systems in place, sport-specific coach development is left largely up to the individual sports to fund and manage (Crawford 2009). This creates a landscape where sports vary greatly in the quality of coaching that they offer to potential participants: while some sport organisations have well-developed coach accreditation systems in place, others do not.

The issue of coach training and education is an important one to consider from a sport development perspective. Often, the most novice coaches – perhaps a parent – work with beginners in the sport. In other words, a sport organisation may have been successful at attracting an individual to their sport, yet in many cases a novice coach is charged with developing a newcomer's skills and nurturing them towards life-long participation in the sport. On the other hand, the very best and most experienced coaches work with the most elite athletes, who arguably need a different focus from the coach beyond skill development. In the case of elite athletes, other aspects of sport, including social and psychological training, may be required for professional athletes to advance their careers. Training and education of a coaching workforce therefore is both complex and multifaceted.

In their study on Australian athletics coaches, Dawson and Phillips (2013) found a distinct lack of policy for coach career development, both within individual sports and nationally, at the highest level of governance of sport in the nation via the ASC. In other words, despite large investments in sport development aimed at ensuring smooth development pathways for athletes, the very individuals who support them – the coaches – are not catered for in ways that recognise the diversity and complexity of coach careers. Practically, for the sport of athletics it is suggested that poor athlete results and organisational issues might partly result due to the lack of attention paid to the development of the vital resource of coaches (Dawson and Phillips 2013).

Case Study 1: educating coaches to deliver modified sport programs: coaching in modified rules in Australian Rules football

Kylie Bellesini and Pamm Phillips

Modified sport programs are an important component of sport development programs as they facilitate opportunities for athletes to play, as well as learn and develop appropriate skills, as we discussed in Chapter 6. In Australia, the AFL has provided a comprehensive set of modified rules for junior Australian Rules football (AF) players to introduce them to the sport and provide age- and skill-appropriate rule reforms to aid in their development. As AF is traditionally played on a very large ground, making it difficult to interact and communicate with beginner U9 participants, one modified rule for that competition has been to allow the coach onto the field of play during competitive play – known as the coach-on-ground rule. The official AFL Junior Match Guide rules state that the coach is allowed on the ground during play 'for the sole purpose of providing immediate feedback to players' (AFL 2015: 17).

Most sports do not allow coaches on the field of play, even in modified sport settings, so the coach-on-ground rule for the U9 group profoundly changes the coaching context. The rule allows coaches to be in close proximity to players throughout competitive play, to follow play around the ground and to provide constant and immediate information to players about their skill execution and performance. In this way, the reader might imagine that this rule provides the opportunity for coaching practice to be very different to what traditionally occurs when coaches are limited to coaching from the sidelines during play, and only have access to players at official breaks in play, such as quarter- or half-time.

Coaches of most AF U9 teams undertake the role voluntarily, and many are parents of the participants. While the AFL – like many other sport organisations nationally and internationally – has mandatory accreditation for all coaches, regardless of level, a study of U9 coaches who utilised the coach-on-ground rule in 2012 found that the coaches were not educated appropriately to use the rule in ways that would maximise the development opportunities that it offers (Dawson and Phillips 2013).

U9 coaches recognised that the main advantage of the rule was that it allowed them to provide immediate feedback to players, which they noted was particularly important when children were developing their skills and their understanding of AF and how it is played. In contrast, when coaches were observed while coaching from the field of play, they did not use the rule in the ways it was intended. Coaches rarely moved around the ground to get into positions from where they could provide immediate feedback to players. They seldom moved with the play; instead, they coached from a standing position in the middle of the ground. In essence, they stood predominantly in one place and yelled instruction and feedback loudly at players who were positioned around the ground (Dawson and Phillips 2013). This is no different to what they would have been limited to doing if they had coached from the sidelines and were not allowed onto the ground.

Further, coaches did not take the opportunity to provide different types of feedback, or more frequent feedback that their proximity to players would allow. Coach feedback was focused mostly on player positioning – where to stand and/or move – and while positive, the opportunity to provide feedback in ways that would assist skill development did not occur (Dawson and Phillips 2013). Therefore, the real advantage of the rule was not realised. This has important implications for the AFL, as a key part of their sport development pathway and processes is missing through the coaches' lack of understanding of how to use the rule modifications. Sport development programming may need reviewing to ensure the appropriate and relevant management and education of coaches to implement the rule and use it to their advantage, to ensure player participation and development.

Further resources

AFL Junior Match Guide: This is Our Game: www.aflcommunityclub.com.au/index.php?id=32

Case study extension activities

1   What should the AFL do to educate coaches of U9 competitions? What elements of coaching are different to what might be expected at elite levels and how would you develop an education program to assist parents who volunteer for such roles?
2   Do modified rules sport programs require different coaching practices? Explain your perspective.
3   Choose a modified sport program that you are familiar with. How are coaches prepared to work in this context?
4   Choose a sport that you are familiar with. How can coaching be modified to assist in SD?

SUPPLEMENTARY EXERCISE

In groups of four or five, create a list of all of the different roles and responsibilities that coaches undertake. This list will be used to design an education framework for coaches. It might be useful to begin by imagining a particular coach such as a professional coach, your own coach, a coach of community sport, a club coach, a high performance coach, or you may be coach and can draw on personal experience. Brainstorm to create a list of things that these coaches do. Next, share your list with another group and collate a master list. What are common elements that all coaches should have skills or accreditation in? How would you teach these to a teenager compared with a parent?

OFFICIALS IN SD

Without officials – umpires or referees – organised sport would not exist. Officials ensure that standard rules of competition are adhered to, and that the sport is played in a safe manner. Similar to the situation described above with coaching, models of SD imply that officials are necessary personnel as part of a comprehensive SD system, but there has been little attention paid to how they are an integrated part of SD pathways, or how officials themselves are developed so that they are effective in SD systems.

Umpire recruitment and retention is a problem for many sports internationally (Kellett and Shilbury 2007). High turnover rate is an expensive human resource problem, and too many sport organisations invest in training and developing umpires who very quickly leave the role (Kellett and Warner 2011). Kellett and Shilbury (2007) noted that it is a common misperception that umpires discontinue largely due to the verbal – and sometimes physical – abuse that they receive. In fact, Kellett and Shilbury (2007) found that for those umpires who continued in the activity, abuse was not something that concerned them; rather, they liked being an umpire for many reasons that rendered any abuse personally meaningless. Extending that study, Phillips and Fairley (2014) found that umpires at the community or club level of Australian Rules football competitions actively engage in umpiring as it is a choice about what to do in their leisure time. That is, individuals who umpire understand umpiring as their sport – in a similar way that another individual might view and understand their participation in playing a sport. Umpires reported that the activity of umpiring had a dual purpose. First, the activity itself kept them fit and active and they felt that they could develop skills and mastery in umpiring if they desired. In this way, umpiring, from the perspective of SD, was no different to how athletes describe their experiences of sport (Phillips and Fairley 2014). Second, for individuals in this study, umpiring was also a social outlet. Umpires understood the activity as an important part of their lives and part of their identity. In this way, umpiring as an activity might be no different to the way in which sport can be used for benefit beyond the field of play – SFD (Phillips and Fairley 2014). However, umpires' pathways and transition opportunities have, until recently, not been considered critically from the perspective of SD and SFD – something that needs to be changed in the future.

CHANGE AGENTS IN SFD

While the terms coach and referee are self-explanatory for anyone interested in sport, the term *change agent* may be less familiar to sport students, and therefore deserves some explanation. In the context of organising and delivering SFD projects, change agents are described as anchormen or mediators between groups of people, and are defined by Schulenkorf (2010: 119) as 'external parties who help (communities) establish contact, open negotiations and develop projects for cooperation and sustainable development'. Change agents are often community workers, youth development professionals, sport coaches or volunteers who work in difficult social contexts to make a positive difference for individuals and their communities. For example, change agents may use sport projects to establish or facilitate contact and engagement between individuals and communities in the context of socially, culturally or ethnically divided societies.

Because of their active involvement on the field of play – as well as their engagement off the field of play – change agents also fulfil many of the roles that coaches and managers hold. At times, they may even act as umpires as they are generally considered impartial facilitators that are trusted and respected (Schulenkorf 2010). In recent years, it has become popular, particularly for young change agents, to combine sport-related development work with overseas travel. More and more students, interns and university graduates embark on a journey to new and challenging destinations and include on their itinerary SFD projects in developing countries in Africa, Asia or the Pacific Islands (see Darnell 2011; Schulenkorf *et al.* 2011; Tiessen 2008). In such cases, these individuals are getting involved as international change agents and their goal is to help disadvantaged communities with the staging of sport projects or events.

When projects are initiated or guided by international change agents, there is, however, the danger of employing a dominant paternalistic approach to management (Botes and van Rensburg 2000; Stiglitz 2002). The international change agent may unconsciously or consciously have the feeling of *knowing what's best* for communities, which may result in local input being undervalued (Midgley 1986; Willmott 1988). The misuse of power and the drift from a *bottom-up* towards a *top-down* approach may prohibit communities from showing and experiencing their own full potential, which in turn might lead to community uncertainty and resistance.

Against this background, several authors have highlighted the importance of establishing cooperative partnerships between change agents and local communities (Schulenkorf 2010; Sugden 2006; Vail 2007). If this can be done, jointly organised SFD projects have the best chances of prospering. On the one hand, change agents are able to instigate and guide the planning, management and delivery of SFD by mobilising support and inculcating an attitude of confidence and cooperation among participating community groups and their respective members. Change agents may foster grass-roots participation and integrate people and communities from different backgrounds, so that they rub shoulders in common tasks and seek common goals. On the other hand, local communities possess important cultural knowledge about the norms and values, customs and traditions of a place or community. Local communities have the requisite cultural work skills within or among given communities, which means that the work of change agents can benefit substantially from local input and participation (see, for example, Craig 2007; Darnell 2007; Guest 2009). It is argued that only a fruitful cooperation between communities and change agents can lead to the empowerment of people and groups that enhances individual and collective capacities and efficacy, as well as social and economic justice and well-being.

In sum, to achieve SFD objectives, change agents should not be serving as a dictating force, but as a supportive enabler and facilitator for projects and partnerships between project stakeholders, including players, residents, management and community organisations (Sanoff 2000; Skinner *et al.* 2008). At the same time – and with the intent of realising a sustainable form of development – local communities need to be empowered by receiving an increased amount of management responsibilities for SFD projects over time. This means that once the local communities have learned the skills necessary to plan, implement and manage projects themselves, change agents should take a step back and gradually reduce their influence on the project. In other words, change agents have succeeded once communities have full ownership of projects, and once they have made themselves redundant.

Case Study 2: SFD change agents working in a war-torn country

Nico Schulenkorf

As a result of historic developments and international influences, the island of Sri Lanka is an ethnically, religiously, linguistically and geographically diverse society. Of the 21 million people living on the island, 74 per cent are mainly Buddhist Sinhalese who speak Sinhala, 18 per cent are Hindu and Christian Tamils who speak Tamil, and 7 per cent are Indian and Sri Lankan Moors – generally labelled and referred to as Muslims in Sri Lanka – who speak either Sinhala, Tamil and/or English (Sri Lankan Department of Census and Statistics 2001).

Intergroup relations within multi-ethnic Sri Lanka have been fraught with difficulties for several decades. The Tamil minority has been distrustful of the country's unitary form of government, believing that the Sinhalese majority would abuse Tamil rights (Dunung 1995). In the 1970s, the Liberation Tigers of Tamil Eelam (LTTE or Tamil Tigers) were formed to fight for self-sovereignty in the north-eastern regions of Sri Lanka, which are considered the areas of traditional Tamil settlement. Seeing themselves as the acting representative of the Tamil people, the LTTE's violent demands culminated in a double civil war with the Sinhalese-dominated Sri Lankan government that lasted from 1983 to 2002 and 2008 to 2009; overall, the wars resulted in a terminal defeat of the Tamil Tigers and led to approximately 100,000 deaths on the island (Witte 2011). In 2015, civil society in Sri Lanka continues to suffer from the social, economic and political consequences of the civil war.

As an impartial change agent, the Asian-German Sport Exchange Program (AGSEP) is an NGO that has been conducting sport-related reconciliation projects in Sri Lanka since 2002. In cooperation with local communities and international donors, the organisation has focused mainly on youth integration projects in rural western Sri Lanka that are designed to make a modest contribution to overcoming intergroup rivalry and reducing ethnic distance on a community level. Thus far, AGSEP has been able to establish a sport complex in the western Sri Lankan town of Nattandiya for regular inter-community SFD activities for local youths. Moreover, a functioning sports event program across the country has been designed to encourage active social and intergroup development of the community at large. All AGSEP initiatives are supported by local community members and international volunteers who act as change agents; the latter are often sport and event management students from European universities who spend several months in Sri Lanka undertaking work experience or internship programs.

Against the background of a deeply divided society, interview-based qualitative research was conducted with SFD stakeholders to find out in detail about the roles and responsibilities of AGSEP's change agents in Sri Lanka (see Schulenkorf 2010). Findings suggested that change agents hold nine key roles and responsibilities in the inter-community SFD process. These are: an agent for community participation; a trust builder; a networker; a leader; a socially responsible advocate; a resource developer; a proactive innovator; a financial supporter; and a strategic planner for the long-term sustainability of SFD projects. The research study suggested that it is important to fulfil all these roles to secure active community participation, to achieve positive sociocultural SFD impacts and outcomes and to provide a strategic framework for inter-community development (Schulenkorf 2010).

Case study extension activities

1 The case study has introduced nine key roles and responsibilities for change agents in SFD. Can you think of examples for practical activities that align with these roles? What kind of activities would you have to engage in to fulfil the nine roles for AGSEP?
2 Do you think all roles and responsibilities are equally important? If you had to rank the nine roles, which ones would you select as the top three? Explain why.
3 Can you think of any additional roles that change agents should take at SFD projects?

The case study discussion highlights the very important roles and responsibilities of change agents in the community development process. Interestingly, to achieve their goals, sport-specific knowledge and expertise are often considered less important than social and youth development skills. This, of course, has consequences for the specific training and education programs that are designed for change agents. While some affinity towards sport is certainly desired in an SFD context, expert sport skills are not a prerequisite for success. Instead, training for change agents focuses more specifically on social skills, providing engagement opportunities, designing specific learning programs and fostering cultural activities, for example. For change agents that work on international projects – particularly for individuals from HICs working in an LIC or LMIC context – additional education, which focuses on local customs, cultural knowledge and community traditions, should be provided. While this is the ideal, unfortunately not all NGOs, development agencies and SFD programs are providing training and experience beyond sport. In contrast – and against the background of increasingly commercialised volunteering and placement programs (Godfrey *et al.* 2015) – there are numerous SFD entrepreneurs who provide fee-paying, volunteer opportunities for sport students to engage as change agents without providing this accurate social and cultural training and education.

SUPPLEMENTARY EXERCISE

In groups of four or five participants, try to design a training and education program for change agents going to work in a football-based SFD project in India. What focus should the education program take and what kind of activities would you include as part of the necessary training activities for change agents?

SUMMARY

This chapter has highlighted the important role that coaches, officials and change agents undertake in both SD and SFD. It notes the irony in having well-defined and developed athlete SD and SFD systems, yet poorly developed SD and SFD systems for the development of coaches, officials and change agents themselves. The chapter has articulated the varied tasks and responsibilities that coaches, officials and change agents can and should undertake as part of their role in SD and SFD. The complexity of the roles that they undertake has emphasised how difficult it is to develop and devise standardised programs and accreditation systems for coach, official and change agent education and training. The two case studies have illustrated the complexity that exists in this space; they have invited the reader to explore the different roles and responsibilities of coaches, officials and change agents, and to consider training and education in the respective social contexts.

DISCUSSION QUESTIONS

1 What is the value of coach education and accreditation in sport development?
2 Who should be responsible for coach education and accreditation?
3 How can a coach education system be designed to account for all of the complexities of the coach's role requirements and the age at which they might study coaching?
4 Which activities would you include in an education or accreditation system for change agents in an SFD context?

REFERENCES

AFL (2015) 'Junior Match Guide: This is Our Game', *AFL*, available at: www.aflcommunityclub.com.au/index.php?id=32 (accessed July 2015).

Banks, J. (2006) 'The role of the coach', in N. Goodman (ed.), *Beginning Coaching*, 4th edn, Canberra: Australian Sports Commission.

Bergmann Drewe, S. (2000) 'Coaches, ethics and autonom', *Sport, Education & Society*, 5(2): 147–62.

Botes, L. and van Rensburg, D. (2000) 'Community participation in development: nine plagues and twelve commandments', *Community Development Journal*, 35(1): 41–58.

Craig, G. (2007) 'Community capacity-building: something old, something new . . .?', *Critical Social Policy*, 27(3): 335–59.

Crawford, D. (2009) *The Future of Australian Sport*, Barton, ACT: Commonwealth of Australia, pp. 1–365.

Darnell, S. C. (2007) 'Playing with race: Right to Play and the production of whiteness in "development through sport"', *Sport in Society*, 10(4): 560–79.

Darnell, S. C. (2011) 'Identity and learning in international volunteerism: "sport for development and peace" internships', *Development in Practice*, 21(7): 974–86.

Dawson, A. and Phillips, P. (2013) 'Coach career development: who is responsible?', *Sport Management Review*, 16(4): 477–87.

Department of Culture, Media and Sport (DCMS) (2002) *The Coaching Task Force: Final Report*, London: Department of Culture, Media and Sport.

Dunung, S. (1995) *Doing Business in Asia*, New York: Lexington Books.

Gilbert, W. and Trudel, P. (2004) 'Role of the coach: how model youth team sport coaches frame their roles', *The Sport Psychologist*, 18: 21–43.

Godfrey, J., Wearing, S. and Schulenkorf, N. (2015) 'Medical volunteer tourism as an alternative to backpacking in Peru', *Tourism Planning and Development*, 12(1): 111–22.

Green, B. C. (2005) 'Building sport programs to optimize athlete recruitment, retention, and transition: toward a normative theory of sport development', *Journal of Sport Management*, 19(3): 233–54.

Guest, A. M. (2009) 'The diffusion of development-through-sport: analysing the history and practice of the Olympic Movement's grassroots outreach to Africa', *Sport in Society*, 12(10): 1336–52.

Kellett, P. (1999) 'Organisational leadership: lessons from professional coaches', *Sport Management Review*, 2(2): 150–71.

Kellett, P. and Shilbury, D. (2007) 'Umpire participation: is abuse really the issue?', *Sport Management Review*, 10(3): 209–29.

Kellett, P. and Warner, S. (2011) 'Creating communities that lead to retention: the social worlds and communities of umpires', *European Sport Management Quarterly*, 11(5): 471–94.

Lynn, A. and Lyle, J. (2010) 'Coaching workforce development', in J. Lyle and C. Cushion (eds), *Coaching: Professionalization and Practice*, Edinburgh: Churchill Livingstone, pp. 193–207.

Midgley, J. (1986) *Community Participation, Social Development and the State*, New York: Methuen.

Phillips, P. and Fairley, S. (2014) 'Umpiring: a serious leisure choice', *Journal of Leisure Research*, 46(2): 184–202.

Pyke, F. S. (2001) *Better Coaching: Advanced Coach's Manual*, 2nd edn, Belconnen, ACT: Australian Coaching Council.

Russell, J. S. (2011) 'The moral ambiguity of coaching youth sport', in A. R. Hardman and C. Jones (eds), *The Ethics of Sports Coaching*, London: Routledge, pp. 87–103.

Sanoff, H. (2000) *Community Participation Methods in Design and Planning*, New York: John Wiley & Sons.

Schulenkorf, N. (2010) 'The roles and responsibilities of a change agent in sport event development projects', *Sport Management Review*, 13(2): 118–28.

Schulenkorf, N., Thomson, A. and Schlenker, K. (2011) 'Intercommunity sport events: vehicles and catalysts for social capital in divided societies', *Event Management*, 15(2): 105–19.

Shilbury, D. and Kellett, P. (2011) *Sport Management in Australia: An Organisational Overview*, Crow's Nest, NSW: Allen & Unwin.

Skinner, J., Zakus, D. and Cowell, J. (2008) 'Development through sport: building social capital in disadvantaged communities', *Sport Management Review*, 11(3): 253–75.

Sotiriadou, P., Shilbury, D. and Quick, S. (2008) 'The attraction, retention/transition, and nurturing process of sport development: some Australian evidence', *Journal of Sport Management*, 22(3): 247–72.

Sports Coach UK (2008) *The UK Coaching Framework*, Leeds: Coachwise Limited.

Sports Coach UK (2012) *Coach Tracking Study: A Four-Year Study of Coaching in the UK*, Leeds: Coachwise Limited.

Sri Lankan Department of Census and Statistics (2001) *Sri Lanka: Statistical Abstract 2001. Chapter 2*, available at: www.statistics.gov.lk/population/index.htm (accessed July 2015).

Stiglitz, J. E. (2002) 'Participation and development: perspectives from the comprehensive development paradigm', *Review of Development Economics*, 6(2): 163–82.

Sugden, J. (2006) 'Teaching and playing sport for conflict resolution and co-existence in Israel', *International Review for the Sociology of Sport*, 41(2): 221–40.

Tiessen, R. (2008) 'Educating global citizens? Canadian foreign policy and youth study/volunteer abroad programs', *Canadian Foreign Policy*, 14(1): 77–84.

Timson-Katchis, M. and North, J. (2008) *UK Coaching Tracking Study: Year One Headline Report*, Leeds: Sports Coach.

Tutko, T. and Richards, J. (1971) *Psychology of Coaching*, Boston, MA: Allyn & Bacon.

USADA (2011) *The Importance of Others – Coaches, Parents, Peers – The TrueSport Report*, available at: www.usada.org/truesport/truesport-report/the-importance-of-others-coaches-parents-peers/ (accessed February 2015).

Vail, S. E. (2007) 'Community development and sport participation', *Journal of Sport Management*, 21(4): 571–96.

Vargas-Tonsing, T. M. (2007) 'Coaches' preferences for coaching education', *International Journal of Sports Science and Coaching*, 2(1): 25–35.

Wehner, K. and Dawson, A. (2010) 'Examining sports coaching philosophy: implications for policy, pedagogy and practice', *ICSSPE Bulletin*, 58: 1–3, Berlin: ICSSPE.

Wiersma, L. D. and Sherman, C. P. (2005) 'Volunteer youth coaches' perspectives of coaching education/certification and parental codes of conduct', *Research Quarterly for Exercise and Sport*, 76(3): 324–38.

Willmott, P. (1988) *Community Initiatives: Patterns and Prospects*, London: Policy Studies Institute.

Witte, C. (2011) 'Kriegsverbrechen: Sri Lanka's Killing Fields', *Deutsche Welle Asien*, 19 July, available at: http://dw.de/p/11yBV (accessed July 2015).

SECTION 5

Sport and social change

CHAPTER 9

Sport and health promotion

Katie Rowe and Katja Siefken

INTRODUCTION

In Chapter 2, the concepts of development *of* sport (SD) and development *through* sport (SFD) were introduced. SD was explained to be related to systems and pathways that are put in place to support athlete progression; while SFD was described as the ways in which sport can be used to contribute to community-related objectives such as peace, social cohesion and health, among others. These definitions provide a useful starting point for this chapter, positioning sport in the context of health promotion, as a vehicle through which health-related objectives can be achieved.

OUTLINE OF THE CHAPTER

In this chapter, the concepts of health, health promotion and physical activity are introduced, and the role of sport in promoting health is considered. Challenges associated with taking action to promote health through sport are introduced and readers are provided with examples of existing initiatives that aim to engage the population in physical activity and/or to use sport as a tool to communicate key health messages.

After completing this chapter, you should be able to:

* define and understand the concepts of health and health promotion;
* explain the role of sport in promoting health across the globe;
* comprehend the interrelated nature of physical activity and sport promotion;
* understand the challenges associated with promoting health through sport, particularly for sport organisations; and
* discuss initiatives that promote health through sport across the globe.

WHAT DOES THE THEORY TELL US?

In many societies, sport participation is seen as a healthy activity if performed in safe settings. This is largely due to the established links that exist between physical activity (PA) and health (WHO 2010). Comprehensive reviews of evidence related to the health benefits of PA have been explained elsewhere; for example, readers may like to review World Health Organization (2010) or Hardman and Stensel (2009). For our purposes in this discussion, however, it should be noted that the benefits of regular PA include reduced risk of cardiovascular diseases, diabetes, osteoporosis and some cancers (Haskell *et al.* 2007; Warburton *et al.* 2006). PA is also a key aspect of obesity prevention, a critical component of energy balance and is associated with positive mental health outcomes (Bull *et al.* 2004).

Despite the known benefits of PA and risks associated with inactivity, global rates of physical inactivity continue to rise (Kohl *et al.* 2012), placing strain on national health systems. While comparisons are difficult to draw, the severity of the impact that physical inactivity is having on population health has been likened to that of smoking or obesity (Lee *et al.* 2012).

To combat recent rises in global rates of physical inactivity, many governments around the world have established PA guidelines to encourage people to be more active in order to receive associated health benefits. Such guidelines are largely informed by the global recommendations for PA provided by the World Health Organization (WHO) and are of relevance to children and adults (WHO 2010).

Conceptualising health and health promotion

Health is a multidimensional concept that extends beyond describing one's physical state of being. A widely accepted definition, provided by the World Health Organization (WHO 1948: 100), contends that health is 'a state of complete physical, mental and social well-being, and not merely the absence of disease'. This definition highlights that health describes more than just one's physical capacity; it also relates to a person's mental well-being, their ability to interact with others and cope in their daily lives. Three dimensions of health that are often discussed in the literature, as noted in the above definition, include physical, mental and social health (WHO 1948), outlined below:

- *Physical health*: the absence of physical disease and having the energy to perform daily tasks – including moderate- to vigorous-intensity activity.
- *Mental health*: the absence of mental disorders and the ability to negotiate daily challenges and social interactions in life without major issues.
- *Social health*: the ability to interact with other people in the social environment and engage in satisfying personal relationships.

When conceptualising health in this way, it can be argued that sport and active recreation has the potential to enhance population health by engaging people in physically active behaviours, encouraging them to strive to achieve personal goals and providing a context for socialisation.

Health promotion is a core function of public health. It is both practical and cost-effective in reducing the global burden of disease and in mitigating the social and economic impact of diseases (WHO 2007). The most accepted definition was provided in the Ottawa Charter for Health Promotion (WHO 1986), wherein health promotion is defined as a 'process of enabling people to increase control over, and to improve their health' (WHO 1986: 1). This definition highlights that health promotion is about giving people the power to achieve positive health outcomes with respect to physical, mental and social health. When considering the role of sport within the context of health promotion, providing people with opportunities to participate in PA and to interact with others in a sporting setting can logically be thought of as ways that positive health outcomes can be achieved.

The World Health Organization: promoting health and physical activity

The WHO has recognised that physical inactivity is a global health risk that is contributing significantly to the non-communicable disease (NCD) burden (WHO 2004). The promotion of PA and sport participation are thus important elements of health promotion action, particularly so in disease prevention (Heath *et al.* 2012). For decades, the WHO has engaged with the sporting world to promote healthy lifestyles and the benefits of regular PA. In 2004, the WHO developed the Global Strategy on Diet, Physical Activity and Health (DPAS) (WHO 2004), which recognises the important links between sport, PA and health, and encourages member states to strengthen the links for reciprocal benefits.

Further, in 2010, the WHO published global recommendations on PA (WHO 2010), aiming to provide national- and regional-level policymakers with guidance on the dose-response relationship between the frequency, duration, intensity, type and total amount of PA needed for the prevention of NCDs. The different WHO regional and country offices provide guidance and technical support on PA promotion and policy development to the multiple sectors, including ministries of health, education and sports, as well as NGOs and other relevant stakeholders. Depending on cultural contexts, various policies, initiatives and programs are supported and implemented with the aim to enhance the physical, social and mental well-being of the citizens.

Sport in the context of health promotion

While clear definitions of health and health promotions have been provided, it can be argued that an agreed definition of the term *sport* has not been reached. Conceptualisations of sport can vary depending on the context in which it is being considered. Drawing on the work of others, Shilbury and Kellett (2011) noted that sport is: play-like in nature; involves elements of competition; is based on physical prowess; involves skill and strategy; has an uncertain outcome; has specific rules; uses specialised equipment and/or facilities; and involves formal sporting leagues based on competition, cooperation and conflict. While the key aspect of PA is embedded in this definition, when considering the role of sport in facilitating health outcomes, definitions of sport are often broader and can encapsulate recreational activities and forms of PA such as walking and dance.

Sport organisations and health promotion

There has been an ongoing debate regarding whether governments should invest more heavily in mass sport participation to achieve community development outcomes related to health and well-being or whether elite athlete development should be the main priority of sport organisations (Jolly 2013). While sport provides opportunities for PA and social interaction, sport participation and club involvement can also be associated with some negative health behaviours and outcomes. For example, sport participation, particularly at the elite level, comes with inherent risks of injury. Furthermore, other potentially negative behaviours and outcomes associated with sport include performance-enhancing drug use, eating disorders, violence, abuse and athlete burnout (Coakley et al. 2011) – each of which can be inadvertently encouraged in high performance sport contexts, given the intense pressure placed on athletes to perform. Sporting clubs often serve alcohol and rely on sales and/or sponsorship from junk food companies in order to generate revenue. So, while sport is considered to be an inherently healthy activity, some aspects of sport can undermine health promotion initiatives, thus compromising the current approach to the integration of sport into health promotion agendas.

Despite some of the negative potential behaviours associated with sport, governments around the world continue to call on sport clubs and associated organisations in efforts to promote PA and health more generally in the community (Casey et al. 2012; Eime et al. 2008). Many health agencies now provide funding to sport clubs in efforts to promote health. However, from a sport development perspective, sport systems have been built to attract participants and establish sporting pathways to enable talented athletes to achieve elite-level success (Sotiriadou et al. 2008). As such, sport organisations are not always equipped, nor resourced, to facilitate the achievement of health promotion objectives (Casey et al. 2009, 2012). Such objectives can be challenging to balance alongside elite athlete development targets. Furthermore, health outcomes can often be more difficult to measure than sport participation and performance outcomes. Herein lies the challenge for sport development professionals: to establish systems, policies and pathways that contribute to population health – while also producing champion athletes – with a limited pool of resources.

Physical activity promotion: theoretical perspectives

While sport participation is a key consideration in the context of sport development literature, efforts to understand and promote sport participation for health benefits can be informed by theoretical understandings provided in the health and behavioural sciences literature (Rowe et al. 2013). Theoretical models and frameworks related to PA participation have been developed to assist researchers in their quests for understanding, given the range of possible participation influences that may impact PA behaviour (Sallis and Owen 1999). Some commonly applied models in the context of PA participation research include the health belief model, the theory of planned behaviour, the theory of reasoned action, the transtheoretical model, social cognitive theory and ecological models. Such models can be useful in shaping interventions to target PA and sport participation. For further details regarding the contribution of such models to PA literature, readers are encouraged to see Sallis and Owen (1999: 111–13).

Although providing some relevant insights, it is important to mention that most of the frameworks listed above were developed in HICs and may have less relevance when applied in alternative cultural contexts (Aggleton 1996). Aggleton (1996) noted that some of these models do not sufficiently take the social context into consideration within which particular actions become meaningful. Importantly, 'efforts to transplant such frameworks to developing countries have encountered difficulties; because social norms, duties and obligations may be different in strength and kind to those encountered in the West [*sic*]' (McKee *et al.* 2000: 6).

IMPLICATIONS OF THEORY FOR PRACTICE

To this point, theoretical understandings have been discussed from the perspectives of sport, health and PA promotion. The role of sport and PA in contributing to health has been explored and issues surrounding relationships between sport and PA, from a participation perspective, have been examined. In the sections that follow, some of the practical considerations related to sport and health promotion are explored.

Health promotion and sport/physical activity in different cultural, social and economic contexts

Target populations for health promotion initiatives – including those related to sport and active recreation – tend to be similar in HICs, LMICs and LICs, with children, adolescents, women, older people, socially disadvantaged groups and the working population being common focal cohorts. But health promotion needs often differ between regions. While urban residents often require more advanced health promotion interventions, for example, the promotion of healthy lifestyle behaviour, PA, healthy eating, occupational health, rural populations – where manual labour and non-motorised transport often remain the norm – require more basic interventions, such as the facilitation of healthcare services, sanitary awareness campaigns, vaccination campaigns and the like. This highlights some of the complexities associated with health promotion action and also the importance of promoting PA and sport participation in different ways in different regions.

Aims and outcomes of health promotion interventions do not differ greatly. Generally speaking, all projects aim to enable people to increase control over, and to improve, their health. More specifically, initiatives intend to increase the physical, mental and social health of their specific target groups. Despite these similarities in target groups and in aims and outcomes, there are differences in health promotion approaches in the different contexts. Lamentably, the differences in health promotion approaches in the different countries have received little attention in the literature, and it is seldom clear how an approach that proved successful in a HIC may differ in the context of a LMIC. Issues relating to context, which must be taken into account, include:

- the relevance of program aims;
- the feasibility of project management; and
- local ownership.

It is essential to carefully develop program aims and to understand how they were decided; further, the project must be seen as a priority *for* and *by* prospective participants; it must fit in the national health plan and it must be culturally relevant and appropriate. Regarding project management, it is important to define and justify the target group and, if the program is an externally generated project, local ownership, maximum participation and sustainability after project completion must be ensured. On this point, the building of local human capacity, knowledge and understanding of project goals and processes, as well as commitment to these goals, is essential. In many cases, the value of a project advisory team or person, such as a cultural adviser, is invaluable in addressing these and other culture related issues that may arise.

Community-based participatory research (CBPR) approaches have increased in popularity over the past decades and have been defined as collaborative approaches 'that equitably involves, for example, community members, organisational representatives, and researchers in all aspects of the research process' (Israel *et al.* 1998: 177). Kirkness and Barnhardt (1991) suggested rules for CBPR methodologies to assist the researcher in conducting culturally sensible and ethically sound research. They put forward the idea of consideration of the four Rs, which are: (a) respect; (b) relevance; (c) reciprocity; and (d) responsibility. For a more in-depth discussion of CBPR, the reader is referred to Israel *et al.* (1998).

Action to promote health through sport

Since physical inactivity is a major risk factor for the development of NCDs, many health promotion-related sport projects emphasise:

* the promotion of healthy lifestyle choices;
* the use of sport as a tool to raise awareness about health in LMICs – for example, through district or national health campaigns supported by athletes and sports competitions; and
* the use of sport as a didactical tool to communicate health-related information.

A great number of goodwill and often successful programs have been initiated over the past years. While not designed to be an exhaustive list, some examples are provided in Table 9.1.

With these initiatives in mind, from a practical standpoint, it can be seen that sport can be integrated into health promotion initiatives. For decades, governments around the world have looked to sport and recreation as health promotion tools; in more recent times, formalised initiatives involving sport organisations, health agencies, private providers and/or community organisations have emerged, perhaps signalling the future of sport participation in the context of health promotion. As people's lives become increasingly busy and sedentary, sport organisations are faced with challenges and opportunities to adapt to changing participant needs and preferences. And as the utility of using sport as a hook to engage people in healthy behaviours – to encourage physical activity, disease prevention and other health outcomes – becomes increasingly recognised, the health-sport nexus will inevitably continue to tighten.

APPLICATION OF THEORY TO PRACTICE

Applying the ideas discussed in the preceding section, the following two case studies present examples of PA and sport interventions that were designed to engage people in

TABLE 9.1 Initiatives to improve health through sport and physical activity

Organisations	Details
• UNICEF • Non-governmental organisation (NGO)	*Right to Play* used sport to raise awareness on immunisation and organised sport events for vaccination campaigns in Zambia against measles. Approximately 5 million children were successfully vaccinated – athlete ambassadors were recruited to reinforce key health messages plastered on posters and billboards. *Right to Play* has partnered with several multilateral agencies and inter-agency programs for vaccination and immunisation. In 2004, Right to Play worked with the Global Alliance for Vaccination and Immunisation (GAVI) and established the GAVI Cup – a tournament that made use of football's popularity to increase vaccination rates in Ghana.
• International cricket teams	During the 2003 Cricket World Cup, the cricket teams from Afghanistan and India together promoted the national polio eradication campaign.
• UNAIDS • International Olympic Committee (IOC)	In 2004, these two organisations collaboratively produced a toolkit on HIV/AIDS prevention for the sports community and established an intensive communication and awareness campaign on HIV/AIDS prevention through sport during the 2004 Olympic Games in Athens.
• FIFA's Medical Assessment and Research Centre (F-MARC)	FIFA shifted its research focus away from *Medicine for Football* to *Football for Health*, the main objectives being to use the popularity of football to encourage more PA among all age groups and to deliver health education to children in LMICs. F-MARC developed the *11 for Health* program – a football-based, health education program for children.
• Canadian not-for-profit organisation • Range of sport and non-sport partners	*ParticipACTION*: not-for-profit organisation formed in Canada to act as the national voice for PA and sport participation. It works with a range of partners, including sport, recreation, PA organisations, governments and corporate sponsors, towards encouraging people to live active lifestyles.
• Nike • American College of Sports Medicine • International Council for Sport and Physical Education	*Designed to Move*: a PA action agenda that brings together information from around the globe to highlight the costs and consequences of PA and thus set an agenda for action. The website provides resources and case studies, encourages champions to lead initiatives and highlights valuable programs seeking public support.

PA and promote health. The first examines a health promotion project in a LMIC, Vanuatu, while the second examines health promotion activities of a governmental agency in a HIC, Australia.

Case Study 1: health development in Vanuatu with *Wokabaot Jalens*

Katja Siefken

Wokabaot Jalens was a culturally centred, research-based health development intervention for female civil servants, implemented in Vanuatu in 2011 with the aim to increase PA and improve health. As a first step, consultations took place with the Ministry of Health to ensure support. Next, program barriers and facilitators were identified, as were potential participants, limitations and opportunities; also at this time, recommendations were provided and management issues elicited.

In order to ensure the design of a locally relevant program, the CBPR approach was applied. Initial formative work found that women were more likely to choose walking for leisure time PA over any other sport or recreational activity (Siefken *et al.* 2014). Focus group members further suggested that they favoured a team approach over individual exercise activities. Barriers identified in the formative stages of the project included financial limitations, time issues, family commitments, environmental aspects and motivational hindrances that limit time and opportunities for healthy lifestyle behaviour; on the other hand, facilitators included more supportive environments, social support mechanisms and the implementation of rigorous health policies (Siefken *et al.* 2014). Taking these insights into account, the Wokabaot Jalens – meaning: walking challenge – was designed in a collaborative way with female Ni-Vanuatu civil servants.

Wokabaot Jalens was based on the simple premise that walking can be increased gradually during the day at work, at home and during leisure time. Emphasis was put on the involvement of the external environment, that is: family and communities.

It was hypothesised that Wokabaot Jalens would increase participants' PA levels and improve health indicators. In addition to the primary outcome – measured steps/day – program effects on health parameters were also measured – waist circumference (cm), blood pressure (BP) (mmHg), fasting serum glucose (mmol/l), cholesterol levels (mg/dl). The study found a stronger change in eating habits (68.9 per cent) than in exercise behaviour (28.2 per cent) (Siefken *et al.* 2015). For a full discussion of the details and findings of Wokabaot Jalens, please see Siefken *et al.* (2014) and Siefken *et al.* (2015).

Further resources

Wokabaot Jalens: http://wokabaot.blogspot.de/

Case study extension activities

In groups of three, discuss the following:

1 What questions would you ask potential participants for a health promotion project that promotes physical activity?
2 What questions would you ask potential participants for a health promotion project that promotes sport?
3 Why is the involvement of local community members essential in developing health promotion projects?
4 Why do you think the study revealed a stronger change in eating habits than in exercise habits?

Case Study 2: VicHealth: supporting sport in Victoria

Katie Rowe

The Victorian Health Promotion Foundation (VicHealth) is a Victorian government agency that exists to promote good health and to take action to prevent chronic disease. The agency is governed by a board whose members are mostly appointed by the Victorian Health Minister. While this agency exists to promote health more broadly, a key vehicle used by VicHealth to achieve health objectives, particularly related to PA participation, is sport and recreation. VicHealth states the following with respect to relationships with sport stakeholders:

> Our long-standing partnership with sport is critical to increasing participation in PA. VicHealth is working to enable the sport sector to lead and innovate; to increase participation rates in sport and create sporting environments that are safe, accessible, inclusive and equitable for all in our community.
>
> (VicHealth 2014a: 1)

The organisation provides a number of relevant programs that aim to support and encourage sport and active recreation participation. In 2014, VicHealth announced its inaugural innovation challenge with a focus on encouraging PA participation. This challenge invited organisations to submit short videos to pitch their innovative ideas designed to engage Victorians in PA. Through this initiative, VicHealth sought to encourage sport organisations and other stakeholder groups to think creatively about new and engaging ways to get the population moving.

Seven winners were funded though this initiative, with money provided to support the translation of these ideas into programs. The VicHealth (2014b) funded programs are listed below:

- Bendigo Orienteers Incorporated – *Go Explore It*: Modification of the treasure hunt concept to encourage people to explore their local neighbourhood.
- City of Melbourne & CoDesign Studio – *Play Streets*: Enables the community to temporarily close local streets and engage in PA.
- Football Federation Victoria – *Fit Football*: Provides modified group fitness training to encourage parents and guardians to participate during their kids' sport.
- Healthy Communities Australia – *Back 2 School Fitness*: Social enterprise that links group fitness training for parents and friends with school fundraising.
- Malvern Harriers Running Club & London Agency – *Pulseraiser*: A charity-giving fitness app incentivising daily PA through charity fundraising.
- Netball Victoria – *CardioNET*: Modified group fitness training targeted at re-engaging people who are no longer involved in netball.
- Victorian Skateboarding Association – *Learn Right Skate School*: Provides skate education in schools and then a safe transition into community skate parks.

It can be seen from these initiatives that there are many different ways to go about engaging people in physical activity, with modified/alternative sport formats and modern technology being popular, innovative choices.

Further resources

VicHealth: www.vichealth.vic.gov.au

Case study extension activities

1 Visit the VicHealth website and choose one of the current initiatives the organisation has in place to promote PA through sport. Identify its purpose and objectives; examine the mechanisms through which active participation is promoted.
2 Consider your own local sport club or a community group you are involved with. Using the above as example concepts, develop a proposal or pitch that outlines how your own sport/community group might take innovative action to engage people in sport and/or PA. You might consider working in a small group to create a short video to pitch this idea (up to two minutes) as applicants of the VicHealth grant example were required to do.

SUPPLEMENTARY EXERCISES

1 Duration: 1 hour. Assume that you want to enter into a community with which you are not familiar in order to help the community become more physically active. Describe this community, and then write a two-page paper highlighting the steps you would take to gain entrance into the community.

2 Duration: 30 minutes. When planning a health intervention, SMART objectives are crucial for success. SMART stands for:

Specific, Measurable, Achievable, Realistic, Time-based

Instructions: Use the following sentence and create a SMART program for a community health intervention:

By [INSERT DATE], [INSERT WHO] will have [INSERT WHAT], resulting in [INSERT RESULTS] by [INSERT DATE].

Once you have written your SMART project objective, test them as a team and ask the following questions:

- Is the objective specific?
  - What are you going to do? With and for whom?
  - Is it clear who is involved?
  - Is the intended outcome clear?
  - Is the objective measurable?
  - How will we know the intended change has occurred?
- Is each objective achievable?
  - Can you get it done in the proposed time frame?
  - Can you do it with the resources available?
- Is each objective relevant?
  - Can the people with whom the objective has been set make an impact on the situation?
  - Do they have the necessary knowledge, authority and skill?
  - Is each objective time-based?
  - When will this objective be accomplished?

Sample objectives

- Physical activity at the workplace: increase the number of employees using an active travel mode to and from work by 10 per cent by [date].
- Sport participation in community: increase the number of female migrant children signing up in district [name] for a sports club by 20 per cent by [date].

Further resources

SMART goal setting: www.udemy.com/blog/goal-setting-worksheet/

SUMMARY

This chapter has considered the theoretical and practical connections that exist between sport, health and health promotion. From a sport development perspective, initiatives that connect sport with health promotion agendas can be considered as being related to the concept of development through sport (SFD). It has been explained that sport is often promoted by governments as a vehicle through which people can improve health outcomes by engaging in adequate amounts of physical activity. Sport can contribute not only to physical health, but also to mental and social health, given its ability to bring people together and support social interaction. In addition to the contribution that traditional sport organisations can, and do, make to health outcomes, other initiatives often take more interventionist approaches to using sport as a vehicle to achieve positive health outcomes. In this regard, care needs to be taken to ensure such interventions are culturally appropriate and suited to the specific needs and preferences of the community. As inactivity levels continue to rise, both SD and SFD professionals are well placed to consider how they might engage with the concept of health promotion and find ways to contribute to population health through sport and physical activity promotion.

DISCUSSION QUESTIONS

1 Why is sport often used to promote health?
2 How is sport currently being used to promote health across the globe?
3 What challenges might sport organisations face in setting and achieving health promotion objectives?
4 What challenges exist with respect to promoting health through sport in HICs, LICs and LMICs?

REFERENCES

Aggleton, P. (1996) 'Global priorities for HIV/AIDS intervention research', *International Journal of STD & AIDS*, 7(2): S13–S16.

Bull, F. C., Armstrong, T. P., Dixon, T., Ham, S., Neiman, A. and Pratt, M. (2004) 'Physical inactivity', in M. Ezzati, A. D. Lopez, A. Rodgers and C. J. L. Murray (eds), *Comparative Quantification of Health Risks: Global and Regional Burden of Disease Attributable to Selected Major Risk Factors*, Geneva: World Health Organization, pp. 729–883.

Casey, M. M., Payne, W. R. and Eime, R. M. (2012) 'Organisational readiness and capacity building strategies of sporting organisations to promote health', *Sport Management Review*, 15(1): 109–24.

Casey, M. M., Payne, W. R., Eime, R. M. and Brown, S. J. (2009) 'Sustaining health promotion programs within sport and recreation organisations', *Journal of Science & Medicine in Sport*, 12(1): 113–18.

Coakley, J., Hallinan, C. and McDonald, B. (2011) *Sport in Society: Sociological Issues and Controversies*, North Ryde, NSW: McGraw-Hill.

Eime, R., Payne, W. and Harvey, J. (2008) 'Making sporting clubs healthy and welcoming environments: a strategy to increase participation', *Journal of Science and Medicine in Sport*, 11(2): 146–54.

Hardman, A. E. and Stensel, D. J. (2009) *PA and Health: The Evidence Explained*, 2nd edn, New York: Routledge.

Haskell, W. L., Lee, I. M., Pate, R. R., Powell, K. E., Blair, S. N., Franklin, B. A., Macera, C. A., Heath, G. W., Thompson, P. D. and Bauman, A. (2007) 'Physical activity and public health: updated recommendation for adults from the American College of Sports Medicine and the American Heart Association', *Medicine and Science in Sports & Exercise*, 39(8): 1423–34.

Heath, G. W., Parra, D. C., Sarmiento, O. L., Andersen, L. B., Owen, N., Goenka, S., Montes, F. and Brownson, R. C. (2012) 'Evidence-based intervention in physical activity: lessons from around the world', *The Lancet*, 380(9838): 272–81.

Israel, B., Schulz, A., Parker, E. and Becker, A. (1998) 'Review of community-based research: assessing partnership approaches to improve public health', *Annual Review of Public Health*, 19(1): 173–202.

Jolly, R. (2013) *Sports Funding: Federal Balancing Act*, Canberra: Commonwealth of Australia, available at: www.aph.gov.au/About_Parliament/Parliamentary_Departments/Parliamentary_Library/pubs/BN/2012-2013/SportFunding (accessed July 2015).

Kirkness, J. and Barnhardt, R. (1991) 'First nations and higher education: the four Rs – respect, relevance, reciprocity, responsibility', *Journal of American Indian Education*, 30(3): 1–15.

Kohl, H. W., Craig, C. L., Lambert, E. V., Inoue, S., Alkandari, J. R., Leetongin, G. and Kahlmeier, S. (2012) 'The pandemic of physical inactivity: global action for public health', *The Lancet*, 380(9838): 294–305.

Lee, I. M., Shiroma, E. J., Lobelo, F., Puska, P., Blair, S. N. and Katzmarzyk, P. T. (2012) 'Effect of physical inactivity on major non-communicable diseases worldwide: an analysis of burden of disease and life expectancy', *The Lancet*, 380(9838): 219–29.

McKee, N., Manoncourt, E., Yoon, C. S. and Carnegie, R. (eds) (2000) *Involving People. Evolving Behavior*, New York: United Nations Children Fund (UNICEF), Southbound Sdn. Bhd.

Rowe, K., Shilbury, D., Ferkins, L. and Hinckson, E. (2013) 'Sport development and physical activity promotion: an integrated model to enhance collaboration and understanding', *Sport Management Review*, 16(3): 364–77.

Sallis, J. F. and Owen, N. (1999) *Physical Activity and Behavioral Medicine*, London: Sage.

Shilbury, D. and Kellett, P. (2011) *Sport Management in Australia: An Organisational Overview*, 4th edn, Crow's Nest, NSW: Allen & Unwin.

Siefken, K., Schofield, G. and Malcata, R. (2014) 'Engaging urban Pacific women in healthy lifestyle behaviour: an outcome evaluation of a workplace-based physical activity intervention in Vanuatu', *Journal of Sport for Development*, 2(3), available at: http://jsfd.org/2014/06/30/engaging-urban-pacific-women-in-healthy-lifestyle-behaviour-an-outcome-evaluation-of-a-workplace-based-physical-activity-intervention-in-vanuatu/ (accessed July 2015).

Siefken, K., Schofield, G. and Schulenkorf, N. (2014) 'Laefstael jenses: an investigation of barriers and facilitators for healthy lifestyles of women in an urban Pacific island context', *Journal of Physical Activity and Health*, 11(1): 30–7.

Siefken, K., Schofield, G. and Schulenkorf, N. (2015) 'Process evaluation of a walking programme delivered through the workplace in the South Pacific island Vanuatu', *Global Health Promotion*, 22(2): 53–64.

Sotiriadou, K., Shilbury, D. and Quick, S. (2008) 'The attraction, retention/transition, and nurturing process of sport development: some Australian evidence', *Journal of Sport Management*, 22(3): 247–72.

VicHealth (2014a) 'Physical activity programs', *VicHealth*, available at: www.vichealth.vic.gov.au/Programs-and-Projects/Physical-Activity/Physical-activity-programs.aspx (accessed December 2014).

VicHealth (2014b) 'VicHealth innovation challenge: physical activity', *VicHealth*, available at: www.vichealth.vic.gov.au/Media-Centre/Media-Releases-by-Topic/Physical-activity/Seven-ideas-get-funding-to-kick-start-a-new-path-for-Victorian-sport.aspx#.VHwlosmnHh7 (accessed December 2014).

Warburton, D. E. R., Nicol, C. W. and Bredin, S. S. D. (2006) 'Health benefits of PA: the evidence', *Canadian Medical Association Journal*, 174(6): 801–9.

World Health Organization (WHO) (1948) 'Preamble to the Constitution of the World Health Organization as adopted by the International Health Conference', New York, 19 June–22 July 1946; signed on 22 July 1946 by the representatives of 61 States (Official Records of the World Health Organization, no. 2, p. 100) and entered into force on 7 April (1948).

World Health Organization (WHO) (1986) *Ottawa Charter on Health Promotion: International Conference on Health Promotion*, Geneva: World Health Organization (WHO), available at: www.who.int/health promotion/conferences/previous/ottawa/en/ (accessed July 2015).

World Health Organization (WHO) (2004) *Global Strategy on Diet, Physical Activity and Health: World Health Assembly 57.17*, Geneva: World Health Organization (WHO), available at: www.who.int/dietphysicalactivity/strategy/eb11344/strategy_english_web.pdf (accessed July 2015).

World Health Organization (WHO) (2007) *Health Promotion in a Globalized World: Report by the Secretariat*, Geneva: World Health Organization (WHO).

World Health Organization (WHO) (2010) *Global Recommendations on Physical Activity for Health*, Geneva: World Health Organization (WHO), available at: www.who.int/dietphysicalactivity/factsheet_recommendations/en/ (accessed July 2015).

CHAPTER 10

Sport and social inclusion

Jon Welty Peachey and Emma Sherry

INTRODUCTION

Throughout history, many groups have been socially excluded from communities and marginalised to the edges of society. Social exclusion refers to the forms of disadvantage suffered by groups identified as disadvantaged in some way (Roberts 2009). A person can be socially excluded if he or she lives geographically in a society but – for uncontrollable reasons – is not able to take part in normal societal activities in which he or she would like to participate (Barry 2002). Individuals can experience social exclusion if they have unequal access to educational, occupational and political opportunities (Barry 2002; Sherry 2010). From persons suffering from homelessness, to racial and ethnic divides, social exclusion – rather than inclusion – has been the norm.

In addition to individuals suffering from homelessness, other socially excluded groups include, but are not limited to, immigrants, individuals with a mental or physical disability, persons of a minority status in their respective regions or countries and – in many parts of the world – young women and girls. As an illustrative point, individuals suffering from homelessness, who sleep in shelters, tents or in other unstable environments, can be excluded from most forms of participation in society, including sport (Barry 2002; Sherry 2010; Welty Peachey et al. 2013a). When individuals have limited access to occupational, political and educational opportunities, there is the risk that they may withdraw from society (Jarvie 2003). In this context, sport is a symbol of broader social access and, as such, social marginalisation can also result in lower participation in and access to sport (Collins 2004). To avoid social exclusion, individuals therefore need a safe and sustainable place to live and engage. Applied to a sporting context, social exclusion can thus be prevented if individuals can develop increased social and cultural capital.

OUTLINE OF THE CHAPTER

This chapter first presents the theory and concepts related to social inclusion; we discuss the concepts that comprise social inclusion with reference to the seminal theorists in the field before providing case studies that demonstrate the theories in real-world contexts, offering insights into the complexities of providing inclusive sporting opportunities.

After completing this chapter, you should be able to:

- understand the factors underpinning social exclusion and inclusion;
- understand the different forms of social capital;
- recognise the ways in which sport participation can address issues of social exclusion and inclusion; and
- be alert to the possible unintended consequences of sport programming.

SPORT AND SOCIAL INCLUSION

There is an inherent assumption here – verified by emerging empirical research – that sport participation will lead to some form of personal change, and subsequently this personal change will result in broader, positive societal impacts (Coalter 2007, 2010). Against this background, sport has recently been advanced as a method for addressing issues of social exclusion (Coaffee 2008; Jarvie 2003; Sherry 2010; Welty Peachey et al. 2013a). As such, social exclusion may be reduced when individuals belong to and interact within groups and organisations; sport programming has the capacity – if designed and managed well – to empower and support disenfranchised and marginalised individuals (Frisby et al. 1997; Sherry 2010; Sherry and Strybosch 2012; Welty Peachey et al. 2013a, 2013b). In other words, sport can be an excellent tool for re-engaging marginalised individuals into society because it can be reflective of the kinds of activities that an individual must be involved in for societal participation (Hartmann 2003); furthermore, sport provides a supportive environment within which to encourage and assist these individuals in their social development and integration.

By supporting connections between various groups and social networks, sport has the ability to promote social inclusion and social mobility for marginalised individuals (Jarvie 2003; Skinner et al. 2008; Spaaij 2009). The social networks that can be built and expanded through sport participation are valuable in fostering social inclusion and helping individuals integrate back into society by again feeling part of the community and developing a sense of belonging (Sherry 2010; Welty Peachey et al. 2013a). Through the enhanced self-esteem and self-confidence that can result through sport participation, historically excluded individuals can begin to feel good about themselves again; they may then take the initiative to form friendships and connections with individuals perhaps different from themselves, which may lead to the ability to integrate to a greater degree into social life (Welty Peachey et al. 2013a). In other words, sport can provide a cornerstone and an environment for the development of relationships within communities that could result in an increase in social and cultural capital.

SOCIAL AND CULTURAL CAPITAL

One way that sport can address issues of social exclusion and social mobility for disadvantaged individuals is to facilitate social and cultural capital development; as mentioned above, sport participation can provide an opportunity to make friends and develop networks, thereby reducing social isolation (Burnett 2006; Cowell 2007;

Sherry 2010; Skinner *et al.* 2008; Spaaij 2009). The three most important theoretical interpreta-tions of social capital have been contributed by Bourdieu (1984, 1986), Coleman (1988) and Putnam (1995, 2000). The three authors have slightly different views on the concept and production and use of social capital.

For Bourdieu, who first formulated thoughts on social capital in the 1980s, social capital is based upon the class struggles of the disadvantaged, unequal access to resources and unequal distribution of power (Coalter 2007). Bourdieu (1986: 248) defined social capital as 'the aggregate of the actual or potential resources which are linked to a durable network of more or less institutionalised relationships and mutual acquaintance and recognition'. According to Bourdieu, social capital is unevenly distributed; it is predicated upon the resources individuals have access to within their networks and is the exclusive property of elites who use it to secure their positions. Thus, Bourdieu focused on actors engaged in struggle and is sceptical about altruistic actions free from the constraints of individual interests. Bourdieu also first articulated the concept of cultural capital, which he defined as the cultural goods, knowledge, experience, education, competencies and skills that an individual possesses and that confer power or status in society (Bourdieu 1984, 1986; Spaaij 2009). Cultural capital even encompasses the social graces, style of dress and appearance of an individual, and – like social capital – is unequally distributed.

Another major social capital theorist is Coleman (1988), who viewed social capital as a more ubiquitous resource instead of as a positional good, property or asset belonging to a social class, as articulated by Bourdieu. For Coleman (1994: 300), social capital is defined as 'the set of resources that inhere in family relations and in community social organisation and that are useful for the cognitive or social development of a child or young person'. Coleman (1988) referenced the mostly neutral aspects of social structure and social relationships, where social capital is a way of explaining how people cooperate through the social processes resulting from free choice to further one's self-interests (Coalter 2007).

The third principal social capital theorist is Robert Putnam (1995, 2000), who places less emphasis on kinship relations and instrumentalism, and more on social capital as a public good that binds communities together. Putnam (1995: 66) defined social capital as the 'features of social organisation such as networks, norms, and social trust that can facilitate coordination and cooperation for mutual benefit'. For Putnam, the key elements of social capital are trust, networks and reciprocity. Once personalised, generalised and institutionalised trust is developed, social networks can be created. Within these networks, an exchange process – reciprocity – can then occur, where one engages in a behaviour with the expectation that another person will return the favour at some point in the future (Putnam 2000). Putnam opined that increased social connectedness will bring about greater social solidarity and social cohesion, particularly through the mechanisms of *bonding, bridging* and *linking* into a larger, collective whole. *Bonding social capital* delineates social networks between homogenous groups, such as kin, neighbours or close friends. Because of the close interaction and familiarity with each other, individuals acquire resources that allow them to get by or to cope with their situations. By contrast, *bridging social capital* occurs when relationships are developed with individuals who are different from oneself, where social ties and bonds may be looser and more diverse in nature. As a result of these bridging relationships, individuals acquire the potential to leverage a broader set of resources than can be provided through bonding social capital alone. Finally, *linking social capital* is focused on vertical relationships between different levels or social strata, where individuals form relationships entirely outside their community (Woolcock 2001). This wider network provides individuals with the potential to more effectively leverage resources and obtain greater access to economic – material wealth – and cultural capital (Coalter 2007).

IMPLICATIONS OF THEORY FOR PRACTICE

A number of studies have investigated the potential of sport to help facilitate social inclusion and develop social capital among marginalised and disenfranchised individuals. Research into street soccer in the US (Welty Peachey *et al.* 2013a, 2015) and Australia (Sherry 2010; Sherry and Strybosch 2012) found that over time, participants were able to leverage social capital to gain access to housing, education and employment support and mechanisms. The upcoming case study of the use of street soccer programming to affect social inclusion for disadvantaged citizens demonstrates the effectiveness and the complexity of such sport programming.

Spaaij (2009) observed that disadvantaged youths' participation in the Sport Steward program in the Netherlands served to modestly increase their cultural, social and economic capital in the short term by linking them to external resources such as jobs and education. Similarly, sport participation was shown to build social capital among the disadvantaged in the UK (Cowell 2007). Studies have also revealed that sport contributed to the development of bonding, bridging and linking social capital of community members by providing an interface between other community spheres to expand networks, develop norms of trust and reciprocity, and foster active citizenship behaviour and community engagement in South Africa and Australia (Burnett 2006; Tonts 2005). Further, research has shown that community sport club participation in Australia helped facilitate Muslim women's sense of belonging and relational inclusion through increased social relationships and leadership opportunities, which in turn led to the ability to access sponsorship, training and funding (Maxwell *et al.* 2013). Paradoxically, however, the close bonding that occurred between Muslim women served to exclude non-Muslim women from club activities (Maxwell *et al.* 2013). Further, in rural communities in Australia, community football clubs (Australian Rules football) have helped with the social inclusion of women and families through developing trust and reciprocity and expanding their social networks through proactive organisational strategies (Frost *et al.* 2013).

While evidence is emerging that sport participation has manifold positive impacts on individuals' lives, it is also important to avoid assumptions about the inherent value of sport participation as additional factors need to be taken into consideration. As stated by Green (2008: 131), 'it is not sport per se that is responsible for particular outcomes; it is the ways that sport is implemented'. With any kind of social intervention, there are unintended consequences – as the research by Maxwell *et al.* (2013), mentioned above, demonstrated – that need to be professionally addressed; Chapter 12 discusses the importance of evidence gathering, planning, design and evaluation to reduce such unintended consequences.

Sport programs aimed at improving inclusion must bear in mind the many potential variables and constraints that might influence implementation and delivery – and therefore outcomes – of the program. For example, in the context of competitive sport, there is the risk that individuals on a losing team might experience negative impacts from participation (Welty Peachey *et al.* 2013a). An improperly designed and implemented program could serve to heighten individuals' sense of defeat or exclusion. For example, research undertaken in Norway examining an alternative sport program – the aim of which was to include traditionally inactive youth – found that in trying to allow youth to generate their own activities, the open sports hall developed a 'distinctly masculine culture which [was] dominated by the older, stronger males and which marginalise[d] young females' (Skille and Waddington 2006: 251). This suggests that a program may well be successful in forging some kinds of social capital, but less so in creating other forms of social capital, meaning that the progression towards inclusion is limited.

In another example, Spaaij (2012) studied Melbourne Giants, a sport initiative for refugees, principally hailing from Somalia, and the development of social capital. Spaaij (2012) noted that bonding capital was developed: the football program was success-ful in improving participants' inclusion within their own community and with other similar communities; for example, teams comprising individuals of the same faith – bonding capital. It was less successful, however, in achieving a sense of inclusion across the football community in general – bridging capital; in fact, the capacity of the program to build bridges between different cultural groups was minimal, with cross-group interactions limited to sporting activities and some participants experiencing race-based conflict and discrimination (Spaaij 2012). These findings confirm Green's (2008) observation that the way in which sport programming is implemented is critical to achieving successful inclusion outcomes and underscores the importance of evidence-based, planned programming.

The following case studies present examples of sport programming with social inclusion as a central element of their design and implementation; the first is an example of an SFD program targeting social inclusion through a program for specific at-risk and marginalised people in the local community. The second case study presents an example of an SD program targeting social inclusion through increased organised sport participation.

Case Study 1: Street Soccer USA

Jon Welty Peachey

Street Soccer USA (SSUSA) is a not-for-profit organisation whose mission is to use football (soccer) to help individuals suffering from homelessness in the US make positive changes in their lives. The organisation was founded in 2005 by Lawrence Cann in Charlotte, North Carolina, and it has since expanded into 20 cities. In their home cities, participants take part in practices and play in local football leagues, with volunteers from the community and local social service providers serving as coaches and facilitators. Football is used as the hook to draw participants into the program, where they can then be connected to other resources needed to improve their situations – that is: their homelessness – and reduce their social isolation. SSUSA also administers a national tournament called the SSUSA Cup. This four-day tournament is the signature event of SSUSA and is held each year for the 20 teams in Washington, DC, New York City or San Francisco. Participants take part in the tournament, stay in dorms, and participate in many ancillary cultural, educational and social activities, such as opening and closing ceremonies, concerts, educational workshops, sightseeing tours and group discussions. At the end of the SSUSA Cup, a men's and women's national team is selected to compete in the Homeless World Cup (HWC).

Research has shown that the SSUSA Cup generally fosters a positive impact for participants by building a sense of community, creating hope, cultivating an outward focus, fostering life goal achievement and enhancing personal development (Welty Peachey et al. 2013a, 2015). In addition, the HWC is instrumental in helping participants reduce their sense of social isolation by building bonding and bridging social capital, and then helping to link participants to other resources in their local communities to assist in improving their life situations. Importantly, this positive impact is facilitated by creating a celebratory and festive space for social interaction and by fostering an inclusive climate where achievement is celebrated (Chalip 2006; Lyras and Welty Peachey 2011). Preliminary research is also showing that participation in the SSUSA local teams throughout the year is having a positive impact on helping individuals reduce their sense of social isolation and exclusion, increase their social capital and improve their life situations by furthering their education, obtaining jobs and moving into sustainable housing (Welty Peachey et al. 2013a).

Unfortunately, the highly competitive nature of the SSUSA Cup has resulted in negative impact on some participants, who – when experiencing lopsided losses of 12–0 or 15–0 – found their self-confidence diminished and the stigma that they could not succeed in life reinforced. For them, the HWC experience perpetuated a sense of social exclusion, rather than facilitating inclusion as desired by organisers (Welty Peachey et al. 2013b). To try to correct this problem, HWC organisers made changes to the competition structure in subsequent iterations of the HWC, paying closer attention to matching teams of similar calibre in the round-robin phase of the tournament, de-emphasising winning, giving all participants medals regardless of whether they won or lost, and focusing much more on the educational and cultural aspects of the event surrounding the competition.

Further resources

Street Soccer USA: http://streetsoccerusa.org/
Homeless Word Cup: www.homelessworldcup.org

Case study extension activities

1 How do potential participants find out about the SSUSA programs?
2 What are the key barriers to sport participation for SSUSA participants? Would these barriers be different in your country?
3 How can an SFD program reduce potential barriers to sport participation?

SUPPLEMENTARY EXERCISE

Undertake a Web search to identify a sport for social inclusion program in your area. What is the aim of the program? Who funds and delivers the program? Who are the target participants?

If you were designing a sport for social inclusion program in your local community, how would you identify your target participant group? What are your target participant group's primary barriers to participation? Which organisations might you partner with to achieve your social inclusion goals?

Case Study 2: Netball for All

Emma Sherry

Netball Victoria (NV) is the state body that governs the provision of netball in Victoria, Australia (NV 2013). It manages the state teams and its 111,210 registered members (NV 2013), as well as countless informal players. Netball – the second most popular sport for female children and the sixth most popular for women in Australia (ABS 2012) – has been a mainstay of girls' and women's sport participation since its introduction to Australian shores at the end of the nineteenth century (Taylor 2001). Sport is argued to be central to the Australian national identity (Mewett 1999), meaning that netball clubs – and their male counterparts, football clubs – have been traditional sites for sport participation and social interaction (Mooney *et al.* 2012). In rural and regional areas, netball continues to play an important social role in communities (Mooney *et al.* 2012); in particular, participation in netball teams affords status and opportunities to foster social and cultural capital for girls in these contexts (Mooney *et al.* 2012).

However, in recent years, NV noted that the sport had ceased to grow, with participation rates remaining static over a period of time (ABS 2012). One reason for this stagnation is theorised to be the changing demographics of Victorian metropolitan centres. Research has shown that sport participation among migrant populations is impacted by a range of factors, including, but not limited to, length of time in the new country, income and employment, level of education, gender, language, family commitments, social support, and divergent understandings and perceptions about the role and value of sport (O'Driscoll *et al.* 2014). In addition, cultural or religious constraints – such as being in mixed-gender settings or uniform requirements – impact on female sport participation (Alamri 2013; Kay 2006). In the case of Victoria – a state with a significant multicultural and diverse community – the growing number of people from a culturally and linguistically diverse (CALD) background appears to be a challenge for the delivery of sport to these communities.

In order to combat the stagnating numbers of participants and to maintain the relevance of the sport, NV initiated a series of programs aimed at improving participation among multicultural, or culturally and linguistically diverse, cohorts. The program,

Netball for All, aimed at improving inclusion in the sport for a range of marginalised groups, including people with a disability and indigenous people (NV 2013). Netball for All was developed by NV in partnership with VicHealth, a Victorian state government body, to provide a more welcoming and inclusive environment for diverse participants. The program addresses the NV primary strategic goal to 'increase participation in the game' through 'making netball attractive, accessible and welcoming for everyone' (NV 2013: 18).

The CALD program was delivered to primary school-age children in areas of Melbourne, Victoria's largest city, identified as having populations with a high rate of cultural diversity. The program was delivered into 12 primary schools, during school hours, by NV coaches, and included a weekly clinic for the duration of one school term, culminating in an interschool competition. The program introduced children to the sport and the weekly training regime was designed to gradually develop technical skills. A modified version of the game was offered in the weekly clinics and children were not required to wear a uniform. Clinics were designed to be introductory, and exercises and activities were developed with novice participants in mind. The focus in the weekly clinics was on having a go at something new and having fun. To assist with achieving the latter, elite athletes, currently representing state and national teams, attended some of the clinics, giving children an opportunity to meet high-profile athletes. An important ambassador for the program was Geva Mentor, an elite athlete from a multicultural background. Children were delighted to meet a national representative, and including time for photographs became a regular feature of Geva's attendance at the clinics.

Evaluation of the program – undertaken midway through the three-year funding period – revealed a high level of support for the program from teachers and other stakeholders, such as LGA representatives (Sherry and Hoye 2015). Further, teachers described the program as well designed, properly delivered and instructive. Children reported enjoying the program very much and excitedly discussed their experiences, in particular the end-of-term competition (Sherry and Hoye 2015).

However, despite positive feedback on enjoyment and support for the program, conversion rates were very low. In other words, very few children attending the weekly school-based clinics went on to take up netball in a club or association setting (Sherry and Hoye 2015). A lack of parental support was cited by all stakeholders and participants as the main barrier to conversion. This arguably has its origins in cultural knowledge and traditions, which may be less likely to encourage female children to participate in sport and/or spend time away from studies or home duties (Hajkowicz *et al.* 2013). Cost, transport and unfamiliarity with recreational sport as a social activity were also cited as barriers, all of which could be viewed as related to parental support. These findings confirm those of previous research (see, for example, O'Driscoll *et al.* 2014). Additional barriers noted were those originating in structural features of netball, such as availability of teams, facilities and perceived inflexibility of clubs and associations (Sherry and Hoye 2015). Results from the midway evaluation will be used to further develop the program to address identified gaps in programming.

Further resources

Netball Victoria 'Netball for All': http://vic.netball.com.au/get-involved/netballforall/

Case study extension activities

1 What additional activities could be implemented/undertaken, in addition to providing clinics in schools?
2 What gaps in inclusion actions can you identify in NV's programming?
3 What are your opinions on gathering all inclusion initiatives under the umbrella of Netball for All?
4 Why do you think there is such a low conversion rate? What steps might you take to address this problem? Undertake an audit of Netball for All to assess its strengths and weaknesses and to identify areas for improvement, specifically focused on converting interest in the school-based program into formal participation.

SUPPLEMENTARY EXERCISE

Visit the Netball Victoria website and examine the information provided there for Netball for All (http://vic.netball.com.au/get-involved/netballforall/). Make note of the extent of the information provided to clubs and associations interested in trying to achieve inclusion. What discrepancies do you notice? Why might these be considered important? How might you address them?

SUMMARY

This chapter has introduced the concepts of social exclusion and inclusion. It has demonstrated how sport can be instrumentalised to assist with improving social inclusion for community members and sport participants, through programs such as in the Street Soccer USA program, which developed participants' relationships, and the Netball for All program, which attempts to engage the Victorian CALD communities in the sport of netball. The chapter further demonstrated that the traditional sport development model of program delivery can adopt inclusion models in order to develop their particular sport, combat decline in participation and remain relevant in a changing society.

DISCUSSION QUESTIONS

1 Identify five different community groups who may experience social inclusion in your city. In what ways do these individuals experience exclusion?
2 Thinking of a disadvantaged group in your community, how would you engage the participants in a sport program?
3 What are the risks of developing a sport for social inclusion program for a sport organisation?
4 Staffing a sport for social inclusion program requires a diverse range of skills and expertise. What types of roles and skills would be required?
5 Many sport for social inclusion programs are delivered via partnerships. What types of organisations could a sport partner with to develop and deliver these programs?

REFERENCES

ABS (2012) *1301.0: Year Book Australia, 2012*, available at: www.abs.gov.au/ausstats/abs@.nsf/Lookup/by%20Subject/1301.0~2012~Main%20Features~Sports%20and%20physical%20recreation~116 (accessed March 2015).

Alamri, A. (2013) 'Participation of Muslim female students in sporting activities in Australian public high schools: the impact of religion', *Journal of Muslim Minority Affairs*, 33(3): 418–29.

Barry, B. (2002) 'Social exclusion, social isolation and the distribution of income', in J. Hills, J. Le Grand and D. Piachaud (eds), *Understanding Social Exclusion*, Oxford: Oxford University Press, pp. 13–29.

Bourdieu, P. (1984) *Distinction: A Social Critique of the Judgement of Taste*, London: RKP.

Bourdieu, P. (1986) 'The forms of capital', in S. Baron, J. Field and T. Schuller (eds), *Social Capital: Critical Perspectives*, Oxford: Oxford University Press, pp. 83–95.

Burnett, C. (2006) 'Building social capital through an "active community club"', *International Review for the Sociology of Sport*, 41(3–4): 283–94.

Chalip, L. (2006) 'Towards social leverage of sport events', *Journal of Sport Tourism*, 11(2): 109–27.

Coaffee, J. (2008) 'Sport, culture and the modern state: emerging themes in stimulating urban regeneration in the UK', *The International Journal of Cultural Policy*, 14(4): 377–97.

Coalter, F. (2007) *A Wider Social Role for Sport: Who's Keeping the Score?* London: Routledge.

Coalter, F. (2010) 'Sport-for-development: going beyond the boundary?', *Sport in Society*, 13(9): 1374–91.

Coleman, J. S. (1988) 'Social capital in the creation of human capital', *American Journal of Sociology*, 94: S95–S120.

Coleman, J. S. (1994) *Foundations of Social Theory*, Cambridge, MA: Belknap Press.

Collins, M. (2004) 'Sport, physical activity, and social exclusion', *Journal of Sport Sciences*, 22(8): 727–40.

Cowell, J. (2007) *Sport and Social Capital in Disadvantaged Communities*, Canberra, ACT: The Winston Churchill Memorial Trust of Australia.

Frisby, W., Crawford, S. and Dorer, T. (1997) 'Reflections on participatory action research: the case of low-income women accessing local physical activity services', *Journal of Sport Management*, 11(1): 8–28.

Frost, L., Lightbody, M. and Halabi, A. K. (2013) 'Expanding social inclusion in community sports organizations: evidence from rural Australian football clubs', *Journal of Sport Management*, 27(6): 453–66.

Green, B. (2008) 'Sport as an agent for social and personal change', in V. Girginov (ed.), *Management of Sports Development*, London: Butterworth-Heinemann, pp. 130–45.

Hajkowicz, S. A., Cook, H., Wilhelmseder, L. and Boughen, N. (2013) *The Future of Australian Sport: Megatrends Shaping the Sports Sector over Coming Decades. A Consultancy Report for the Australian Sports Commission*, Canberra: CSIRO.

Hartmann, D. (2003) 'Theorizing sport as social intervention: a view from the grassroots', *Quest*, 55(2): 118–40.

Jarvie, G. (2003) 'Communitarianism, sport and social capital', *International Review for the Sociology of Sport*, 38(2): 139–53.

Kay, T. (2006) 'Daughters of Islam: family influences on Muslim young women's participation in sport', *International Review for the Sociology of Sport*, 41(3–4): 357–73.

Lyras, A. and Welty Peachey, J. (2011) 'Integrating sport-for-development theory and praxis', *Sport Management Review*, 14(4): 311–26.

Maxwell, H., Foley, C., Taylor, T., Burton, C., Doherty, A. and Cousens, L. (2013) 'Social inclusion in community sport: a case study of Muslim women in Australia', *Journal of Sport Management*, 27(6): 467–81.

Mewett, P. G. (1999) 'Fragments of a composite identity: aspects of Australian nationalism in a sports setting', *The Australian Journal of Anthropology*, 10(3): 357–75.

Mooney, A., Casey, M. and Smyth, J. (2012) '"You're no-one if you're not a netball girl": rural and regional adolescent girls' negotiation of physically active identities', *Annals of Leisure Research*, 15(1): 19–37.

Netball Victoria (NV) (2013) *Annual Report*, Melbourne: Netball Victoria.

O'Driscoll, T., Banting, L., Borkoles, E., Eime, R. and Polman, R. (2014) 'A systematic literature review of sport and physical activity participation in culturally and linguistically diverse (CALD) migrant populations', *Journal of Immigrant and Minority Health*, 16(3): 515–30.

Putnam, R. D. (1995) 'Bowling alone: America's declining social capital', *Journal of Democracy*, 6(1): 65–78.

Putnam, R. D. (2000) *Bowling Alone: The Collapse and Revival of American Community*, New York: Simon & Schuster.

Roberts, K. (2009) *Key Concepts in Sociology*, Basingstoke: Palgrave Macmillan.

Sherry, E. (2010) '(Re)engaging marginalized groups through sport: the Homeless World Cup', *International Review for the Sociology of Sport*, 45(1): 59–71.

Sherry, E. and Strybosch, V. (2012) 'A kick in the right direction: longitudinal outcomes of the Australian Community Street Soccer Program', *Soccer & Society*, 13(4): 495–509.

Sherry, E. and Hoye, R. (2015) *'Netball for All' Program Evaluation: Final Report Prepared for Netball Victoria*, Centre for Sport and Social Impact, Latrobe University, Melbourne.

Skille, E. Å. and Waddington, I. (2006) 'Alternative sport programmes and social inclusion in Norway', *European Physical Education Review*, 12(3): 251–71.

Skinner, J., Zakus, D. H. and Cowell, J. (2008) 'Development through sport: building social capital in disadvantaged communities', *Sport Management Review*, 11(3): 253–75.

Spaaij, R. (2009) 'Sport as a vehicle for social mobility and regulation of disadvantaged urban youth', *International Review for the Sociology of Sport*, 44(2–3): 247–64.

Spaaij, R. (2012) 'Beyond the playing field: experiences of sport, social capital, and integration among Somalis in Australia', *Ethnic and Racial Studies*, 35(9): 1519–38.

Taylor, T. (2001) 'Gendering sport: the development of netball in Australia', *Sporting Traditions: Journal of the Australian Society for Sports History*, 18(1): 57–74.

Tonts, M. (2005) 'Competitive sport and social capital in rural Australia', *Journal of Rural Studies*, 21(2): 137–49.

Welty Peachey, J., Borland, J., Lobpries, J. and Cohen, A. (2015) 'Managing impact: leveraging sacred spaces and community celebration to maximize social capital at a sport-for-development event', *Sport Management Review*, 18(1): 86–98.

Welty Peachey, J., Lyras, A., Cohen, A. and Borland, J. (2013a) 'Street Soccer USA Cup: preliminary findings of a sport-for-homeless intervention', *ICHPER-SD Journal of Research*, 8(1): 3–11.

Welty Peachey, J., Cohen, A., Borland, J. and Lyras, A. (2013b) 'Exploring the initial motivations of individuals to volunteer with a sport-for-homeless initiative', *International Journal of Sport Management*, 14(1): 103–22.

Woolcock, M. (2001) 'The place of social capital in understanding social and economic outcomes', *Canadian Journal of Policy Research*, 2(1): 1–17.

CHAPTER 11

Sport for conflict resolution and peace building

Nico Schulenkorf, John Sugden
and Jack Sugden

INTRODUCTION

Fundamentally, sport development is about providing opportunities for individuals and communities to engage in sport and physical activity. When appropriately conceived, managed and promoted, sport allows participants to optimise their physical fitness levels (see Chapter 9); it also has the capacity to provide people of varying ages and backgrounds with valuable social experiences that contribute to feelings of inclusion and social capital (see Chapter 10). As we will see in this chapter, the purposes, values and desired outcomes of sport development are not static; indeed, the recent focus on sport for development and peace (SFDP) indicates a fundamental move away from sport participation per se. Under the SFDP banner, sport has increasingly been used as a new and potentially powerful vehicle to achieve conflict resolution between disparate communities and peace building in divided societies. In these contexts, the principal goal of sport managers is the deployment of sport and physical activity programs to engage people from varying ethnocultural and socio-economic backgrounds to improve interpersonal engagement, reduce intergroup conflict and pave the way for peaceful intergroup relations.

OUTLINE OF THE CHAPTER

This chapter begins with a discussion of how sport became a significant player in global efforts towards conflict resolution and peace building. It then examines contemporary concepts and theories that underpin SFDP today, drawing on international literature and current research from around the globe. The chapter also provides practical examples and case studies of SFDP that are based on fieldwork conducted in Fiji and the fiercely contested Israel/Palestine region. The chapter is therefore divided into four key sections: (1) the origins and evolution of the SFDP movement; (2) sport, intergroup relations and peace-building theory; (3) application of theory to practice, including two contemporary case studies; and (4) implications of theory for SFDP practice. Finally, conclusions are drawn, a summary is provided and discussion questions are posed.

After completing this chapter, you should be able to:

*   understand the history and development of the SFDP movement;
*   apply the theory of intergroup relations to conflict settings;
*   appreciate the importance of cultural context and the different social issues impacting sport for conflict resolution and peace-building initiatives;
*   critically analyse the planning and management of SFDP in divided societies; and
*   identify challenges and limitations of sport in achieving lasting peace.

THE ORIGINS AND EVOLUTION OF THE SFDP MOVEMENT

SFDP is a relatively new stream within the field of international development: it utilises sport as a development tool, particularly in divided societies and/or seriously disadvantaged communities (Kidd 2008). Despite the different contexts in which SFDP projects have been implemented, the concept itself evolved out of the common belief that well-designed, sport-based initiatives incorporating appropriate values from within sport can be powerful, practical and cost-effective tools to achieve development goals and contribute something towards peace objectives (Coalter 2010; Schulenkorf 2010a; Sugden 2010). The importance of this new field is reflected in the creation of the official United Nations Office on Sport for Development and Peace (UNOSDP) in 2001. With offices in Geneva and New York, the mandate of the UNOSDP is to coordinate the efforts undertaken by the UN to promote sport in a systematic and coherent way as a means to contribute to positive social change (see UN 2015).

The creation of the UNOSDP in 2001 was a first but highly significant step towards official recognition and legitimacy for the SFDP movement. Subsequent assertions – such as the Magglingen Declaration in 2003 and the United Nations International Year of Sport and Physical Education in 2005 – further raised awareness of SFDP. Using sport programs as vehicles towards achieving reconciliation and peace building, numerous sport associations, aid agencies, development bodies, sponsoring organisations and NGOs have since established a plenitude of local and international SFDP projects. According to advocates, when people are engaged in appropriately organised SFDP projects and programs, they are provided with opportunities to interact in an environment that promotes intergroup trust and the cultivation of respect. Indeed, according to Dyreson (2003), sport is a de facto language that virtually all people in the world can speak and understand, and which – if appropriately structured – has the capacity to positively engage diverse groups.

In this context, Chalip (2006) contended that sport projects have the potential to promote dialogue, solidarity, understanding, integration and teamwork – even in conflict-ridden contexts where other forms of social and political negotiation have been unsuccessful. For a long time, these perspectives were largely anecdotal and – according to critics – idealistic (Coalter 2010). In other words, it was difficult to find evidence of SFDP projects that demonstrated sustainable outcomes in terms of reconciling or reuniting disparate communities. However, over the past 10 years, as the number of grass-roots initiatives has risen, there have been growing calls for evidence-based, independent reporting of the outcomes of SFDP projects; further, project organisers have been called on to not only commit to, but actually meet, KPIs. It has become noticeable, therefore, that funding bodies now expect improved monitoring of SFDP programs and project organisers are required to demonstrate their operational effectiveness (Lyras and Welty Peachey 2011). A detailed overview of a variety of SFD projects, their purpose, goals, objectives and approaches can be found on the website of the International Platform on Sport and Development (www.sportanddev.org). The platform is orchestrated by the Swiss Academy for Development, an NGO focused on applying practice-oriented research and knowledge to current topics in the areas of intercultural dialogue, youth engagement and SFD. An examination of the reporting requirements discussed on the platform demonstrates the increased requirements for demonstration of organisational effectiveness.

SUPPLEMENTARY EXERCISE

Go to the website of the International Platform on Sport and Development (www. sportanddev.org) and identify one of the projects that engage in SFD. What exactly are the goals and objectives of the project, and how are the organisers trying to achieve them? Considering the financial, sociocultural and geographical context in which the project is situated, what could be some of the challenges for local and international people working on combined projects? Provide some suggestions on how the project may be further developed or improved.

SPORT, INTERGROUP RELATIONS AND PEACE BUILDING

When discussing the rapidly developing field of SFDP, it is important to remind ourselves what the word *peace* actually means. In its most limited meaning, peace equals the absence of war. However, in the case of SFDP, the word needs to be given a broader definition and include connotations of personal and community well-being, as well as the absence of conflict and tension between antagonistic groups. While peace is a policy goal that receives almost universal endorsement, it is extremely hard to sustainably achieve, particularly in areas that have historically suffered from ethnic or cultural hostilities and violent conflicts between opposing groups (Schulenkorf and Edwards 2010). Examples of long-standing intergroup conflict and hostilities can be found in various parts of the world, such as Northern Ireland, Cyprus, Yemen, Kenya, Rwanda, Indonesia, East Timor, Papua New Guinea and – probably the best-known example – Israel and Palestine. Even in the small Pacific Island nation of Fiji – generally known for its tropical beaches and luxury holiday resorts – there have been ongoing debates around peace, reconciliation and social justice between indigenous and non-indigenous communities, as the following case study demonstrates.

Case Study 1: Fiji – trouble in paradise

Nico Schulenkorf, John Sugden and Jack Sugden

With a population of over 850,000 people spread across 332 islands, 110 of which are inhabited, Fiji is the Pacific's most populous nation, known for its sandy beaches and breathtaking scenery. However, less known is that Fiji suffers from a history of political, ethnic and social division. The island nation has undergone four military coups since independence from British rule in 1974; the coups were, for the most part, driven by ethnic nationalism and an inability of some indigenous factions to cede power to the sizeable population of Indian Fijians (Robertson 2012).

Many Indian Fijians are descended from indentured labourers brought over by the British; they often worked in terrible conditions on Fiji's large sugar plantations. Today, Indian Fijians make up around 38 per cent of the total population and, while their political influence in Fiji remains insignificant, they dominate the country's business sector.

When the British departed in 1974, they left behind a legacy of division but also a sporting culture dominated by football and rugby. Rugby, first, is the most popular sport in Fiji and is culturally enmeshed within indigenous tribal life. This is reflected in rugby participation, which – similar to the government and military – is overwhelmingly indigenous (Kanemasu and Molnar 2013). Football, on the other hand, the second most popular sport in Fiji, is played by both groups, but organised and governed exclusively by Indian Fijians. Unlike rugby, football enjoys only minimal support from the Fijian national government and its Ministry of Sport. Overall, there are significant tensions and issues at the macro, meso and micro levels of sport in Fiji.

At the macro level, the most recent government sport policy recognises the uniqueness of Fiji's somewhat problematic and polarised plurality in stating: 'At a society level sports contribute to an environment for social interaction, unification and reconciliation that is essential' (Naupoto 2012). However, this rather vague statement merely recognises the potential of sport to foster unity outside of narratives of racial assignations; it does not provide a call to action to engineer sporting contexts that would bring about the so-called 'essential unification and reconciliation'.

At the civil society – or meso – level, unity and reconciliation is hampered by the deeper meanings and pseudo-identities attached to some of Fiji's NSOs. For example, rugby's popularity in Fiji from its very beginning has been interwoven with indigenous tribalism and governance. The Prime Minister in 2015 is indigenous Fijian Admiral Voreqe Bainimarama, who is also head of the Fijian Rugby Union. Next, the Fijian Football Association (FFA) is similarly important to cultural identity for Indian Fijians as it began life as the Fiji Indian Football Association – a racial organisation for Indians only. Although the FFA has now dropped the 'Indian' from its title, the organisation is undoubtedly dominated by Indian Fijians (Prasad 2013).

Finally, at the community – or micro – level, the Fijian national rugby team enjoys multi-ethnic support across the country. However, there is a distinct lack of Indian Fijian representation on the field on all levels – from grass-roots to professional rugby. Teams and players reflect tribal loyalties that are played out, quite literally, on the field, and it is this organic fusion that creates significant barriers to interethnic participation (Kanemasu and Molnar 2013). Football, on the other hand, does not have the same interwoven cultural meaning to Indian Fijians, neither is it so closed and mono-ethnic in terms of participation. Nevertheless, the Indian Fijian community certainly feels a sense of ownership of the game, which has been serving as a cultural centre and social meeting point for generations (Prasad 2013).

Further resources

Fiji Times: www.fijitimes.com/section.aspx?s=sport

Discussion questions and extension activities

1 In what way does sport in Fiji reflect and/or encourage ethnic division?
2 Why does the organisation of football in Fiji continue to be dominated by Indian Fijians despite its mixed participation?
3 How could sport in Fiji be employed strategically to reduce ethnic division?
4 Examine the sport page of Fiji's main national newspaper, *The Fiji Times*. What do you note about differences in coverage of rugby and football?

When discussing SFDP and its opportunities and challenges in contributing to conflict resolution and peace building, it is important to engage with the *theory of intergroup relations*. However, before analysing intergroup relations in greater depth, we need to define and explain what the term *group* actually stands for. According to Brown (1988: 2–3), who undertook an extensive review of the literature, a group exists when 'two or more people define themselves as members of it and when its existence is recognised by at least one other'. Lewin (1997) added that a group is a set of human beings whose behaviour is partially patterned, interdependent and cooperative. Often, people are oriented towards something that motivates them and they form groups according to their shared interests – football fans of the same team or self-help groups are examples of this. Other relevant large-scale groups include cultural or ethnic communities, where members identify with the group through factors such as interests, faith or shared values.

Once identified with their group, one of the first things people do when they meet others is to locate them on their social map; in other words, individuals categorise and identify other individuals in terms of the group, or groups, they may belong to. This categorisation then accentuates the contrast between *us* and *them* (Simon 1999). When social distance is small, there is a feeling of communality, closeness and shared experiences. But when social distance is large, people perceive and treat *others* as belonging to a different group or category (Alba and Nee 2003). Think of a situation in a football stadium where you feel connected closely with other fans of your favourite team. When your team scores, you cheer and celebrate together – when the opposition scores, you all share a sense of frustration or sadness. And if the social distance to the opposing team is large – for example, as might occur between the main rivals in the league – your feelings may even be more extreme and may turn against *the others*, both verbally and physically. Chants against opposition fans and fights in stadiums are evidence of this.

The group categorisation process – and hence the nature of interaction between groups – can be both positive and negative, as it is determined by the specific interests and overall goals of all groups involved. In particular, *intergroup hostilities* stem from incompatible interests between groups – with the incompatibility fostered by scarcity of resources, such as money, an area of land or status and prestige; *intergroup friendships*, on the other hand, stem from work or belief in a common good (Sherif and Sherif 1966, 1979). In other words, intergroup relations, attitudes and behaviours reflect the interdependent relations between groups. Ultimately, the goal for people involved in SFDP is to find ways to reduce social distance and intergroup conflict.

Most of the SFDP projects in conflict-ridden societies or post-war contexts build on the seminal work of Allport and his highly influential contact hypothesis (1954). The hypothesis holds that contact between opposing groups – through sport or any other medium – is not automatically sufficient to improve intergroup relations. Rather, for contact between groups to reduce conflict and achieve intergroup harmony, four conditions must be present: (1) equal status within the contact situation; (2) intergroup cooperation; (3) common goals; and (4) support of authorities, law or custom. Allport (1958: 489) later suggested that:

> to be maximally effective, contact and acquaintance programs should lead to a sense of equality in social status . . . and if possible enjoy the sanction of the community in which they occur. The deeper and more genuine the association, the greater its effect.

APPLICATION OF THEORY TO PRACTICE

Examples of SFDP projects that build on Allport's (1954) contact theory to advance intergroup relations between conflict parties are now easily found. One example of a football-based conflict resolution program that has been implemented for over a decade is Football 4 Peace (F4P), the subject of an upcoming case study. The roots of sport-based coexistence program F4P are buried deep in the bitter sectarian conflicts that blighted Belfast and the north-east corner of Ireland for much of the twentieth century. It was in this context that the prototype for F4P – a football-based, community relations project, then called Belfast United – was born and nurtured in the 1980s and 1990s. The founding rationale for this sport-based development project was quite simple. The founder of Belfast United, John Sugden, was a university lecturer, soccer player and coach. In these capacities, he witnessed bonds of friendship grow and endure between Catholic and Protestant football players in Northern Ireland; in other walks of life, these players would never have had the opportunities to meet and get to know and even like each other in the then deeply divided society. As Sugden watched and became increasingly dismayed by the worst excesses of sectarian hatred and violence being played out on the streets of the city that surrounded him, he and a few like-minded teachers and soccer coaches wondered if there was anything they could do to translate their positive experiences of sport into programs that might build bridges between the otherwise polarised communities. Thus, Belfast United was born as a program that brought together young people from different communities in Belfast, integrating them into common teams and coaching groups.

Given the deep-seated nature of Northern Ireland's divided sectarian cultural geography, it would be foolish to overstate the positive and life-changing impact of F4P as it was a relatively small-scale and fleeting sport and integration experiment. Nevertheless, early research showed that at certain levels, these short-lived opportunities for contact across sectarian boundaries could have memorable and enduring influences on the participants (Sugden and Bairner 1993). Soon after Sugden left Belfast to join the University of Brighton in 1996, he was approached by his new colleagues and private individuals who were in the early stages of trying to organise sport-based peace-building projects in Israel. In this new environment, Sugden was not only able to bring his Belfast experiences to the table; he was also, in his role as a lecturer in a sport and physical education department, able to provide access to other specialist physical education teacher trainers and sport coaches, as well as a pool of student volunteers. Thus it was that Belfast United evolved into the World Sport Peace Project (WSPP) and later into F4P.

After the first few years of delivering projects that brought together Arab and Jewish communities in northern Israel, early evaluations carried out by the key project facilitators in Israel determined that sport-based contact alone was insufficient to promote enduring mutual understanding. With a commitment to peaceful and sustainable coexistence, it was decided that more could and should be done with the quality and content of the sport-based contact experience. This led to the development of an innovative approach to coaching and training that was based not so much on skill acquisition and competition, but on the apprehension and enactment of a set of key values that were believed to promote more tolerant attitudes towards inter-community relations. The four key values are: respect, trust, responsibility and equality/inclusivity. On this basis, the core delivery team designed a dedicated practical sport coaching curriculum that prioritised these key values, and which required participants to demonstrate understanding of these values – both on the field of play and outside it – once the contact program was over.

The activities of the F4P curriculum are closely aligned with Allport's (1954) contact hypothesis. First, for positive intergroup relations to be established, the F4P administrators and coaches in Israel set the scene and designed sport-related activities that provided *equal status* for Jewish and Arab administrators: no group or individual was given privileges, mutual agreement for all activities was pivotal, and all voices and concerns were heard and respected to establish a level playing field. Moreover, on the football pitch, the children had equal amount of playing time and opportunities to play. Second and third, *intergroup cooperation* was actively sought by organisers and children to achieve *common goals*. The administrators asked the respective sport authorities and community representatives from Jewish and Arab backgrounds to cooperate to achieve their common goal of staging F4P activities. In short, these requirements meant that without the contributions and support from both groups, there would be no F4P program. On the field, the children were put into mixed teams made up of Jewish and Arab players – so that intergroup cooperation was needed to achieve their superordinate goal of playing together and scoring goals. The approach was also complemented with outdoor education activities that specifically focused on contact and engagement between children from the two communities. Here, the focus was on combining social engagement with physical engagement – in other words:

combining body and mind for inclusive development. Finally, *support of authorities, law and custom* was achieved by partnering with leaders and representatives from all participating local communities, as well as influential international organisations and institutions in Israel, including the Israeli Sports Authority, the English Football Association and the German Football Association. Here, the local leaders were instrumental in teaching the international group how to best respect cultural norms and traditions. For example, communities advised on specific requirements related to the timing of sport activities, provision of culturally appropriate food and drinks and the inclusion of particular customs at sport functions – such as cultural symbols, speeches and rituals at opening and closing ceremonies.

SUPPLEMENTARY EXERCISE: THE HUMAN KNOT

Get together in a circle of about 10 participants. Put your right hands in the air and reach over and grab the hand of someone on the other side of the circle; do the same with your left hands, thus forming a tight knot of hands. Try to untangle yourself without letting go, by climbing over, under and through other pairs of hands. Notice how difficult it is to extricate yourself from the circle. Notice too how some folks end up facing outwards – what might this tell us about strong links with specific others in the face of many interrelationships?

Case Study 2: Football 4 Peace – the role of international volunteers

Nico Schulenkorf, John Sugden and Jack Sugden

With many SFDP projects taking place around the world, one commonality is the need for a facilitator or change agent (Schulenkorf 2010b). There are many reasons for this, including the fact that SFDP projects rarely spring up organically, particularly within volatile and/or deeply divided societies. Like F4P, many of these projects are dreamt up, funded and facilitated by organisations from HICs; moreover, many use international volunteers to help implement sport sessions. Although not overly familiar with the project environment, these volunteers are often skilled coaches and well known to such organisations. In the context of F4P, there were many advantages but also some disadvantages regarding project implementation through international volunteers.

The first advantage is neutrality; in any conflict – from a fight in a school playground to an international war – the search for peaceful resolution often requires a neutral party to facilitate the process of reconciliation. In sport-for-peace work, the facilitator or coach is essentially a neutral agent of behaviour change. Within complex social environments, such as Israel/Palestine, community division is extremely salient and negative prejudices are inherent on both sides. This suggests that – although empowerment of local people is important for the sustainability of projects in the long run – to get the ball rolling, the neutrality of an international volunteer is key to bringing people from conflicting groups together.

Second, an international volunteer or coach is exactly that: international. For the different F4P projects, the international factor added a certain amount of star quality to the projects, which helped to attract key participants to the program. This international star quality acts as bait on the hook of sport itself. In other words, star quality, coupled with a high level of coaching experience, is an effective combination in reconciliation and peace-building work.

With these advantages come many disadvantages. For example, one major challenge with F4P in Israel/Palestine was language. During the football sessions, participants were combined into mixed groups of Hebrew- and Arabic-speaking participants. This meant that all instructions had to be translated twice by one or two local coaches – for reasons of both understanding and equity. On a practical level, the language barrier made training and engagement difficult and the international volunteer coaches had to adapt their teaching styles; they had to use demonstrations and be more physically expressive, for example.

The lack of linguistic understanding is part of the wider disadvantage of limited contextual awareness of international volunteers. Although very able sport coaches, the facilitators were not political historians, and their lack of local knowledge meant that their approaches at times lacked sensitivity and cultural understanding. On the other hand, a local volunteer could fill these gaps in cultural knowledge; accordingly, F4P's international volunteers were continually flanked by at least one local volunteer. Training and empowerment of local volunteers is central to the sustainability of any sport-for-peace work. In F4P projects, local volunteers not only acted as translators, but also became students of the value-based development approach practised through the F4P curriculum.

Further resources

Football 4 Peace: www.football4peace.eu/

Discussion questions and extension activities

1 Can you name any further advantages of using international volunteers in SFDP, other than those listed above?
2 How would you go about combating the disadvantages associated with using international volunteers in SFDP?
3 What are the potential problems in empowering local volunteers to carry out sport-for-peace work?
4 Search the term 'ripple effect' in peace-building work. How does this concept apply to sport projects, such as F4P?

IMPLICATIONS FOR THEORY OF PRACTICE

The establishment of representative organisations – such as the UNOSDP, and other political assertions, such as the 2003 Magglingen Declaration and the 2005 United Nations Year of Sport and Physical Activity – have been important to put sport on the agenda as a potentially valuable tool for wider development efforts. However, it is the efforts of grass-roots sport organisations, communities and volunteers that are going to make the difference on the ground.

It seems important to highlight that both lobbying at the representative level and the active work on the ground are important arms of SFDP. In the case of the latter, F4P has been both influential and sustainable. In the context of contributing to intergroup relations and peace building, it took F4P several years before its programs were firmly established in communities in northern Israel. Only then did F4P slowly begin to influence other organisations and actors and extend its reach into neighbouring regions of conflict – such as Palestine and Jordan – as well as areas with related development needs – such as southern and western Africa, the Korean peninsula and parts of Eastern Europe. It was over a decade after the first F4P project started in Israel in 2002 that F4P slowly started to expand. However, concurrently, international F4P staff were, and are, still involved in project planning and delivery. It takes a long time – and significant commitment from organisers, funders and communities – to make SFDP projects work. Today, the F4P organisation has started to advocate a more devolutionary approach, whereby the recruitment, training and capacity building of local people and expertise are prioritised over top-down and externally designed and imposed delivery models. In other words, F4P realised that a careful and well-supported transfer of control and ownership is central to the sustainability and long-term viability of programs.

Clearly, the development towards local ownership of projects is not an easy process and presents challenges to both local and international stakeholders. Critically, it is the responsibility of the international organisers to determine suitable timing to begin the process of transferring knowledge, skills, responsibility and, ultimately, control to the local communities. This knowledge, skills and power transfer process will never be completed in short-term projects that are funded for one or two years only. Research examining knowledge and ownership transfer revealed that if the power transfer process is initiated at too early a stage, disparate communities will revert to socially exclusive practices and perhaps even violence between groups; however, if the process starts too late, communities may lose interest in the peace-building projects and/or may develop a dependent relationship with the international organisers that undermines any development outcomes (see Schulenkorf 2010b). Overall, while the way towards community empowerment and ownership of SFDP projects may be a long and challenging one, it contributes to culturally adequate preparations before the projects, higher participation and satisfaction during the projects, and sustainable community empowerment afterwards.

SUMMARY

SFDP is a relatively new discipline within the field of international development that uses sport-based initiatives as potentially powerful, practical and cost-effective tools to achieve development outcomes. SFDP programs are able to create fresh spaces for intergroup contact and peace building, where people from different backgrounds get the chance to work, learn, collaborate and celebrate with each other. If managed professionally and designed in accordance with local traditions and customs, SFDP projects have the potential to reduce conflict and social distance between groups, and can result in local empowerment and sustainable development for participating communities. However, SFDP is not a panacea for all social and cultural problems in the world, and should therefore be interpreted as just one kind of initiative among a suite of community-focused initiatives – that may include music, dance, festival and arts projects – all of which share the common goals of intercultural engagement and mutual understanding, ultimately leading to improved social cohesion.

This chapter has introduced SFDP in the context of projects in areas of social conflict and/or divided societies. In such contexts, the big challenges for local and international stakeholders are: to reconcile diversity among communities; help transfer sport management knowledge; and assist in creating an exciting SFDP atmosphere that meets the needs of all participating groups. Football 4 Peace was introduced as an example of a reconciliation and peace-building program that adheres to Allport's (1954) four necessary conditions for positive intergroup contact: (1) equal status within the contact situation; (2) intergroup cooperation; (3) common goals; and (4) support of authorities, law or custom.

Three key lessons learnt from over a decade of F4P are that: (1) strong commitment and hands-on contributions are needed to establish the positive social contact required to make a positive difference between members of conflict communities; (2) SFDP programs benefit from strong partners – both local and international – in designing, managing and growing projects; and (3) long-term commitment and community involvement is needed to have any real chance of making a sustainable difference in divided societies.

DISCUSSION QUESTIONS

1 Sport has often been praised for its ability to connect people from different backgrounds. Why is sport considered so special, and do you think other activities may have similar ability to connect communities? Discuss critically.
2 Do you agree with Nelson Mandela, who famously said that 'sport has the power to save the world'? Why?
3 After 10 years of operation in Israel, international F4P organisers are still involved in program delivery and organisation. What are the benefits and challenges of this ongoing involvement?
4 The F4P program now advocates a devolutionary approach, which aims at transferring control and responsibility to local administrators, coaches and volunteers. When do you think SFDP organisations should actively step back and give power to local communities? What are the challenges in this process?
5 How can positive intergroup relations created during SFDP projects be grown and leveraged beyond the boundaries of the sporting grounds?

REFERENCES

Alba, R. and Nee, V. (2003) *Remaking the American Mainstream: Assimilation and Contemporary Immigration*, Cambridge, MA: Harvard University Press.

Allport, G. W. (1954) *The Nature of Prejudice*, Cambridge, MA: Addison-Wesley.

Allport, G. W. (1958) *The Nature of Prejudice* (abridged), Garden City, NY: Doubleday.

Brown, R. (1988) *Group Processes: Dynamics within and between Groups*, Oxford: Blackwell.

Chalip, L. (2006) 'Towards social leverage of sport events', *Journal of Sport and Tourism*, 11(2): 109–27.

Coalter, F. (2010) 'The politics of sport-for-development: limited focus programmes and broad gauge problems?', *International Review for the Sociology of Sport*, 45(3): 295–314.

Dyreson, M. (2003) 'Globalizing the nation-making process: modern sport in world history', *The International Journal of the History of Sport*, 20(1): 91–106.

Kanemasu, Y. and Molnar, G. (2013) 'Problematizing the dominant: the emergence of alternative cultural voices in Fiji rugby', *Asia Pacific Journal of Sport and Social Science*, 2(1): 14–30.

Kidd, B. (2008) 'A new social movement: sport for development and peace', *Sport in Society*, 11(4): 370–80.

Lewin, K. (1997) *Resolving Social Conflicts: Field Theory in Social Science*, Washington, DC: American Psychological Association.

Lyras, A. and Welty Peachey, J. (2011) 'Integrating sport-for-development theory and praxis', *Sport Management Review*, 14(4): 311–26.

Naupoto, V. Hon. (2012) *National Sports Policy*, Ministry of Youth & Sports, Fiji, available at: www.youth.gov.fj/index.php/policies/policies-3?download=26:national-sports-policy (accessed July 2015).

Prasad, M. (2013) 'Sidelines and solidarity: race and cultural hegemonies in the transition from mission to national soccer in Fiji and South Africa', *The Journal of Pacific Studies*, 33(1): 26–43.

Robertson, R. (2012) 'Cooking the goose: Fiji's coup culture contextualised', *The Round Table*, 101(6): 509–19.

Schulenkorf, N. (2010a) 'Sport events and ethnic reconciliation: attempting to create social change between Sinhalese, Tamil and Muslim sportspeople in war-torn Sri Lanka', *International Review for the Sociology of Sport*, 45(3): 273–94.

Schulenkorf, N. (2010b) 'The roles and responsibilities of a change agent in sport event development projects', *Sport Management Review*, 13(2): 118–28.

Schulenkorf, N. and Edwards, D. (2010) 'The role of sport events in peace tourism', in O. Moufakkir and I. Kelly (eds), *Tourism, Progress and Peace*, Oxford: CABI International, pp. 99–117.

Sherif, M. and Sherif, C. W. (1966) *Groups in Harmony and Tension*, New York: Octagon Books.

Sherif, M. and Sherif, C. W. (1979) 'Research on intergroup relations', in W. G. Austin and S. Worchel (eds), *The Social Psychology of Intergroup Relations*, Monterey, CA: Brooks/Cole, pp. 7–18.

Simon, B. (1999) 'A place in the world: self and social categorisation', in T. R. Tyler, R. M. Kramer and O. P. John (eds), *The Psychology of the Social Self*, Mahwah, NJ: Lawrence Erlbaum Associates, pp. 47–70.

Sugden, J. (2010) 'Critical left-realism and sport interventions in divided societies', *International Review for the Sociology of Sport*, 45(3): 258–72.

Sugden, J. and Bairner, A. (1993) *Sport, Sectarianism and Society in a Divided Ireland*, Leicester: Leicester University Press.

United Nations (UN) (2015) *United Nations Sport for Development and Peace*, available at: www.un.org/wcm/content/site/sport/ (accessed July 2015).

SECTION 6

Monitoring and evaluation

CHAPTER 12

Evaluating sport development

Emma Sherry, Nico Schulenkorf and Pamm Phillips

INTRODUCTION

To ensure that sport programs achieve their intended outcomes, monitoring and evaluation (M&E) are crucial activities. Evaluation of program outcomes ensures that the organisational mission is adhered to and that the program is delivered in the intended manner, at the intended time and with the intended participants (Coalter 2013a). Developing a clear and informed understanding of the success – or failure – of a program in achieving its intended outcomes provides vital information. By analysing why a program was successful or not, lessons can be learned about the context, the approach, the tools and the intent of the program, which can also facilitate the design of future initiatives. The planning, management and development of sport programs represent considerable investments in both time and money, and it is imperative that organisations regularly monitor and evaluate their progress and outcomes. In other words, M&E ensures that resources and funding are being well spent (Houlihan 2011).

Organisations that provide SD or SFD programs require funding to design, create and implement them. Funding organisations may be a government body or a major state, national or international sporting organisation, such as the IOC. Sometimes, program funding will be provided by a collaboration of private philanthropic and government agencies; for example, the Grootbos Foundation is a conservation organisation that teamed up with Barclays and ABSA banks and the Western Cape Department of Cultural Affairs and Sport to create the Football Foundation of South Africa (FFSA), an organisation delivering programs aimed at providing a sporting infrastructure legacy from the 2010 FIFA World Cup, held in South Africa (Swart *et al.* 2011).

In a sporting context, competition for funding is generally high (Houlihan 2011), meaning that funding organisations are required to prove that they have directed and used funds appropriately (Coalter 2011). Each external funding organisation has its own strategic goals and objectives (Coalter 2011); therefore, sports organisations seeking to acquire funds through these sources need to demonstrate how their program meets those strategic targets. As we discovered in Chapter 7, inter-organisational relationships are critical to the delivery of SD and SFD programs. In the case of the FFSA, multiple funding organisations were involved, each with their own strategic objectives as diverse as athlete development, urban regeneration and improvement of local sporting infrastructure. Moreover, each of the partners involved in providing funding for FFSA's programs had differing priorities within the region, and FFSA needed to serve them through their sport programming (Swart *et al.* 2011). Regular monitoring and evaluation of the programs is key to examining how these objectives have been met or addressed. At the same time, monitoring and evaluation can demonstrate the proper acquittal of those funds and, further, may help to secure ongoing funding.

OUTLINE OF THE CHAPTER

This chapter discusses the role of monitoring and evaluation in sport development and sport for development programs. It introduces and contextualises the challenges and opportunities for evaluating programs and provides an overview of evaluative tools, approaches and theory.

After completing this chapter, you should be able to:

• understand the value and importance of monitoring and evaluation;
• understand how evaluation must be part of program design;
• recognise that planning and establishing metrics influence program outcomes; and
• determine the best methods of evaluation to answer specific research question(s).

WHAT DOES THEORY TELL US?

Evaluation of outcomes begins with program design (Coalter 2013a). Research in the sport development field has demonstrated that while this sounds like a simple enough statement, it is in fact more complicated than it first appears (Houlihan 2011). In particular, managers of programs must identify the specific outcomes they desire from the program and, simultaneously, consider how they will measure the success of those outcomes (Coalter 2013a; Long 2011).

An example of an SFD program aimed at reducing crime in a disadvantaged neighbourhood can demonstrate the complexity of this task. Many factors influence how such a program might be designed. One of the first considerations is the participants. Who is the program aimed at? How has this cohort of participants been selected? The identification of target participants is key to ensuring that the desired impacts are achieved; in our example, it would be necessary to understand who is committing the crime in the neighbourhood by gathering evidence. At the same time, information about the neighbourhood itself – the social context – is important to make informed decisions.

A second consideration is to understand the intended outcomes. In other words, what – specifically – is the program hoping to achieve? Crime reduction is a desired overall outcome, but how will the program achieve that end? Will it be through improving individuals' well-being with the intent that improved self-esteem will lead to a reduced desire to commit crimes? Perhaps it will be through providing a place for disaffected people to spend time, keeping them occupied and involved in a social setting in which they can make friends and social connections, which will in turn reduce the desire to engage in antisocial behaviours? Perhaps it will be by providing a place to learn new skills and develop talents that could open new pathways?

If the aim of our SFD program is to improve well-being, key questions from an evaluation perspective include:

- How will well-being be measured and defined?
- How will improvements in well-being be measured?
- How will the activities that are likely to lead to improved well-being be determined?
- Given the subjective nature of well-being, how is a program that impacts positively on a cohort of individuals' well-being designed appropriately?
- Is the chosen determination of well-being commensurate with that of our intended participants? In other words, might our own personal understanding of the necessary conditions for well-being differ from those of intended participants?

Similarly, an SD program might seek to grow the sport into specific regions or cohorts. If this is the case, key questions from an evaluation perspective might include:

- How might the intended groups be identified?
- What are the specific conditions surrounding these cohorts' non-participation?
- Are there financial constraints – such as residing in a socioeconomically disadvantaged area?
- Are there locational or geographic constraints – such as remoteness?
- Perhaps the sport is broadly considered a masculine sport, meaning females struggle to participate?
- Are there cultural constraints? Perhaps the sport is not well known in a particular cultural group; perhaps in that culture, sport participation is considered inappropriate for one gender?
- Are there personal physical constraints, such as a disability?
- The intended outcomes must also be considered: does the program seek to develop individual athletes or is it aimed at raising overall participation?

The answers to questions such as these can facilitate program design in that they can act as a guide for managers to ensure that program aims for specific outcomes are evidence-based, measurable, achievable and repeatable.

PROGRAM THEORY

Program theory offers a framework through which to understand the relationship between program design and program outcomes. Adoption of a theory-based approach to sport programming enables sound evaluation and closes the gap between policymakers, practitioners and researchers by providing opportunities for collaboration and conversation (Coalter 2013a). Through discussion, the finer details of program intents are brought into the light, allowing assumptions to be examined and a clearer picture of the issues, the situation and the intent to be developed, which facilitates and supports evaluation (Coalter 2013a). Coalter (2013a) discusses the theory in terms of *inputs, outputs, impacts* and *outcomes*, as Figure 12.1 demonstrates.

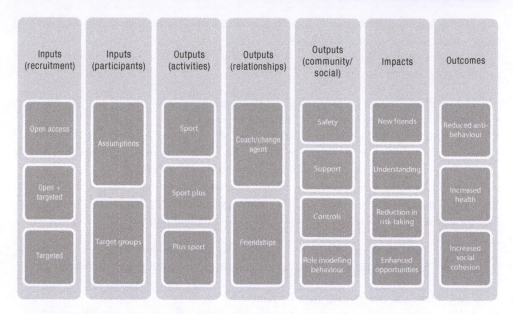

FIGURE 12.1 Program logic model

Source: Adapted from Coalter (2013a).

The first input is derived from the methods of *recruitment* (Coalter 2013a); these can range from open access, through self-selecting, to targeted and via referral. The program might be free, subsidised or paid for by the participant. Each recruitment method will result in a different participant cohort; the recruitment method should be designed to garner the appropriate participants. Gathering sufficient information on the nature, extent, severity and distribution of the issues that are the desired focus of the program determines the best recruitment method, which in turn ensures that the correct participants are recruited (Long 2011).

Further, gathering sufficient evidence on which to base program planning decisions is important to ensure that the program will be relevant, useful and have the desired outcomes for its intended participants (Houlihan 2011). There is a danger that organisations seeking to address an identified issue will impose their own understandings of a situation onto developing solutions (Coalter 2011). This is illustrated in the context of international SFD programs that are managed by staff from HICs seeking to address social, cultural, educational or health-related issues associated with local communities in LICs and LMICs (Schulenkorf 2012). In such cases, dominant ideologies – more relevant to the organisation's country of origin – can be imposed on program design and delivery. For example, Darnell (2011) demonstrated that interns working in Commonwealth Games Canada's (CGC) International Development through Sport (IDS) program understood their role as one that would facilitate the development of participants' leadership skills. The underpinning philosophy was that sport would facilitate personal development by creating individualised understandings of success and achievement for the participants, thereby leading to empowerment. Implicit in this philosophy is the notion that persons experiencing disadvantage have failed to achieve self-actualisation, an individualist notion that emanates from the neo-liberal philosophies of HICs and fails to account for the manifold pressures influencing an individual's development, such as war, poverty and disease (Darnell 2011). Researchers caution strongly against the wholesale imposition of neo-liberal philosophies, arguing that for sport for development programs to be effective – and to not just become another arm of global hegemony – design must begin in situ and with a proper assessment of the local understandings of desired outcomes (Coalter 2013a; Darnell 2011; Houlihan 2011; Schulenkorf *et al.* 2014).

The second input is *participants* (Coalter 2013a). Leading SFD scholars, such as Sugden (2010) and Coalter (2011, 2013a), warn against making assumptions about the inherent positive impact of sport and advocate the development of a clear understanding of the context, nature and distribution of the specific issues in focus. In the absence of adequate information and evidence about the issues that a program seeks to address, managers of programs run the risk of adopting a deficit view of participants that is based on environmental determinist assumptions that assume homogeneity in the cohort. Evidence-based planning ensures that measurable performance indicators are set (Coalter 2013a).

Further, consideration of performance indicators facilitates decisions around what tools will be used to evaluate the program, as some outcomes are more suited to measurement by some tools than others (Houlihan 2011). For example, in an SD context, quantitatively measuring an athlete's BMI pre- and post-program will be a more effective method than qualitatively interviewing the athlete about how much body fat he or she thinks they might have lost through participation. Similarly, in an SFD context, discovering the impacts of participation on an individual's development of social connections is better achieved through qualitative methods that allow discussion of what participation has meant to him or her in terms of their social situation. Tools for evaluation are discussed later in this chapter.

The first output varies depending on *the nature of the program* (Coalter 2013a), represented in Figure 12.1 by outputs (activities). For example, an SD program that offers sporting opportunities might be aimed at increasing participation in the sport, or developing mastery of the sport, or becoming proficient in the rules of the sport, or all three. On the other hand, an SFD program uses sport as the context, or the site, in which participants have the opportunity to gain desired skills or behaviours through their participation in the program. In both SD or SFD contexts, outcomes are derived not simply from the assumption that sport is good for you. Rather, it is the combination of the context and the specific activities included in the design of the program – such as attaining a coaching certificate or collaboratively developing a community sport event – that work towards achieving program outcomes. The choice of sport can be influential (Agans and Geldhof 2012); for example, an SFD program seeking to improve social skills might consider whether a team sport or an individual sport would be most effective for achieving the intended outcomes for the particular cohort.

The second output concerns *social relationships* (Coalter 2013a), represented in Figure 12.1 by outputs (relationships). The relationships with the personnel delivering the program, in combination with the type of program, have been shown to be a critical aspect of program effectiveness (Vella *et al.* 2013). In an SD context, the primary social relationship is with the coach; this relationship is typically constrained to sport-related activities and opportunities for developing closer personal relationships are limited. However, in an SFD context, the development of social relationships is often key to the success of the program (Coalter 2013b; Sherry 2010). For example, in the context of an SFD program seeking to address issues of gang membership, racism and at-risk youth, research has demonstrated that participants' outcomes are enhanced when trusting, respectful and reciprocal relationships are formed between participants and personnel (Coalter 2013b; Schulenkorf 2013).

The third output is the *social climate* (Coalter 2013a), represented in Figure 12.1 by outputs (community/social). This refers to the social environment in which the program is conducted. In an SD program, there might be an emphasis on understanding and abiding by the rules, learning cooperation or teamwork. In an SFD context, the social climate might be more directed towards creating a safe and accepting environment in which the participants are comfortable and able to speak, listen and self-reflect (Spaaij and Schulenkorf 2014).

According to program theory, the impacts are about *providing a foundation for changing attitudes and behaviours* and *changing values and attitudes* (Coalter 2013a), the final column in Figure 12.1. In other words, the combination of the social relationships, the social climate and the activities create a context in which participants can develop the respect, trust and reciprocity required to achieve change. In an SD context, the foundation might be the combination of the acquired technical skills and adoption of the necessary attitude that enable the participant to perform at a high standard. In an SFD setting, this foundation of respect, trust and reciprocity might take the form of the participants seeking to not disappoint the coach, their team members or communities, and to conform to expectations. In terms of changing values and beliefs, varying with the nature of the program, the ability to achieve the desired changes depends on the inputs, outputs and on the receptiveness and suitability of the participants. SFD programs often seek to affect a change; for example, in attitudes towards people from other cultures. SFD programs thus emphasise the importance of understanding the implications of negative behaviours – both in a sporting context and elsewhere – in the hope that they will assume responsibility for their actions and adopt the desired changes.

Outcomes obviously vary depending on the nature of the program. An SD program might see the addition of a new team into a tournament or the development of a new league (see, for example, Swart *et al.* 2011); an SFD program might see a reduction in violence or antisocial behaviour (see, for example, Kelly 2013).

IMPLICATIONS OF THEORY FOR PRACTICE

Up to this point, this chapter has discussed SD and SFD programs as if they are two distinct activities. This was done to demonstrate the variety in programming and the divergent outcomes intended from sport programming. However, it is helpful to think of SD and SFD as occupying either end of a continuum, as there are many similarities between the two. For example, programs with a sport-for-development focus can serve to develop the sport, and programs seeking to develop the sport can also have positive community and personal development outcomes.

Monitoring and evaluation of a program's success is achieved in part through measurement of outcomes; however, as seen through an examination of program theory in this chapter, evaluation is threaded throughout the planning and design process. From identification of the program's objectives, to recruitment of participants and program delivery, there is a constant need for M&E to determine the relevance and utility of program intent, delivery approach and desired outcomes. Rather than seeing M&E as something that occurs once the program is complete, evaluation needs to be embedded in design and considered throughout the process as it is influential in decision-making along the way.

Evaluation, then, is both a *formative* part of the initial planning stages of programming and also serving to shape and improve programming through amendment. It is also *summative*, providing useful feedback on completion of the program, to prove what was and was not successful (Houlihan 2011). Formative evaluation includes: *needs assessment*, in which the need for the program is assessed; *evaluability assessment*, to determine the feasibility of the evaluation; *structured conceptualisation*, in which stakeholders define the target population, the program, the approaches and methods for delivery, and possible outcomes; *implementation evaluation*, which monitors program delivery; and *process evaluation*, where delivery processes are monitored for possible improvements (Trochim 2006). Summative evaluation includes: *outcomes evaluation*, which investigates whether the program had demonstrable effects in the areas targeted; *impact evaluation*, which looks for broader effects of the program, intended and unintended; *cost-effectiveness and cost-benefit analysis* evaluates the efficiency of resource use; *secondary analysis*, in which alternative methods are considered; and *meta-analysis*, which brings together a range of research evaluating the same question (Trochim 2006).

Tools for evaluation

Consideration of evaluation affects decisions about the kind of tools and research approach that will be taken to measure the outcomes of a program. As was mentioned earlier, there is a variety of research tools used in evaluation; determining the desired outcomes of a program facilitates decision making about how to measure the progress and success of a program. This section presents a brief overview of the tools used in evaluation.

Qualitative methods enable the voices of program participants to be heard (Corbin and Strauss 2008) and provide in-depth information about individuals' experiences (Thomas 2006). Qualitative tools include interviews, semi-structured interviews and focus groups, as well as journaling and observation (Corbin and Strauss 2008).

The focus of qualitative evaluation is on understanding, rather than generalisability, which is often the focus of quantitative evaluation (Creswell 2007). Qualitative methods often use purposive sampling, in which selection is made based on knowledge about the sample (Creswell 2007); this is in order that the garnered information is relevant and that the sample is sufficiently knowledgeable about the topic or issue that he or she is able to offer insights.

In order to collect appropriate information, interview schedules – which outline what should be asked of participants – and research protocols – which provide structure regarding what information might be observed or collected – are developed with the gathering of specific information in mind (Kvale and Brinkmann 2009). In other words, interview schedules and research protocols should reflect the specific outcomes that are being measured. Vague questions will likely encourage the sharing of information with limited utility or relevance to the issues under examination (Kvale and Brinkmann 2009).

Qualitative evaluation typically uses inductive analysis in which detailed readings of raw data – for example, interview transcripts or researcher observation notes – are used to draw out themes, concepts or a model (Thomas 2006). In this way, a theory emerges from the data (Strauss and Corbin 1998), allowing evaluation of the programming from a participant's point of view.

Quantitative methods are well suited to measurement of change. Causality and generalisability underpin quantitative evaluation, making it particularly useful for summative evaluation (Clarke and Dawson 1999). Change as a result of programming can be measured quantitatively. An SFD program aimed at reducing crime, for example, could measure the outcome in terms of crime statistics. On the other hand, an SD program might measure increases in participation rates. It is argued that quantitative techniques avoid research bias as the method design precludes the need for lots of interpretation (Punch 2014).

Quantitative tools include surveys, questionnaires, pre- and post-tests, and statistical information (Punch 2014); samples are typically much larger than those found in qualitative evaluation as the aim is to provide generalisable results (Long 2011). A range of quantitative instruments, scales and measures, designed to measure specific aspects of individuals' experiences, can be used in SD and SFD contexts. For example, the Positive Youth Development Inventory (Arnold *et al.* 2012) measures youths' psychological development, and could be used pre- and post-program to evaluate outcomes of participation on participants' positive development.

APPLICATION OF THEORY TO PRACTICE

The following case studies demonstrate evaluation in practice. The first case study presents an example of evaluation of a sport for development program, while the second one focuses on a sport development initiative.

Case Study 1: Timor Leste study

Katherine Raw

Timor Leste is a half-island nation with a population of 1.2 million, located north of Australia. Following 450 years of Portuguese occupation, Timor Leste was occupied by Indonesia for 24 years and, during that period, approximately one-quarter of the Timorese population were killed (Millo and Barnett 2004). In 2002, with the assistance of the UN, Timor Leste gained independence and is now considered to be one of the world's youngest countries (Millo and Barnett 2004; Robinson 2011). Since 2000, the UN, various NGOs and government groups have worked collaboratively to reduce poverty and violence, with the intention of promoting stability and progressive development throughout Timor Leste (McGregor 2007; Silove *et al.* 2009). However, with 53 per cent of the population under the age of 18 (UNICEF 2011), disengaged youth (Robinson 2011) and violence were key barriers to reducing social tensions and establishing peace (Goldsmith 2009; Scambary 2009).

In 2010, the Australian Catholic University (ACU) developed and implemented the Future in Youth (FIY) program in Timor Leste's second biggest town, Baucau. The program was coordinated in partnership with a handful of Baucau's local community leaders. Program development was centred on a community that had often been disrupted by hostility, primarily at the instigation of martial arts youth gangs, with high attrition rates from school, high levels of youth unemployment and disengaged youth. This SFD program used football as the sporting activity, and aimed to improve the health, well-being and life skills of youth and to build the capacity of the community. An additional long-term goal of the program is for the citizens of Baucau to have ownership of the program and sustain it independently of ACU.

Assessing these particular objectives of the program was the primary focus of M&E activities that were supposed to be conducted regularly. However, by the time the FIY program was in its fourth year of operation in 2013, it had not instigated any formal M&E. The only form of assessment that had been undertaken was done directly by the program's Australian operators, largely in an informal manner. Therefore, in accordance with current recommendations from SFD research, the FIY program implemented M&E by engaging an independent researcher, not affiliated with the program. Community leaders and coaches involved with the FIY program (n = 24) were invited to share their views and opinions regarding the program and its impacts. Qualitative data were gathered through semi-structured interviews with community leaders and focus groups with coaches.

A question guide was developed to provide an overall framework summarising the content to be covered during discussions. As opposed to a more controlled approach, the question guide was developed with the idea of allowing questions to be asked in any order with minimal fixed wording and answered with various time allowances (as per Morgan and Guevara 2008). To reduce the potential for prompting or bias, the FIY program's aims were not directly included within the question guide; however, if participants broached these topics, they were allowed to discuss them. The final question guide for this study comprised several open-ended questions asking participants about their opinions regarding the FIY program, with the option of using more targeted questions to explore topics as necessary. Once finalised, the primary interpreter translated the question guide into the local language of Tetum; it was then two-way translated from Tetum back into English – without prior viewing of the English questions – by a second interpreter in order to minimise the potential for concepts to become lost in translation (Muthoni and Miller 2010; Squires 2009).

While not specifically a part of formal data collection, reflexive journaling was also undertaken to enhance the depth of data that emerged through semi-structured interviews and focus groups. These processes occurred at the completion of the FIY program, and again three months later to examine whether the program was achieving and sustaining its identified outcomes. Following the completion of interviews and focus groups, data were translated, transcribed and pooled. Analysis of data was done using thematic analysis techniques, which involved identifying, analysing and then reporting on themes that emerged from the data. A hierarchal structure of themes emerged, allowing the discovery and investigation of patterns in the data, which were related back to the question guide and therefore, in turn, assessed in relation to the research questions. To enhance the dependability of data analysis, two researchers undertook this process separately and compared the emergent themes.

Positive links were found between the FIY program and the health, well-being and life skills of the program's youth participants, coaches and community leaders. To an extent, sport-specific community capacity was also developed through football and coaching skills. The findings regarding program sustainability were mixed, with the majority of participants expressing that the program was sustained for four years in a largely unstructured manner by the youth who had participated in the program with little input from the coaches. However, there were some community leaders and coaches who indicated their willingness to take more responsibility to ensure the program would be sustained in the future. This particular point was instrumental in moving the FIY program forward in terms of sustainability, as these individuals have since become key facilitators of improvements in local program sustainability in 2014.

The results gathered through the initial bout of M&E in 2013 highlighted the value and necessity of the evaluation process to program organisers and funders. This understanding was solidified again in 2014 with a second year of M&E that produced an even greater depth of information and honesty from participants. As a result, ongoing M&E was implemented the following year and will continue to be a permanent practice into the future.

Further resources

Evaluation and Program Planning (an open-access Elsevier journal devoted to evaluation research): www.sciencedirect.com/science/journal/01497189
Innovation Network 2014, Point K: Practical Tools for Planning, Evaluation and Action: www.innonet.org/index.php?section_id=4&content_id=16

Case study extension activities

1 What are the possible benefits and disadvantages of having M&E undertaken by independent researchers?
2 In what ways do you think evaluation research outcomes were served by the data being examined by two independent researchers?
3 Why do you think the M&E process was even more enlightening in the second year it was conducted?
4 How might you incorporate opportunities for M&E into program design?

Case Study 2: Hockey Victoria

Angela Osborne

Hockey Victoria (HV) is a state body charged with oversight of hockey in the Australian state of Victoria. Hockey is a mixed-gender sport with some 22,000+ members registered in Victoria (HV 2014). HV had noted that the participation rate for girls was steadily dropping and that girls in the 16–19-year-old bracket were quitting the sport, resulting in a talent gap beginning to form in the elite levels as insufficient numbers of girls were going on to play senior hockey. In 2010, HV received funding from state government body VicHealth to put into place a suite of inclusion programs aimed at improving the participation and retention rates of women and girls in hockey (HV 2014).

In addition to improving retention and increasing participation rates of junior girls, the program sought to raise awareness of the contributions of women and girls in hockey, both in the sport and in individual clubs. To achieve these strategic aims, HV developed a range of programs, each of which was directed towards addressing specific issues, with specific outcomes in mind.

Inclusion awareness training was offered to HV staff and board and was intended to raise awareness of the issues facing diverse communities within the sport of hockey and to garner broad organisational support for the inclusion strategy.

The pilot club program brought several clubs together regularly to discuss issues and solutions; a range of speakers offered club representatives ideas and information on how to improve the participation of girls and women. Clubs developed different kinds of initiatives and discussed their implementation; HV provided support and resources for clubs seeking to affect change in their club. In addition, HV developed and delivered a range of courses and programs aimed at addressing specific aspects of the identified issues.

A coaching program was established that offered girls and women an opportunity to learn new coaching skills and to get their coaching certificate. This program was developed with the intent of raising the visibility of women and girls in hockey. HV found that girls can be intimidated by male officials, which made them unlikely to seek assistance for problems and had an indirect influence on decisions to leave the sport. The coaching program was a long-term strategy to achieve gender balance in officials with a view to improving retention.

A junior leadership program was developed with the intent of establishing and consolidating girls' sense of ownership and belonging within their club. This program sought to empower girls to encourage them to remain in the club through the critical 16–19-year-old period.

A governance workshop offered club representatives ways to address inequity in their club at the governance level; for example, by ensuring that the board was representative of club membership – it had been noted that many clubs had very few, or no, female board members.

A coaching workshop devoted to coaching girls was offered. Coaches and club representatives were provided with training about gender differences and on how to adapt their coaching practices to ensure that girls feel, and are, included as valuable members of the team.

A mentoring program was established that matched current junior elite players with older, more experienced elite players. This program sought to provide elite athletes with an avenue for discussion about their hockey and life experiences. The underpinning intent was to offer additional support to elite athletes – which would not impact on selection or standing within their clubs – with the intent of encouraging retention and transition into senior elite hockey.

Evaluation of the suite of programs was undertaken halfway through the three-year funding period and again at the end of the funding period. Mixed methods were used to evaluate different aspects of the suite of programs. Qualitative evaluation questioned program participants' understandings of inclusion, their experiences in the specific program they were involved with, how their clubs had changed following participation and recommendations for further improvement. Overall, the qualitative evaluation sought to ascertain the extent to which the principles underpinning the programming had been understood and embedded into practice; thus, qualitative evaluation was necessary to properly understand the range and depth of the impact on the hockey community.

For the qualitative evaluation, an interview schedule was developed that addressed the research questions and encouraged discussion of the aspects of the programs related to increasing visibility and improving retention of women and girls in hockey. The questions on the interview schedule were all crafted to garner information about a specific aspect of the programming and its underpinnings. For instance, in order to assess the adoption of the principles of inclusion, research participants were asked to discuss their opinions on creating a safe, welcoming and inclusive environment. Responses to this question provided information about the extent to which the ideas underpinning the programs had been understood and incorporated into practice; responses offered information about possible gaps in understanding, which can then be used to develop further programs.

Participants for the qualitative evaluation included program participants, HV staff and the HV board. HV provided a complete list of program participants, all of whom were invited to take part in the evaluation. Contact was initially made via email; the response rate to the invitation was 73 per cent. Research participants provided their phone contact details and a researcher conducted a telephone interview at a time of their choosing. Interviews were recorded and transcribed. A qualitative software management program, NVivo, was used to manage and sort the data; thematic analysis was used to uncover themes within the data.

Through the process of qualitative evaluation, HV received information about the impact and outcomes of programs, with which it was then possible to determine the success of the programming. For example, evaluation revealed that: the pilot club model was successful and had begun to have results, with an increase in the numbers of junior girls noted across pilot clubs; women and girls felt that their status within clubs had improved; and the focus of the suite of leadership, governance and coaching programs was having a positive impact on retention as girls felt supported, encouraged and empowered to continue their hockey participation through the critical period.

Moreover, evaluation undertaken midway through the three-year funding period enabled HV to adjust programs to better meet the needs of participants. For example, evaluation of the mentor program midway revealed that participants who were geographically distant struggled to meet, thereby reducing the effectiveness of the program. Amendments were made on the strength of this finding, and subsequent participants were paired with geographic proximity in mind. Similarly, midway evaluation found that some mentors – particularly those employed in a coaching role – felt unsure about the precise nature of the relationship; this information allowed HV to provide clarification about the nature of the role and how it differed from that of a coach. The second cohort of mentors was clearer about their role and no such problems were encountered.

The summative evaluation provided information on how to better HV programming. For instance, evaluation of the governance workshop revealed that while regional clubs were benefited by the inward-looking, club-focused governance activities, metropolitan clubs would have preferred an outward-looking, whole-of-sport focus that examined strategic direction for the sport. Metropolitan clubs, by virtue of their location and surrounding populations, had been concerned with inclusion – either directly or indirectly – for some time, meaning that their needs around governance and inclusion differed markedly from those of clubs in regional areas. This revelation enabled HV to develop programming more suited to the needs of the participants. Further, the finding provided HV with crucial information delineating the experiences of metropolitan and regional clubs, enabling better understanding of how programming and strategy might be developed in a more targeted fashion that accounts for these variations in experience in the future.

Further resources

Hockey Victoria (HV): www.hockeyvictoria.org.au/

Case study extension activities

1 Why do you think the evaluations adopted a qualitative approach?
2 Why would it be important for HV to garner an in-depth understanding of program participants' experiences?
3 How might quantitative approaches have been used?
4 What would be the benefits and challenges of each kind of evaluative approach for M&E of HV's suite of programs?

SUMMARY

This chapter has examined the role of evaluation in sport programming. It has demonstrated that evaluation is necessary and useful at all stages of planning, implementation and delivery in order to ensure program outcomes are relevant, useful and successful for intended cohorts. It has provided a framework with which to embed evaluative practice in program design and has demonstrated the commonalities and differences between monitoring and evaluation in sport for development and sport development programs.

DISCUSSION QUESTIONS

1 Identify and discuss the difference between quantitative, qualitative and mixed-method research approaches.
2 You are developing an SD program aimed at developing individual athletes in a specific sport. What should be taken into account in the research design process when developing an evaluation plan? List the factors and state why these are important.
3 Imagine you are developing an SFD program aimed at reducing truancy in your city or region. What should be taken into account in the research design process when developing an evaluation plan? List the factors and state why these are important.
4 Why do funders and stakeholders require monitoring and evaluation to be undertaken for sport programs? What are the possible implications of failure to do so?
5 Evaluation can be undertaken within the program or by external experts – discuss the pros and cons of each approach.

REFERENCES

Agans, J. P. and Geldhof, G. J. (2012) 'Trajectories of participation in athletics and positive youth development: the influence of sport type', *Applied Developmental Science*, 16(3): 151–65.

Arnold, M. E., Nott, B. D. and Meinhold, J. L. (2012) *The Positive Youth Development Inventory (PYDI)*, Corvallis, OR: Oregon State University 4-H Youth Development Program.

Clarke, A. and Dawson, R. (1999) *Evaluation Research: An Introduction to Principles, Methods and Practice*, London: Sage.

Coalter, F. (2011) 'Sport development's contribution to social policy objectives: the difficult relationship between politics and evidence', in B. Houlihan and M. Green (eds), *The Routledge Handbook of Sports Development*, London: Routledge, pp. 561–78.

Coalter, F. (2013a) *Sport for Development: What Game Are We Playing?* London: Routledge.

Coalter, F. (2013b) '"There is loads of relationships here": developing a programme theory for sport-for-change programmes', *International Review for the Sociology of Sport*, 48(5): 594–612.

Corbin, J. and Strauss, A. (2008) *Basics of Qualitative Research*, Thousand Oaks, CA: Sage.

Creswell, J. W. (2007) *Qualitative Inquiry and Research Design: Choosing among Five Approaches*, Thousand Oaks, CA: Sage.

Darnell, S. C. (2011) 'Identity and learning in international volunteerism: "sport for development and peace" internships', *Development in Practice*, 21(7): 974–86.

Goldsmith, A. (2009) '"It wasn't like normal policing": voices of Australian police peacekeepers in Operation Serene, Timor-Leste 2006', *Policing and Society*, 19(2): 119–33.

Hocky Victoria (HV) (2014) *Annual Report*, available at: www.hockeyvictoria.org.au/Portals/15/2014%20Media%20Uploads/2014HVAnnualReport-Website.pdf (accessed July 2015).

Houlihan, B. (2011) 'Introduction: the problems of policy evaluation', in B. Houlihan and M. Green (eds), B. Houlihan and M. Green (eds), *The Routledge Handbook of Sports Development*, London: Routledge, pp. 557–60.

Kelly, L. (2013) 'Sports-based interventions and the local governance of youth crime and antisocial behavior', *Journal of Sport and Social Issues*, 37(3): 261–83.

Kvale, S. and Brinkmann, S. (2009) *InterViews: Learning the Craft of Qualitative Research Interviewing*, 3rd edn, Los Angeles, CA: Sage.

Long, J. (2011) 'Researching and evaluating sports development', in K. Hylton and P. Branham (eds), *Sports Development: Policy, Process and Practice*, 2nd edn, London: Routledge, pp. 236–57.

McGregor, A. (2007) 'Development, foreign aid and post-development in Timor-Leste', *Third World Quarterly*, 28(1): 155–70.

Millo, Y. and Barnett, J. (2004) 'Educational development in East Timor', *International Journal of Educational Development*, 24(6): 721–37.

Morgan, D. and Guevara, H. (2008) 'Interview guide', in L. Given (ed.), *The Sage Encyclopaedia of Qualitative Research Methods*, Thousand Oaks, CA: Sage, pp. 470–1.

Muthoni, H. and Miller, A. (2010) 'An exploration of rural and urban Kenyan women's knowledge and attitudes regarding breast cancer and breast cancer early detection measures', *Health Care for Women International*, 31(9): 801–16.

Punch, K. F. (2014) *Introduction to Social Research: Quantitative and Qualitative Approaches*, 3rd edn, London: Sage.

Robinson, G. (2011) 'East Timor ten years on: legacies of violence', *The Journal of Asian Studies*, 70(4): 1007–21.

Scambary, J. (2009) 'Anatomy of a conflict: the 2006–2007 communal violence in East Timor', *Conflict, Security & Development*, 9(2): 265–88.

Schulenkorf, N. (2012) 'Sustainable community development through sport and events: a conceptual framework for sport-for-development projects', *Sport Management Review*, 15(1): 1–12.

Schulenkorf, N. (2013) 'Sport-for-development events and social capital building: a critical analysis of experiences from Sri Lanka', *Journal of Sport for Development*, 1(1): 25–36.

Schulenkorf, N., Sugden, J. and Burdsey, D. (2014) 'Sport for development and peace as contested terrain: place, community, ownership', *International Journal of Sport Policy*, 6(3): 371–8.

Sherry, E. (2010) '(Re)engaging marginalized groups through sport: the Homeless World Cup', *International Review for the Sociology of Sport*, 45(1): 59–71.

Silove, D., Brooks, R., Bateman Steel, C. R., Steel, Z., Hewage, K., Rodger, J. and Soosay, I. (2009) 'Explosive anger as a response to human rights violations in post-conflict Timor-Leste', *Social Science & Medicine*, 69(5): 670–7.

Spaaij, R. and Schulenkorf, N. (2014) 'Cultivating safe space: lessons for sport-for-development projects and events', *Journal of Sport Management*, 28(6): 633–45.

Squires, A. (2009) 'Methodological challenges in cross-language qualitative research: a research review', *International Journal of Nursing Studies*, 46(2): 277–87.

Strauss, A. L. and Corbin, J. M. (1998) *Basics of Qualitative Research: Techniques and Procedures for Developing Grounded Theory*, Thousand Oaks, CA: Sage.

Sugden, J. (2010) 'Critical left-realism and sport interventions in divided societies', *International Review for the Sociology of Sport*, 45(3): 258–72.

Swart, K., Bob, U., Knott, B. and Salie, M. (2011) 'A sport and sociocultural legacy beyond 2010: a case study of the Football Foundation of South Africa', *Development Southern Africa*, 28(3): 415–28.

Thomas, D. R. (2006) 'A general inductive approach for analyzing qualitative evaluation data', *American Journal of Evaluation*, 27(2): 237–46.

Trochim, W. (2006) *Research Methods Knowledge Base*, available at: www.socialresearchmethods.net/kb/index.php (accessed July 2015).

UNICEF (2011) 'At a glance: Timor-Leste', *UNICEF*, available at: www.unicef.org/infobycountry/Timorleste_statistics.html (accessed July 2015).

Vella, S. A., Oades, L. G. and Crowe, T. P. (2013) 'The relationship between coach leadership, the coach-athlete relationship, team success, and the positive developmental experiences of adolescent soccer players', *Physical Education and Sport Pedagogy*, 18(5): 549–61.

Glossary

ableist 'Discrimination in favour of able-bodied people; prejudice against or disregard of the needs of disabled people' (OED 2015). See Chapter 3 in this book.

Active-After-Schools Community program A program funded by federal government was developed in 2004 with the aim of increasing participation among primary school children. See Chapter 4 in this book.

advocacy coalition framework A type of policy framework. See Cairney (2015) and Chapter 4 in this book.

advocacy coalitions Groups of policy actors that are aligned around particular interests. See 'policy actors' in this glossary. See Chapter 4 in this book.

agency An individual's ability to act on his or her own power. See Chapter 3 in this book.

Agitos Foundation The Agitos Foundation was created by the IPC in 2012, and its purpose is to assist in the development and promotion of physical activity and sport programs, parasport, for those with a physical disability, while also focusing on the Paralympic movement's primary global objective of moving towards a more inclusive society. See Chapter 3 in this book.

airport meet-and-greet high performance system An imperfect situation wherein minority sports elite athletes only meet their team for the first time shortly before competition. See Chapter 5 in this book.

American Development Model An athlete training model developed by US Hockey that values practice and proper training above all else. The model is built on the notion: 'The more they play it, the better chance that they'll love it. And when you combine a passion for the game with increased puck time, kids will start to excel at it. Play, love, excel. That's ADM' (ADMKids 2015). See Chapter 2 in this book.

ANZ Tennis Hot Shots Tennis Australia's official junior starter program. See Chapter 5 in this book.

ATRN An SD model based on attraction, retention/transition and nurturing of athletes. See Chapter 5 in this book.

Auskick A modified sport program operated by the AFL.

Australia's Winning Edge 2012–2022   The ASC's sport development strategy. See Chapter 4 in this book.

Back 2 School Fitness   A health promotion sport intervention funded by VicHealth. See Chapter 9 in this book.

bonding social capital   Delineates social networks between homogenous groups, such as kin, neighbours or close friends. See Chapter 10 in this book.

bridging social capital   Occurs when relationships are developed with individuals who are different from oneself, where social ties and bonds may be looser and more diverse in nature. See Chapter 10 in this book.

CardioNET   A health promotion sport intervention funded by VicHealth. See Chapter 9 in this book.

change agents   'External parties who help (communities) establish contact, open negotiations and develop projects for cooperation and sustainable development' (Schulenkorf 2010: 119). See Chapter 8 in this book.

Clean Clothes Campaign   'The Clean Clothes Campaign is dedicated to improving working conditions and supporting the empowerment of workers in the global garment and sportswear industries' (www.cleanclothes.org). See Chapter 3 in this book.

collaboration   Occurs 'when a group of autonomous stakeholders of a problem domain engage in an interactive process using shared rules, norms, and structures, to act or decide on issues related to that domain' (Wood and Gray 1991: 146). See Chapter 7 in this book.

Community Play   Tennis Australia's community-focused, attraction program. See Chapter 5 in this book.

competition   Competition emerges when there is demand for limited resources by multiple organisations (Barman 2002). See Chapter 7 in this book.

coopetition   Coopetition combines two opposite logics – the competitive paradigm (that is: competing interests) with the collaborative paradigm (that is: common interests). Coopetition is particularly evident in sports leagues – teams compete on the field, but also cooperate with each other on a large number of off-field matters (Robert *et al.* 2009). See Chapter 7 in this book.

dose-response relationship   Direct association between a stimulus and a desired outcome (for example, quantity of physical activity and good health). See Chapter 9 in this book.

economic status   There are various ways to refer to countries with differing levels of economic development. In the past, terms such as the Global North/South, Western/non-Western and developed/developing have been used to describe the status of various countries, often interchangeably. Each of these terms is problematic in its own way; for example, Australia could easily be classed as a developed country but it is neither in the global North, nor is it in the West. Further, the terms developed/developing do not capture the difference between nation states in differing levels of development, which can be substantial. The WTO does not have official definitions for these terms: instead, countries self-report their developing/developed status (WTO 2015), which has clear implications in terms of variant understandings of the term. Finally, the use of terms such as the Global North/South implies that the countries therein referred to share some kind of unity, which is inaccurate. To avoid inaccurate assumptions and implicit generalisations, this book uses World Bank terminology, based on countries' reported gross national income (GNI). The terms used throughout this book are: low-income country (LIC); lower middle-income country (LMIC); upper middle-income country (UMIC); and high-income country (HIC) (World Bank 2015).

engagement   Engagement is a quality of IORs, characterised by frequent and open communication (knowledge-sharing routines) and regular meetings. See Chapter 7 in this book.

exchange relationships   Exchange relationships exist between buyers and sellers. See Chapter 7 in this book.

Fit Football   A health promotion sport intervention funded by VicHealth. See Chapter 9 in this book.

Football Against Racism in Europe   'FARE is an anti-discrimination and social inclusion network that counters inequality and exclusion in football through coordinated action and common efforts' (FARE 2015). See Chapter 3 in this book.

FTEM framework   A sport development model that conceptualises athletes' training stages in terms of Foundations, Talent, Elite, Mastery and is not age-based. See Chapter 2 in this book.

Future in Youth program   SFD football program, implemented by ACU, with the aim of improving the health, well-being and life skills of youth and to build the capacity of the community. See Chapter 12 in this book.

Go Explore It   A health promotion sport intervention funded by VicHealth. See Chapter 9 in this book.

governmentalisation   The process whereby mimicry of structures and processes common to the commercial sector is encouraged by governments through the imposition of targets and performance indicators. Over time, these processes serve to homogenise organisations through the need for compliance. See Chapter 2 in this book.

gross domestic product   'The monetary value of all the finished goods and services produced within a country's borders in a specific time period, though GDP is usually calculated on an annual basis. It includes all of private and public consumption, government outlays, investments and exports less imports that occur within a defined territory' (Investopedia 2015).

gross national income   'Gross national income is defined as the sum of value added by all producers who are residents in a nation, plus any product taxes (minus subsidies) not included in output, plus income received from abroad such as employee compensation and property income' (Investopedia 2015).

health promotion   A 'process of enabling people to increase control over, and to improve their health' (WHO 1986)

heterogeneity   The quality of being diverse and not comparable in kind. See Chapter 5 in this book.

high-income country   This term is used throughout this book to refer to the economic status of a country. See 'economic status' in this glossary.

Homeless World Cup   'The Homeless World Cup is a unique, pioneering social movement which uses football to inspire homeless people to change their own lives' (HWC 2015). See Chapter 10 in this book.

homogenisation   The act of making something uniform in composition. See Chapter 5 in this book.

Human Development Index   'A summary measure of average achievement in key dimensions of human development: a long and healthy life, being knowledgeable and have a decent standard of living . . . The HDI was created to emphasise that people and their capabilities should be the ultimate criteria for assessing the development of a country, not economic growth alone. The HDI can also be used to question national policy choices, asking how two countries with the same level of GNI per capita can end up with different human development outcomes. These contrasts can stimulate debate about government policy priorities' (UNDP 2015). See Chapter 3 in this book.

inter-organisational relationships   Formal arrangements that bring together any combination of tangible and intangible assets of two or more legally independent organisations with the aim to create additional value. See Chapter 7 in this book.

interlocking directorate   An interlocking directorate occurs when one person is a director of two organisations. See Chapter 7 in this book.

international governing body   An organisation charged with responsibility for provision of an activity; for example, the International Olympic Committee.

international non-governmental organisation   An NGO (see 'non-governmental organisation' in this glossary) whose activities are international in scope.

International Olympic Academy   'The aim of the International Olympic Academy is to create an international cultural centre in Olympia, to preserve and spread the Olympic Spirit, study and implement the educational and social principles of Olympism and consolidate the scientific basis of the Olympic Ideal, in conformity with the principles laid down by the ancient Greeks and the revivers of the contemporary Olympic Movement, through Baron de Coubertin's initiative' (IOA 2015).

International Paralympic Committee   'The International Paralympic Committee (IPC) is the global governing body of the Paralympic Movement. Its purpose is to organise the summer and winter Paralympic Games and act as the International Federation for nine sports, supervising and coordinating World Championships and other competitions. The vision of the IPC, run by 200 members, is 'To enable para-athletes to achieve sporting excellence and inspire and excite the world' (IPC 2015). See Chapter 3 in this book.

International Relations Committee   The International Relations Committee (IRC) was formed to facilitate and promote relationships between IOC and benefitting organisations such as NOCs, governments and public authorities. Together, the IRC and its partners develop and implement SFD programs. See Chapter 3 in this book.

joint venture   A joint venture occurs when two or more organisations create a third organisation. Both original organisations retain their own identity and the new organisation reflects the distinctive competencies and interests of each parent organisation. See Chapter 7 in this book.

Learn Right Skate School   A health promotion sport intervention funded by VicHealth. See Chapter 9 in this book.

Lillehammer Olympic Organising Committee   The local Norwegian committee responsible for the 1994 bid to hold the Winter Games and the organisation that first conceived of an Olympic charity fund to support SFD. See Chapter 3 in this book.

linking social capital   Is focused on vertical relationships between different levels or social strata, where individuals form relationships entirely outside their community. See Chapter 10 in this book.

low-income country   This term is used throughout this book to refer to the economic status of a country. See 'economic status' in this glossary.

lower middle-income country   This term is used throughout this book to refer to the economic status of a country. See 'economic status' in this glossary.

LTAD model   Essentially, the LTAD model uses sport science to specify four (for early specialisation sports) or five (for late specialisation sports) necessary training stages, broken down into age and gender, that an athlete must master to reach elite levels. See Chapter 2 in this book.

Melbourne Giants   An Australian sport initiative for refugees, principally hailing from Somalia, aimed at the development of social capital. See Chapter 10 in this book.

memorandum of understanding   'A formal document embodying the firm commitment of two or more parties to an undertaking, and setting out its general principles, but falling short of constituting a detailed contract or agreement' (OED 2015).

mergers and acquisitions   Mergers and acquisitions represent total integration of organisations. One organisation will likely experience a complete loss of identity. See Chapter 7 in this book.

Millennium Development Goals   A series of global goals developed as a result of an agreement entered into in 2000 by world leaders to address the dehumanising effects of poverty. The eight millennium goals are: eradicate extreme poverty and hunger; achieve universal primary education; promote gender equality and empower women; reduce child mortality; improve maternal health; combat HIV/AIDS, malaria and other diseases; ensure environmental sustainability; and develop a global partnership for development. See Chapter 3 in this book.

multiple streams framework, path dependency   A type of policy framework. See Cairney (2015) and Chapter 2 in this book.

National Olympic Committees National Olympic Committees are responsible for organising their country's participation in the Olympic Games and are controlled by the International Olympic Committee. NOCs are also responsible for the promotion of development of athletes, training coaches and officials, and for nominating cities to host future Olympic Games.

national sporting organisation A national body charged with the management and delivery of particular sports. This includes the provision of appropriate facilities for individuals to have an opportunity to participate; programs that offer appropriate experiences depending on age, skill and other factors; pathways so that participants can transition to various programs at different levels to meet their needs; and personnel to facilitate the delivery of programs and the development of participants.

neocolonialism 'The use of economic, political, cultural, or other pressures to control or influence another country; *esp.* the retention of such influence over a developing country by a former colonial power' (OED 2015).

Netball for All An Australian sport development program run by Netball Victoria, aimed at CALD communities and people with a disability. See Chapter 10 in this book.

non-governmental organisation 'A non-governmental organization (NGO) is a non-profit, citizen-based group that functions independently of government. NGOs, sometimes called civil societies, are organized on community, national and international levels to serve specific social or political purposes, and are cooperative, rather than commercial, in nature. Examples of NGOs include those that support human rights, advocate for improved health or encourage political participation . . . While the term NGO has various interpretations, it is generally accepted to include private organizations that operate without government control and that are non-profit and non-criminal. Other definitions further clarify NGOs as associations that are non-religious and non-military' (Investopedia 2015).

observer status 'Non-Member States, entities and organizations [*sic*] that have received a standing invitation to participate as observers in the sessions and the work of the United Nations General Assembly' (UN 2015). See Chapter 3 in this book.

Olympic Aid See 'Right to Play' in this glossary.

Olympic Development Program (US Youth Soccer) 'The US Youth Soccer Olympic Development Program was formed in 1977 to identify a pool of players in each age group from which a National Team will be selected for international competition; to provide high-level training to benefit and enhance the development of players at all levels; and, through the use of carefully selected and licensed coaches, develop a mechanism for the exchange of ideas and curriculum to improve all levels of coaching' (US Youth Soccer 2015).

Olympic Movement 'The Olympic Movement is the concerted, organised, universal and permanent action, carried out under the supreme authority of the IOC, of all individuals and entities who are inspired by the values of Olympism. It covers the five continents. It reaches its peak with the bringing together of the world's athletes at the great sports festival, the Olympic Games. Its symbol is five interlaced rings.

The goal of the Olympic Movement is to contribute to building a peaceful and better world by educating youth through sport practised in accordance with Olympism and its values. Belonging to the Olympic Movement requires compliance with the Olympic Charter and recognition by the IOC' (IOC 2015).

Olympic Solidarity Commission The branch of the IOC charged with reinvesting broadcast revenue into global participation programs. 'The aim of Olympic Solidarity is to organise assistance for all the National Olympic Committees (NOCs), particularly those with the greatest needs, through multi-faceted programmes prioritising athlete development, training of coaches and sports administrators, and promoting the Olympic ideals (Olympic Charter, rule 5)' (OSC 2015).

Olympism for Humanity Alliance (O4H) O4H is a global venture that seeks to build a bridge between theory and practice, and aims to promote integrated applied Olympism teaching, research and community service.

Paralympic Games The competition for athletes with a disability that runs parallel to the Olympic Games.

Paralympic Movement A term referring to the establishment, development and consolidation of the Paralympic Games. See Chapter 3 in this book.

parasport Sport played by persons with a physical or intellectual disability; sports may be adapted for play by persons with a disability.

partnership Partnerships are stable and enduring relationships between organisations that offer opportunity for inter-organisational integration. See Chapter 7 in this book.

Play 60 Program 'NFL PLAY 60 is the National Football League's campaign to encourage kids to be active for 60 minutes a day in order to help reverse the trend of childhood obesity' (NFL 2015). See Chapter 2 in this book.

Play Streets A health promotion sport intervention funded by VicHealth. See Chapter 9 in this book.

policy actors Individuals and groups, both formal and informal, that seek to influence the creation, development and implementation of public policy. See Chapter 4 in this book.

policy broker Policy brokers mediate between the various policy actors to seek compromise and achieve policy outcomes. See Chapter 4 in this book.

policy entrepreneur Policy 'entrepreneurs may be elected politicians, leaders of interest groups or merely unofficial spokespeople for particular causes. They are people with the knowledge, power, tenacity and luck to be able to exploit windows of opportunity and heightened levels of attention to policy problems' (Cairney 2015) in order to promote their preferred policy solution. See Chapter 4 in this book.

Policy Networks framework The Policy Networks framework suggests that policy-making in a particular area may be characterised by loose and diverse issue networks or tighter and more exclusionary policy communities (Marsh and Rhodes 1992). See Chapter 4 in this book.

Program theory   A framework through which to understand the relationship between program design and program outcomes. See Chapter 12 in this book.

Pulseraiser   A health promotion sport intervention funded by VicHealth. See Chapter 9 in this book.

punctuated equilibrium   A type of policy framework. See Cairney (2015) and Chapter 4 in this book.

RBI program   A baseball initiative. See Chapter 2 in this book.

Read to Achieve program   'The NBA's Read to Achieve program is a year-round campaign to help young people develop a life-long love for reading and encourage adults to read regularly to children' (NBA 2015).

reciprocity   Reciprocity is the process of responding favourably to another by returning benefits for benefits. See Chapter 7 in this book.

residency high performance system   A centralised high performance training system whereby athletes live and train in a central facility. See Chapter 5 in this book.

Right to Play   Right to Play is 'a global organisation, using the transformative power of play to educate and empower children and youth. Through playing sports and games, we teach children essential life skills that will help them overcome the effects of poverty, conflict and disease so that they can create better futures and drive lasting social change in their communities and beyond' (Right to Play 2015). See Chapters 2 and 9 in this book.

spillover   Spillover occurs when a policy aimed at achieving specific outcomes has consequences in another policy domain. See Chapter 4 in this book.

sport development   Sport development (SD) aims to create pathways for professional participation and talent identification. SD aims at improving the sport-related skills of particular athletes. In SD, individuals and groups participate with the focus on achieving mastery and potentially excellence in the sport.

sport for development   Sport for development (SFD) focuses on the role that sport can play in contributing to specific social outcomes and overall community well-being. SFD refers to improvement of sport and other skills achieved through sport. In SFD, individuals and groups participate to achieve more than just physical outcomes: they also participate with aspirations to realise certain social, cultural, psychological, educational and/or economic goals.

Sport Steward program   A Dutch SFD program aimed at increasing citizens' cultural capital. See Chapter 10 in this book.

sporting mega-event   A large scale, international sporting event; for example, the Olympic Games, FIFA World Cup or the Paralympic Games.

Sporting Schools   A participation-focused program delivered by the ASC aimed at school-aged children. See Chapter 4 in this book.

strategic alliance   Strategic alliances require each organisation to sacrifice an element of autonomy to access the advantages provided by the common efforts of both organisations. See Chapter 7 in this book.

Street Soccer USA   A not-for-profit organisation whose mission is to use soccer to help individuals suffering from homelessness in the US make positive changes in their lives. See Chapter 10 in this book.

structural hole   A gap between two organisations with complementary resources or information. See Chapter 7 in this book.

theory of intergroup relations   Explains the underpinnings and reasons for the different ways groups interact, why conflict arises, how friendships form. See Chapter 11 in this book.

trust   Inter-organisational trust is the expectation between partners' intent to meet their obligations. Trust is both subjective and dynamic. Trust influences the nature of the relationship and the amount and quality of information and knowledge exchange. See Chapter 7 in this book.

upper middle-income country   This term is used throughout this book to refer to the economic status of a country. See 'economic status' in this glossary.

Urban Youth Academy   A baseball initiative. See Chapter 2 in this book.

vicious cycle   A recurring cycle of events; the result of each increases the deleterious effect of the next. See Chapter 4 in this book.

virtuous cycle   A recurring cycle of events; the result of each increases the beneficial effect of the next. See Chapter 4 in this book.

western   Throughout this book, the terms 'western' or the 'west' are presented in lower case in order to remove any implicit suggestion that there is unity between countries traditionally referred to in this way.

Wokabaot Jalens   A health-focused sport development program in Vanuatu. See Chapter 9 of this book.

REFERENCES

ADMKids (2015) *American Development Model*, available at: www.admkids.com (accessed July 2015).

Barman, E. A. (2002) 'Asserting difference: the strategic response of nonprofit organizations to competition', *Social Forces*, 80(4): 1191–222.

Cairney, P. (2015) '1000 words: key policy theories and concepts in 1000 words', *Paul Cairney: Politics & Public Policy*, available at: https://paulcairney.wordpress.com/1000-words/ (accessed July 2015).

FARE (2015) *Football Against Racism in Europe*, available at: www.farenet.org (accessed July 2015).

Homeless World Cup (HWC) (2015) 'About', *Homeless World Cup*, available at: www.homeless worldcup.org/about/ (accessed July 2015).

Investopedia (2015) 'Dictionary', *Investopedia*, available at: www.investopedia.com/ (accessed July 2015).

IOA (2015) 'International Academy of Olympism', *IOC*, available at: www.ioa.org.gr/ (accessed July 2015).

IOC (2015) 'The Olympic Movement: introduction', *Olympic.org: Official Website of the Olympic Movement*, available at: www.olympic.org/content/the-ioc/governance/introductionold/ (accessed July 2015).

IPC (2015) *International Paralympic Committee*, available at: www.paralympic.org/ (accessed July 2015).

Marsh, D. and Rhodes, R. A. W. (1992) 'Policy communities and issue networks: beyond typology', in D. Marsh and R. A. W. Rhodes (eds), *Policy Networks in British Government*, Oxford: Oxford University Press, pp. 249–68.

NBA (2015) 'Read to Achieve', *NBA*, available at: www.nba.com/features/rta_index.html (accessed July 2015).

NFL (2015) 'Play 60 Program', *NFL*, available at: www.nflrush.com/content/6468 (accessed July 2015).

OED (2015) 'ableist', 'neo-colonialism', 'memorandum of understanding', Oxford English Dictionary Online, available at: www.oed.com/ (accessed July 2015).

OSC (2015) *Olympic Solidarity Commission*, available at: www.olympic.org/olympic-solidarity-commission (accessed July 2015).

Right To Play (2015) *Right To Play*, available at: www.righttoplay.org/ (accessed July 2015).

Robert, F., Marques, P. and Le Roy, F. (2009) 'Coopetition between SMEs: an empirical study of French professional football', *International Journal of Entrepreneurship and Small Business*, 8(1): 23–43.

Schulenkorf, N. (2010) 'The roles and responsibilities of a change agent in sport event development projects', *Sport Management Review*, 13(2): 118–28.

UN (2015) 'Observers', *United Nations*, available at: www.un.org/en/ga/about/observers.shtml (accessed July 2015).

UNDP (2015) 'Human Development Index (HDI)', *United Nations Development Programme*, available at: http://hdr.undp.org/en/content/human-development-index-hdi (accessed July 2015).

US Youth Soccer (2015) 'Olympic Development Program', *US Youth Soccer*, available at: www.usyouthsoccer.org/programs/olympicdevelopmentprogram/ (accessed July 2015).

Wood, D. and Gray, B. (1991) 'Towards a comprehensive theory of collaboration', *Journal of Applied Behavioral Science*, 27(2): 139–62.

World Bank (2015) 'Country and lending groups', *World Bank*, available at: http://data.worldbank.org/about/country-and-lending-groups#Low_income (accessed July 2015).

World Health Organization (WHO) (1986) *Ottawa Charter on Health Promotion: International Conference on Health Promotion*, Geneva: WHO, available at: www.who.int/healthpromotion/conferences/previous/ottawa/en/ (accessed July 2015).

World Trade Organization (WTO) (2015) 'Development: definition: who are the developing countries in the WTO?', *World Trade Organization*, available at: www.wto.org/english/tratop_e/devel_e/d1who_e.htm (accessed July 2015).

Index

advocacy coalition framework (ACF) 46–7
Agitos Foundation 36–7, 42
Allport, G. W. 152–3, 157
American Development Model (ADM) 19–21, 24
attraction, retention/transition and nurturing (ARTN) 63, 67, 70–1
Australia 94, 104, 107–11, 129–30, 169, 171–3; community sport 78–9, 81, 83–7; development policy 45, 51–3, 56–7; high performance development pathways 64–5, 68, 71–2; social inclusion 138–9, 141–4
Australian Football League (AFL) 85–7, 101–3, 109–12
Australian Rules football *see* Australian Football League

Balyi, I. 13
Barnhardt, R. 126
baseball 22–4
basketball 18, 22–4
Bellesini, K. 85–7
Berlin, R. 23
Big Issue 104
Blatter, S. 48
Bourdieu, P. 137
Bowers, M. T. 12–24
Brinkerhoff, J. 100
Brouwers, J. 63–75

Cairney, P. 46
Campbell, S. 50
Canada 19, 109, 127, 164
Cann, L. 139
capitalism 17–19; neocapitalism 34
Chalip, L. 82, 148
change agents 107, 112–15
charity 38–9
children 4, 13, 21, 52, 80, 82, 85–6, 110
China 55
coaching 13, 86, 107–11, 116, 171–3

Coalter, F. 14, 48, 165
Coleman, J. S. 137
collaboration 97
commercialisation 4–5, 14, 69, 115
Commonwealth Games 68
community-based participatory research (CBPR) 126, 128
community engagement 8, 86, 138
community sport 77–88
competition 97, 139, 140
competitive advantage 98–9
complementary resources/capabilities 99
conflict resolution 147–57
contact theory 152–3, 157
contingency theory 97
continuity 56
cooperation 96–8, 100, 112–13
coopetition 97
Corbett, B. 72–4
Côté, J. 13
cricket 95, 127
cultural capital 135–8

Darnell, S. C. 164
Dawson, A. 108–9
De Bosscher, V. 14, 63–75
developing countries 38, 113, 125
development of sport (SD) 6–8, 10, 34, 93, 101–2, 121, 139; coaches/officials/ change agents 107–8, 111–12, 116; community sport 77–83, 85–6, 88; evaluation 161, 163, 165–6, 168; high performance development pathways 63, 69; policy 45–6, 48, 56–7; theory 13–14, 16, 18, 20, 22
disabilities 36–7, 80–1, 142
discrimination 139
doping 69–70, 101
Dowling, M. 5
Dyer, J. H. 98
Dyreson, M. 148

ecology theory 97
economic capital 138
elite facilities 5
elite sport 48, 51, 57, 95, 124, 142
elite sport development 13, 49–50, 52–6, 123;
  pathways 63–75
England 4, 45, 49–51, 56–7, 95
evaluating outcomes 161–74
exchange relationships 94, 99

Fairley, S. 112
Farrelly, F. 101
FIFA 48, 55, 127
FIFA World Cup 55
Fiji 147, 149–51
football 18, 82, 104, 138–9, 142, 150–1,
  153–6
for-profit sector 93
Fordin, S. 23
Foundations, Talent, Elite, Mastery (FTEM)
  framework 13
funding 8, 73, 101–2, 109, 161–2, 173

gender 13, 32, 57, 141, 163, 171–2
Germany 36, 78
globalisation 14, 31, 33–6, 40
global-local nexus 31–5, 37
government 5, 8, 35, 47–50, 52–3, 55–6, 152;
  centralised 16; governmentalisation 14
grass-roots sport 50, 52–3, 57, 63, 77–88
Green, B. C. 12–25, 49, 82, 138–9

Hardman, A. E. 122
Hay, J. 13
health 4, 79, 121–32, 170
heterogeneity 65
high-income countries (HICs) 18, 39, 64, 68,
  115, 124–5, 154, 164–5
high performance development pathways *see* elite
  sport development
hockey 19–21, 24, 171–3
homelessness 100, 104, 135, 139
homogeneity 13, 65, 165
Houlihan, B. 13–14, 45–6

ice hockey 19–22
ideology 8, 164
infrastructure 34, 55, 77–80, 101
instrumentalism 137
inter-organisational networks 94–7
inter-organisational relationships (IORs) 93–105
international federations (IF) 37
international governing organisations (IGOs) 31,
  41, 69
International Olympic Committee (IOC) 31, 34–5,
  38–41, 69, 103, 106, 127

International Paralympic Committee (IPC) 36–8
international sport development 31–42
internationalisation 32
Israel 147, 149, 153–6
Israel, B. 126

Jeanes, R. 45–58
joint ventures 95

Kellett, P. 112, 123
Kennelly, M. 94
key performance indicators 67–8, 149
Kirkness, J. 126
knowledge-sharing routines 99
Kolb, M. 98

Lewin, K. 151
Lihaya, H. 45–58
Lindsey, I. 45–58
local government authorities (LGAs) 78–9, 82–4,
  142
local ownership 125, 156, 169
local partnerships 50
long-term athlete development (LTAD) 13, 19
low-income countries (LICs) 39, 68, 115, 125,
  164
lower middle-income countries (LMICs) 39, 68,
  115, 125–6, 128, 164
Lyras, A. 15

Magdalinski, T. 52
Magglingen Declaration 148, 156
Major, J. 49
Major League Baseball (MLB) 22–4
marginalisation 135–6
market-driven approach 17–21
Martel, K. 20
Maxwell, H. 138
mental health 122–3
Mentor, G. 142
mergers and acquisitions 95
meso-level frameworks 46–8
Minikin, B. 68
Misener, L. 31–42
modified rules 80–1, 85–7, 109–11
monitoring and evaluation (M&E) 161, 167,
  169–70
multiculturalism 79, 141–2
multiple streams framework 46, 48

national academies (NA) 71
National Anti-Doping Organisations (NADOs)
  70
national governing bodies (NGBs) 17, 49–50,
  67, 69
national identity 48, 141

National Olympic Committees (NOCs) 39, 67, 69
National Paralympic Committees (NPCs) 37
national sport organisations (NSOs) 6, 19–21, 52, 81–2
neo-liberalism 165
neocolonialism 39–40
netball 141–3
Netherlands 138
New Zealand 95, 101–3
Newland, B. 83–4
non-communicable diseases (NCDs) 123, 126
non-governmental organisations (NGOs) 35, 41, 101, 114–15, 123, 127, 148–9, 168
Northern Ireland 152–3
not-for profit sector 93, 127

obesity 50, 52, 79, 122
officials 107, 111–12, 116
Olympic Development Academies (ODAs) 73–4
Olympic Games 4, 16, 49, 51, 53, 64, 68
opportunity costs 100

Palestine 147, 149, 153–5
Palm, J. 80
Paralympics 36–8, 80
participation levels 50–2, 78–9, 111, 125, 129, 141
path dependency 46, 49
Patriksson, M. 15
peace building 147–57
Pfeffer, J. 100
Phillips, P. 3–10, 77–88, 107–16, 161–74
physical activity (PA) 121–9, 132
physical education (PE) 50, 55
plus sport 14
policy 45–58
policy actors 47–8
power relations 31–2
praxis 10, 16, 18–19, 24, 35
private sector 35
professional athletes 4, 86
professionalisation 5–6, 82
program design 162
program theory 163–6
programming 77, 80, 142
public relations (PR) 22
punctuated equilibrium 46
Putnam, R. D. 137
pyramid analogy 13, 63

qualitative methods 167–9, 172
quantitative methods 168

rationality 46–7
Raw, K. 168–70

reciprocity 97, 99, 123, 137
recruitment 13, 164
referees see officials
refugees 139
relational rent 98
relationship-specific assets 99
resource-based view (RBV) 98
resource dependency theory 100
Right to Play 38–9
Robinson, L. 68
Rowe, K. 121–32
rugby 72–4, 94–5, 150–1

Salancik, G. 100
Schulenkorf, N. 3–10, 15, 107–16, 147–57, 161–74
Sherry, E. 3–10, 135–44, 161–74
Shilbury, D. 112, 123
Siefken, K. 121–32
Singh, H. 98
soccer see football
social capital 135–9
social contexts 4, 124, 162, 165–6
social health 122–3
social inclusion 14, 135–44
social interaction 7, 122, 124, 132, 140, 141, 150
social investment 50
social network analysis (SNA) 95–7
social welfare 15
Somalia 139
Sotiriadou, P. 13, 63–75
South Africa 138, 161–2
Spaaij, R. 138–9
Special Olympics 80
sponsorship 55, 100–1
sport for development and peace (SFDP) 147–9, 151–2, 154–7
sport for development (SFD) 6–8, 10, 93, 107–8, 112–16, 139, 161–6; community sport 77–80, 82–3, 85–6, 88; health promotion 121, 132; high performance development pathways 63, 69; inter-organisational relationships 100–1, 104; international 31, 34–5, 37–40; policy 45–6, 48, 53, 56–7; theory 13–16, 18, 22–4
sport plus 14
Sri Lanka 107, 114–15
stakeholders 17, 19, 53, 63–4, 66, 70, 113–14, 123
Stensel, D. J. 122
strategic alliances 94–5
strategic planning 78
Sugden, Jack 147–57
Sugden, John 147–57, 165
support services 13, 101

sustainability 31, *55*, 112, 126, 157, 170
Switzerland 149
Swyngedouw, E. 34
systems theory 63

Tanzania 45, 54–7
tennis 71–2, 81
theory of intergroup relations 151–3, 157
Timor Leste 168–70
Toohey, K. 94
transnational corporations 14, 33
transnationalisation 33
triathlon 79, 83–4
trust 99–100, 137
Turner, P. 79

UK 64, 109, 138
umpires *see* officials
United Nations (UN) 31, 34–5, 39–41, 168;
    International Year of Sport and Physical

Education 148, 156; Office on Sport for
    Development and Peace (UNOSDP) 148,
    156; UNAIDS 127; UNICEF 127
USA 16–24, 72–4, 83, 139–40, 143

Vanuatu 128
volunteers 82, 85, 108, 114–15, 139,
    153–5

Wales 95
Warner, S. 77–88
Wasser, K. 31–42
Wehner, K. 108
Welty Peachey, J. 15, 135–44
Whitlam, G. 51
Wicker, P. 78–9
World Anti-Doping Agency (WADA) 69–70
World Championships 64
World Cup *see* FIFA World Cup
World Health Organization (WHO) 122–3